Triumph Toledo 1970-75 Autobook

By Kenneth Ball

and the Autobooks team of Technical Writers

Triumph Toledo 1300 1970-75
Triumph Toledo 1500 1970-75

Autobooks Ltd. Golden Lane Brighton BN1 2QJ England

The AUTOBOOK series of Workshop Manuals is the largest in the world and covers the majority of British and Continental motor cars, as well as all major Japanese and Australian models. For a full list see the back of this manual.

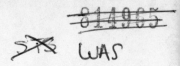
**This book is to be returned on or before
the last date stamped below.**

18.

30. APR 87

30. DEC

21. MAY

20. 87

02. AUR

23. 87

30. 87

13.

04.

CONTENTS

ISBN 0 85147 550 7

First Edition   1972
Second Edition, fully revised   1973
Reprinted   1974
Third Edition, fully revised   1975
Reprinted   1975

975

Printed and bound in Brighton England for Autobooks Ltd by G. Beard & Son Ltd

ACKNOWLEDGEMENT
We wish to thank Standard-Triumph International Ltd. for their co-operation and also for supplying data and illustrations. Considerable assistance has also been given by owners, who have discussed their cars in detail, and we would like to express our gratitude for this invaluable advice and help.

INTRODUCTION

This do-it-yourself Workshop Manual has been specially written for the owner who wishes to maintain his car in first class condition and to carry out his own servicing and repairs. Considerable savings on garage charges can be made, and one can drive in safety and confidence knowing the work has been done properly.

Comprehensive step-by-step instructions and illustrations are given on all dismantling, overhauling and assembling operations. Certain assemblies require the use of expensive special tools, the purchase of which would be unjustified. In these cases information is included but the reader is recommended to hand the unit to the agent for attention.

Throughout the Manual hints and tips are included which will be found invaluable, and there is an easy to follow fault diagnosis at the end of each chapter.

Whilst every care has been taken to ensure correctness of information it is obviously not possible to guarantee complete freedom from errors or to accept liability arising from such errors or omissions.

Instructions may refer to the righthand or lefthand sides of the vehicle or the components. These are the same as the righthand or lefthand of an observer standing behind the car and looking forward.

CHAPTER 1

THE ENGINE

1 : 1 Description

A 1300cc power unit is fitted to all the Toledo models distributed in the UK. Some exported cars are fitted with a 1500cc engine with a choice of either single or twin carburetters.

The engines are almost identical in design except for some slight technical differences in the 1500cc, which gives it a higher power ratio. The fitting of twin carburetters to the 1500cc boosts the power ratio even higher. Details of bore, stroke and other engine specifications are given in **Technical Data** at the end of this manual.

The engine is a four cylinder 'in-line' with No. 1 cylinder leading, that is, nearest to the fan. All models have pushrod-operated overhead valves actuated by the camshaft which runs in four white-metal bearings. The camshaft is driven by the crankshaft using the sprockets and chain system. A keeper plate controls the end float of the camshaft. Integral with the camshaft is a gear that is constantly meshed to a distributor drive gear; this gear drives the oil pump as well as the distributor. An eccentric cam on the camshaft operates the fuel pump which is bolted to the side of the crankcase.

The crankshaft is supported and revolves in three steel-backed alloy shell bearings, the big-end bearing shells are made of the same material. All the bearing shells are renewable, either as standard or in undersizes. End float in the crankshaft is contained by thrust washers located at the rear of No. 3 main bearing.

The oil is contained and cooled in the sump and is drawn from the sump by the oil pump. The pressure from the oil pump is limited by a non-adjustable relief valve which returns excess oil to the sump. The oil is then passed through a fullflow oil filter before entering the fore and aft oil gallery on the lefthand side of the engine. Internal passages lead the oil to the crankshaft main bearings and camshaft bearings. Drilled oilways in the crankshaft take the oil from the main bearings to the big-end bearings. A scroll on the front of the camshaft allows oil to seep out and lubricate the camshaft sprocket as well as the timing chain. The rocker gear requires only a small supply of oil and this is metered by a scroll and two flats on the rear end of the camshaft. After lubricating the rockers the oil runs down the pushrod tubes to lubricate the camshaft followers before finally returning to the sump. The pistons, small ends and

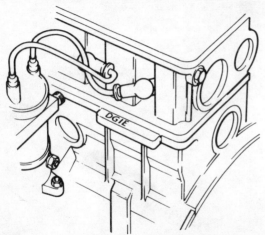

FIG 1:1 Location of engine number. A suffix HE after the engine number denotes 'high compression', a suffix LE denotes 'low compression'

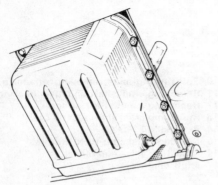

FIG 1:2 The engine sump drain plug 1 is situated on the lefthand side of the sump case

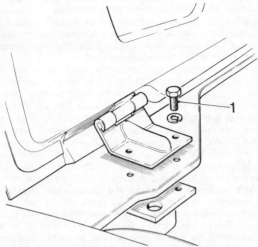

FIG 1:3 To detach the bonnet, remove the four set-screws 1 indicated

cylinder bores are lubricated by oil splash from the crankshaft.

The crankcase ventilation is the closed-circuit type, with a pipe connecting the rocker cover to the air intake filter.

The only task that cannot be done with the engine in the car is removing and replacing the crankshaft. However, if major work is to be carried out it will probably be easier to have the engine removed from the car and on the bench.

The engine number is stamped on a small platform at the rear of the cylinder block on the lefthand side (see **FIG 1:1**). The suffix HE after the engine number denotes a standard high compression engine while the suffix LE indicates that it is a low compression engine, usually for use in countries where high octane fuel is unobtainable. The engine number should be quoted with the commission number when ordering spares from the service garage.

Every 6000 miles (10,000 kilometres) the engine oil should be drained and the engine replenished with new oil of the approved grade. The drain plug 1 shown in **FIG 1:2** is on the lefthand side of the sump case. Unscrew the plug slowly until the oil begins to escape, then as the flow lessens, remove the plug completely. The operation is best carried out when the engine is warm.

The oil filter element should be renewed every 12,000 miles (20,000 kilometres). Instructions on how to do this are given in **Section 1:14**.

1:2 Removing and refitting the engine and gearbox

The gearbox can be removed separately (see **Chapter 6, Section 6:2**), but if the engine is to be removed it is easier to remove them both as a unit and then separate the gearbox from the engine. The combined unit is removed from above the car but certain operations will have to be carried out under the car. If a pit is not available, securely raise the front of the car on stands. Any support holding the car must be safe and secure otherwise the car may drop, causing serious injury to anyone working underneath it, apart from the obvious dangers of mechanical damage.

If the operator is not a skilled automobile mechanic, it is suggested that he will find much useful information in 'Hints on Maintenance and Overhaul' at the end of this Manual, and that he should read it before starting work.

1 Detach the bonnet from the car by unscrewing and removing the four front hinge setscrews (see **FIG 1:3**).
2 Refer to **FIG 1:4** and disconnect and remove the battery.
3 Drain the cooling system (see **Chapter 4**).
4 Refer to **FIG 1:2**, remove the drain plug and drain the engine sump.
5 Disconnect the top and bottom hoses between the radiator and the engine and the hose from the expansion tank.
6 Remove the radiator as described in **Chapter 4**.
7 Slacken the clips and disconnect the two small bore heater hoses at the rear of the engine.
8 Refer to **Chapter 2** to disconnect the throttle linkage of either the single or twin carburetters.

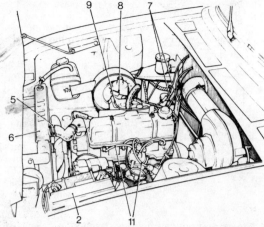

FIG 1:4   Detaching engine connections

Key to Fig 1:4   2 Battery   5 Radiator top hose and expansion tank hose   7 Heater hoses   8 Throttle cable linkage   9 Choke cable   11 Distributor high and low tension leads

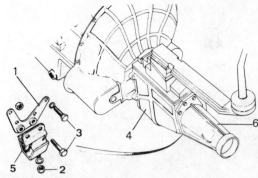

FIG 1:5   Engine rear mountings

Key to Fig 1:5   1 Gearbox attachment bracket   2 Securing nut   3 Bolts   4 Gearbox   5 Engine mounting bracket   6 Gearbox extension

9 Disconnect the choke cable from the securing bracket on the rocker gear cover.

10 Unscrew and remove the three nuts which secure the exhaust pipe to the manifold, collect also the three spring washers and the gasket.

11 Disconnect the high and low-tension leads to the distributor.

12 Remove the nut and spring washer which secure the starter cable to the terminal post and detach the cable. Disconnect the multi-socket connector from the alternator, the oil pressure switch connecting wire, the water temperature transmitting wire and the earth lead from the alternator mounting bracket.

13 Before disconnecting the fuel feed pipe at the petrol pump obtain a plug to block the end of the pipe to prevent the fuel siphoning from the tank and dirt entering the system. A spring-loaded clothes peg clipped to the end of the pipe may suffice. Disconnect the pipe.

14 From underneath the car, uncouple the propeller shaft from the gearbox drive flange. It may be necessary to raise one rear wheel off the ground in order to turn the propeller shaft and move the securing bolts to a more accessible position. Mark the position of the flanges before finally parting.

15 Refer to **Chapter 6** to remove the gearlever from the gearbox extension.

16 Place a small jack under the gearbox extension and interspace with a piece of wood before taking the weight. Refer to **FIG 1:5** and remove the nut 2 which secures the rear engine mounting to the subframe.

17 Remove the nut and bolt which secures the exhaust pipe to its support arm from the gearbox. If necessary refer to **FIG 2:28**.

18 Unscrew the speedometer cable knurled nut from the gearbox extension.

19 Refer to **Chapter 5** for guidance and remove the two bolts which secure the clutch slave cylinder to the gearbox. Move the cylinder away from the gearbox and bring it into the engine compartment.

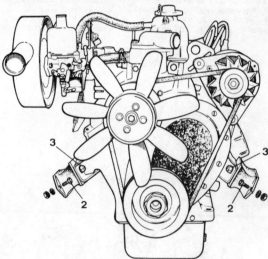

FIG 1:6   Engine front mountings

Key to Fig 1:6   2 Mounting to frame securing bolts   3 Mounting to engine securing nuts

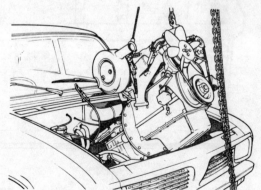

FIG 1:7   Lifting the engine and gearbox out of the frame

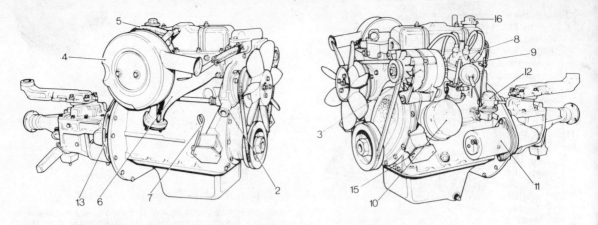

FIGS 1:8 and 1:9   Removing ancillary equipment (necessary when renewing engine only)

Key to Figs 1:8 and 1:9   2 Water pump housing complete with thermostat housing, water pump, fan, pulley and belt
3 Alternator and mounting brackets   4 Air cleaner   5 Carburetter(s) and breather pipe   6 Inlet and exhaust manifolds
7 Dipstick   8 Distributor and HT leads   9 Sparking plugs   10 Oil filter   11 Starter motor   12 Fuel pump   13 Clutch
housing complete with gearbox   15 Engine mounting rubbers   16 Oil filler cap

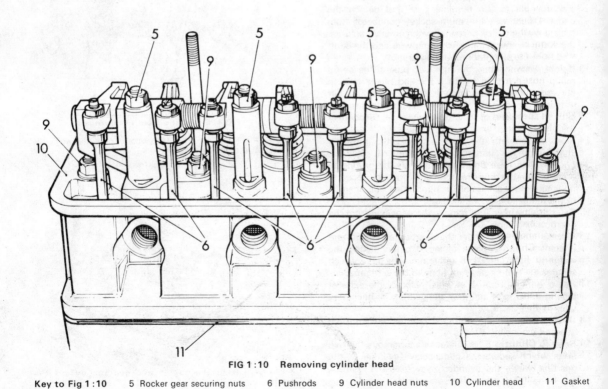

FIG 1:10   Removing cylinder head

Key to Fig 1:10   5 Rocker gear securing nuts   6 Pushrods   9 Cylinder head nuts   10 Cylinder head   11 Gasket

20 Attach the lifting equipment to the engine lifting eyes. Refer to **FIG 1 : 6** and remove the nuts and bolts 2 securing the front engine mounting to the subframe. Lift the engine slightly to clear the rear engine mounting from the subframe and also to raise the sump clear of the subframe. Raise the engine slowly, make checks to ensure all the connections have been detached and manoeuvre the engine and gearbox upwards and out of the frame (see **FIG 1 : 7**).

Refitting the engine and gearbox:

21 Complete the removal operations in the reverse order making sure that pipes and wires are not trapped between the engine and frame. Make sure that all the mountings are secured correctly and the securing nuts and bolts are tightened to the correct torques (see **Technical Data**). Refill the cooling system and engine sump and check the gearbox oil level. After the engine has run for a while, top up the radiator coolant and check for leaks.

Engine renewal:

22 If the engine has been removed for factory reconditioning, the ancilliary equipment will have to be removed. These items are shown and listed in **FIGS 1 : 8** and **1 : 9** but refer to the relevant sections in this manual for guidance when detaching them.

1:3 Removing, refitting the cylinder head

1 Disconnect the terminals from the battery. Drain the cooling system to the instructions given in **Chapter 4.**
2 Remove the carburetter(s) as described in **Chapter 2.**
3 Unscrew and remove the three nuts which secure the exhaust pipe to the manifold, collect also the three spring washers and the gasket.
4 Disconnect the throttle linkage from the induction manifold (single or twin) and clear the linkage and cables away from the cylinder head. Disconnect the servo hose from the inlet manifold, if fitted. Remove the induction and exhaust manifolds and collect the gasket.
5 Pull off the sparking plug connectors and remove the distributor cap. Remove the rocker gear cover and gasket.
6 Refer to **FIG 1 : 10** and unscrew the four nuts 5 to remove the rocker gear, collect the flat washers. Pick up the pushrods 6 and mark their location for the subsequent reassembly.
7 Loosen the clips and disconnect the hoses on the water pump and thermostat housing. Pull off the Lucar connector and wire from the temperature transmitting switch.
8 Refer to **Chapter 4** and remove the fan belt.
9 Refer to **FIG 1 : 11** and unscrew the union nut to release the heater bypass pipe.
10 Refer to **FIG 1 : 12** and remove the three bolts securing the water pump housing to the engine. Push the fuel feed and vacuum pipes clear and detach the water pump housing complete with water pump and fan.
11 Refer to **Chapter 11** and remove the alternator.
12 Refer to **FIG 1 : 10** and slacken and remove the ten cylinder head nuts 9 in the **reverse** order of tightening to the sequence shown in **FIG 1 : 13**.

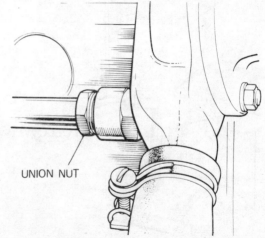

FIG 1 : 11 Heater bypass pipe connection

13 Lift the cylinder head squarely up the studs to remove it. If the head is difficult to free, try tapping on the sides using a wooden block to hammer on. Alternatively, turn the engine by pushing the car in gear and use the cylinder compression to free the head.
14 Take off the cylinder head gasket and scrap it, do not use it again.
15 Refer to **FIG 1 : 14** and lift out the eight cam followers, mark them so that they can be positioned correctly when reassembling.

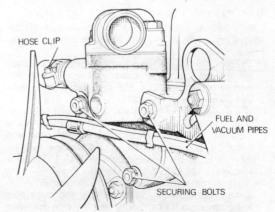

FIG 1 : 12 Removing water pump housing

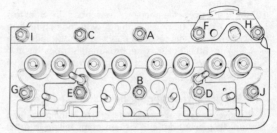

FIG 1 : 13 Cylinder head nut tightening sequence **A** to **J**

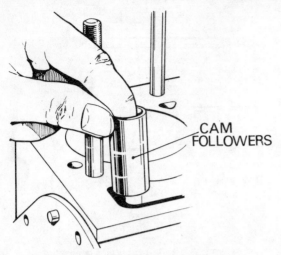

FIG 1:14   Removing cam followers

FIG 1:15   Take out the crosshead screw 1 to free the rear pedestal from the shaft

Refitting cylinder head:

Refitting the cylinder head is the reversal of the removal procedure, with special attention to the following points:

16 Examine the cam followers and renew them if they are chipped, cracked or excessively worn. Refit them in their correct positions and ensure that they rotate and slide freely in their bores.

17 Use a new cylinder head gasket smearing it lightly on both sides with grease to act as an extra seal. Make sure that mating surfaces of the cylinder head and block are scrupulously clean. Tighten the cylinder head nuts, in the order shown in FIG 1:13, to a torque of 38 to 45 lb ft (5 to 6 kg m).

18 Slacken the adjusters on the rocker assembly to prevent them bending the pushrods, and make sure the pushrod ends fit correctly into the cam followers and rocker adjusters. Progressively tighten the four rocker securing nuts to a torque of 26 to 34 lb ft (3.5 to 4.7 kg m).

19 Set the valve clearances as described in **Section 1:16**. After 1000 miles running, with the engine hot, slacken each cylinder head nut in turn in the sequence given in FIG 1:13, by approximately one flat and retighten to the correct torque. Reset the valve clearances.

1:4 Servicing the cylinder head and valve gear

Remove the cylinder head as described in the preceding section. To prevent dirt and carbon chips falling into the engine, block off the oil and water passages with scraps of clean non-fluffy rag. Make sure the pieces are large enough to prevent them falling through or being forgotten when the head is replaced. Scrape the carbon from the combustion chambers before removing the valves, so as to avoid damaging the valve seats or guides. Use a blunt tool to remove the carbon. A rotary wire brush in an electric drill is ideal for cleaning out the inlet and exhaust ports, but take great care not to damage the valve seats or grind away the valve guides. If any abrasive is used in cleaning the cylinder head, make sure that the head is completely dismantled and that all the parts are thoroughly washed in petrol or paraffin so as to remove all particles of abrasive.

Use a long metal straightedge to check that the faces of the cylinder head and block are true and undistorted. Grinding on a surface grinder is the only cure for distortion.

Before cleaning the carbon from the pistons, smear a little grease around the tops of the bores. Turn the engine until one pair of pistons is nearly at TDC and use a soft blunt tool (such as sharpened stick of solder) to scrape away the carbon. Leave the carbon around the periphery of the piston and the tops of the bores as it acts both as an oil seal and as a heat protector for the piston rings. Do not use any abrasive on the pistons as particles may easily remain to work their way into the bores and cause expensive scoring or damage.

Turn the engine to bring the other pair of pistons to TDC. After decarbonizing the pistons the carbon chippings and dust will stick to the grease and the dirty grease can easily be wiped away from the tops of the bores.

1 The rocker assembly is shown in FIG 1:15. The assembly is dismantled by removing the cotterpins at the ends and sliding off the pedestals, springs and

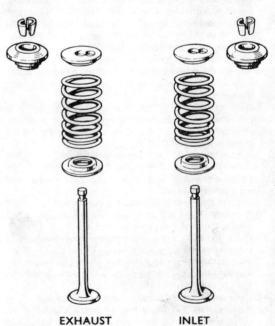

EXHAUST   INLET

FIG 1:16   Exhaust and inlet valve assembly

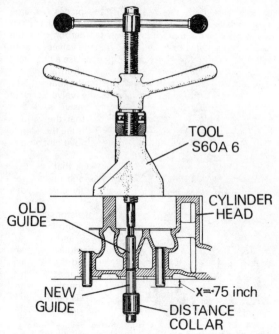

FIG 1:17 Extracting old guide and inserting new guide with tool S60A-6

rockers. The rear pedestal is secured to the shaft by a Phillips-head screw. Clean all the parts in petrol and renew any worn ones. If the working faces of the rockers are slightly worn they may be cleaned up with a fine carborundum stone but any deeper wear necessitates renewal. When reassembling ensure that the parts are replaced in their original positions, and use new cotterpins.

2 The valves are shown in **FIG 1:16**. To remove them, hold the head and compress the spring with a valve spring compressor. Lift out the collets and slowly release the compressor. Mark the valves and store them with their associated parts in the correct order for reassembly.

3 Insert a new valve into each valve guide in turn. Raise the valve slightly and check that the diametric movement on the head does not exceed .020 inch (.508 mm). If this dimension is exceeded then the valve guides are excessively worn and will have to be renewed. **FIG 1:17** shows the method of changing the guides using tool No. S.60A-6 which pulls the new guide in and pushes the old guide out simultaneously. The distance collar ensures that the protrusion **X** is correct at .75 inch (19.05 mm). If the special tool is not obtainable, use a stepped drift, of which the bottom inch fits snugly inside the guide, to drive the guides, chamfered end leading, down into the combustion chamber.

After fitting new valve guides have the valve seats recut to ensure concentricity.

4 Valve stems should show no signs of wear or 'picking up', nor should they be bent. If satisfactory, but the valve seats are excessively pitted, have the seats reground at a garage. Do not attempt to remove deep

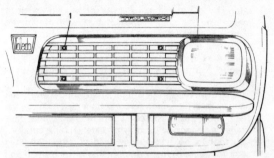

FIG 1:18 Removing lefthand front grille
Key to Fig 1:18   1 Securing nuts

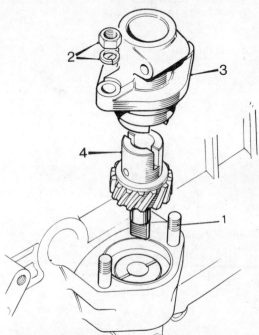

FIG 1:19 Removing distributor pedestal and drive gear
Key to Fig 1:19   1 Studs   2 Nut and washer
3 Pedestal   4 Drive gear

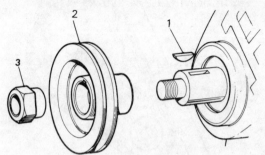

FIG 1:20 Removing crankshaft pulley
Key to Fig 1:20   1 Woodruff key   2 Pulley
3 Securing nut

pitting by using grinding paste as this will only remove metal from the seat in the head as well. Recut the seats in the head if they are badly worn or pitted. If the seats are then too wide they may be reduced by using a 15 deg. facing cutter. Head seats which are beyond recutting can be restored by having inserts fitted.

5 To grind-in valves put a light spring under the head and use medium-grade carborundum paste, unless the seats are in very good condition, in which case fine-grade paste may be used immediately. Use a suction-cup tool to hold the valve head and grind with a semi-rotary movement, letting the valve rise off the seat occasionally by the pressure of the spring under the head. Use the grinding paste sparingly, and when the pitting has been removed, clean away the old paste and transfer to fine-grade paste. When the seats have a matt grey even finish clean away every trace of

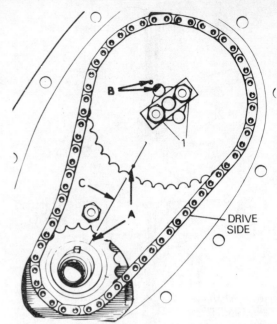

FIG 1 : 23   Aligning the timing marks before removing the sprockets and chain

grinding paste from the valves and ports. If the thickness of the valve head above the ground seat is less than $\frac{1}{32}$ inch (.8 mm) then the valve should be renewed.

6 Check the free length of the valve springs against the dimensions given in Technical Data. Renew the set of valve springs if any are shorter than the dimensions given, as they will all have weakened with service.

7 When reassembling the cylinder head, make sure it is absolutely clean and free from abrasive particles. Lubricate the valve stems and rocker assembly with clean engine oil.

After the cylinder head has been refitted, run the car for approximately 500 miles and then retighten the cylinder head nuts to the correct torque and reset the valve clearances (see **Section 1 : 16**). Tightening the cylinder head nuts will affect the valve clearances so always check the valve clearances after checking the head nuts.

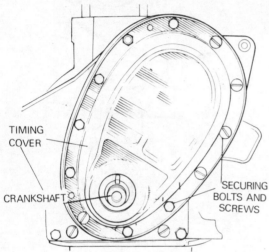

FIG 1 : 21   Removing the timing cover

1 : 5 Removing timing gear and camshaft

1 Disconnect the battery. Drain the coolant and remove the radiator as described in **Chapter 4.**

2 Refer to **FIG 1 : 18** and remove the lefthand front grille. Remove the four nuts 1, extract the bolts and collect the plain washers. Withdraw the grille and rim. On earlier Toledo models the grille and rim are separated, also to remove the grille an additional two rivets must be drilled out.

3 Take off the cylinder head (see **Section 1 : 3**) and remove the cam followers.

4 Remove the distributor as described in **Chapter 3.** Refer to **FIG 1 : 19** and take off the two nuts and washers 2 and lift off the pedestal 3 and gasket. Extract the drive shaft and gear 4.

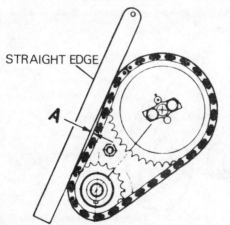

FIG 1 : 22   Checking the timing chain tension with a straightedge

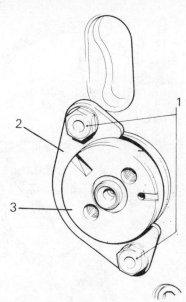

FIG 1:24   Unscrew the two securing nuts to release the camshaft location plate

Key to Fig 1:24   1 Securing nuts   2 Location plate
3 Camshaft

5 Remove the fuel pump as described in **Chapter 2.**

6 Remove the fan belt and fan blades (see **Chapter 4**).

7 Place the car on a ramp or over a pit. Alternatively, jack up the front of the car but make sure it is well supported.

8 Working below the car and referring to **FIG 1:20** unscrew the crankshaft pulley retaining nut 3. Withdraw the pulley. It may be necessary to use an extractor to remove the pulley, if so, loosely replace the nut and use it as a bearing surface for the extractor screw. Remove the Woodruff key 1.

9 Refer to **FIG 1:21** and unscrew the six bolts, five screws and a single nut which secure the cover to the cylinder block. Remove the cover, complete with gasket. Remove the oil thrower off the crankshaft.

10 Refer to **FIG 1:22** and check the chain tension by placing a straightedge along the slack run of the chain. If the slack at point **A** exceeds .4 inch (10 mm) the chain should be renewed.

11 Refer to **FIG 1:23** and turn the engine until the mark **A** is in line with the scribe mark **C**. The marks **B** must also correspond. Bend back the lock tabs and remove the two bolts 1. Slide off both sprockets complete with timing chain.

12 Refer to **FIG 1:24,** unscrew the two bolts 1 and take off the camshaft location plate.

13 Support the front of the engine with a jack, interspaced with a block of wood, and remove the lefthand and righthand front engine mounting bolts (see **FIG 1:6**).

14 Jack up the engine just sufficiently to enable the camshaft to be withdrawn from the engine and through the grille aperture. Be very careful when withdrawing the camshaft to avoid damaging the bearings.

Inspection:

15 Examine the camshaft bearing surfaces for pitting, scoring or wear. Slight score marks can be honed off the cams with a very fine oil stone.

16 Check the crankshaft and camshaft sprocket teeth for wear, if either one is unserviceable renew them as a pair irrespective of the condition of the other. Renew the timing chain also. If new sprockets are obtained they will be unmarked and this will require a complete retiming of the valves and punch-marking the sprockets to correspond (see operations 23 to 26).

17 Check the alignment of the sprockets by referring to the method shown in **FIG 1:25.** Correct any misalignment by fitting selective shims behind the crankshaft sprocket as shown in **FIG 1:26.**

18 Renew the oil seal in the timing chain cover taking care not to damage the cover as the seal is removed.

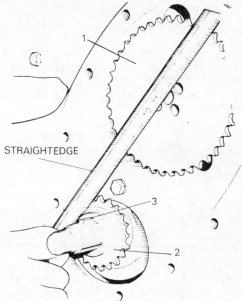

FIG 1:25   Checking the face alignment of sprockets

Key to Fig 1:25   1 Camshaft sprocket   2 Crankshaft sprocket   3 Pulley key

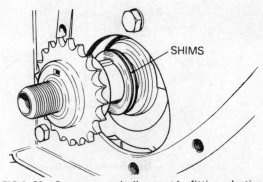

FIG 1:26   Correct any misalignment by fitting selective shims behind the crankshaft sprocket

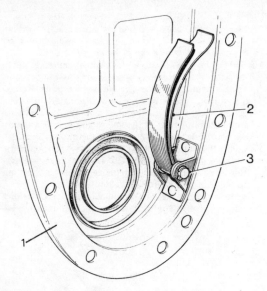

FIG 1:27 To remove the tensioner, prise open the blades and slide them off the anchor pin

Key to Fig 1:27   1 Timing cover   2 Tensioner blades
3 Anchor pin

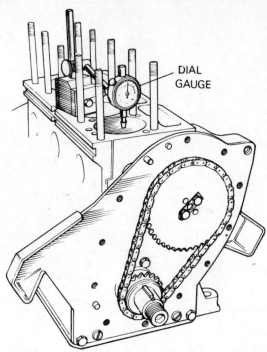

FIG 1:29 Obtaining a true TDC with the help of a dial gauge

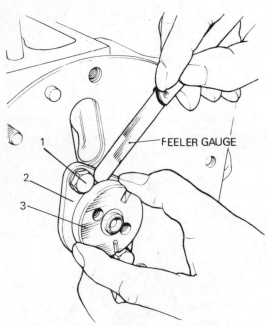

FIG 1:28 Checking camshaft end float

Key to Fig 1:28   1 Securing nuts   2 Location plate
3 Camshaft

FIG 1:30 Use two feeler gauges and move the camshaft to obtain an identical clearance

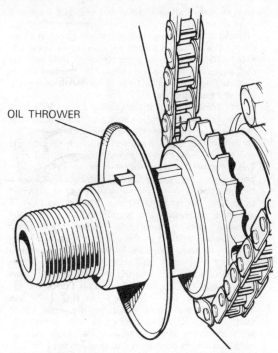

OIL THROWER

FIG 1:31 Fit the oil thrower with its dished periphery facing the timing cover

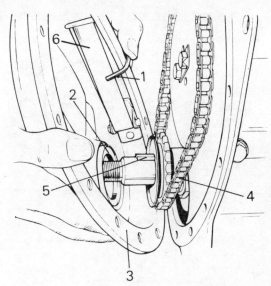

FIG 1:32 Fitting the timing chain cover

Key to Fig 1:32   1 Allen key   2 Oil seal   3 Cover
4 Chain   5 Key   6 Tensioner

Smear the new seal with oil before refitting and locate it inside the cover with the cavity face towards the engine. Ensure that it is pressed into position squarely and fully.

19 If it is necessary to renew the chain tensioner inside the cover, refer to **FIG 1:27**, prise open the blades 2 and slide the tensioner off the anchor pin 3.

Reassembling:

20 Liberally oil the camshaft and carefully insert it into the cylinder block through the front grille. Following this stage the engine jack can be lowered and the engine reclamped into its mountings. Refit the camshaft locating plate.

21 Refer to **FIG 1:28** and check the camshaft end float. Insert a feeler gauge between the locating plate and the inner flange of the sprocket mounting. The end float should be between .0042 and .0085 inch (.110 to .216 mm). If necessary, fit a new location plate to bring the end float within the dimensions.

Retiming the valves:

22 If the engine has been turned, reset it to bring No. 1 piston to TDC. Use a dial gauge to obtain an accurate positioning (see **FIG 1:29**). Do not turn the engine again until the valve timing has been completed.

23 Lubricate the cam followers and replace them in their respective bores. Refer to **Section 1:3** and complete operations 17 and 18 only. Adjust the valve clearances on No. 7 and 8 valves only, to a working clearance of .05 inch (.397 mm) to the method described in **Section 1:16**.

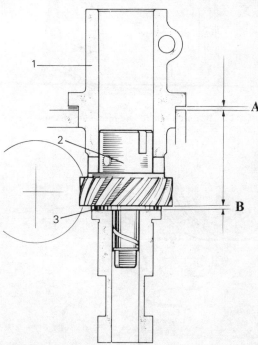

FIG 1:33   Determining the distributor drive gear end float

Key to Fig 1:33   1 Pedestal   2 Drive gear   3 Trial washer   A=End float gap   B=Thickness of trial washer

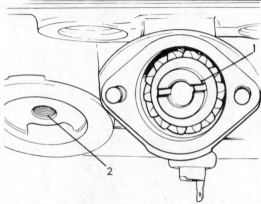

FIG 1 : 34   Aligning the distributor drive gear

Key to Fig 1 : 34   1 Small crescent   2 Thread hole for oil filter

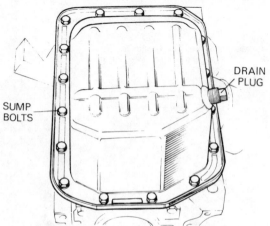

FIG 1 : 35   Draining the oil and removing the sump case

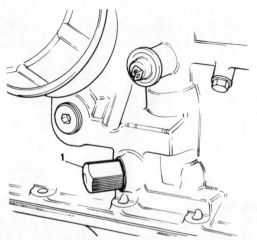

FIG 1 : 36   Location of oil pressure relief valve

24 Turn the camshaft until the valves of 7 and 8 are at a state of equalibrium, that is, the inlet valve 7 is just opening and the exhaust valve 8 is just about to close. Check this by using two feeler gauges as shown in **FIG 1 : 30** and oscillating the camshaft until the two clearances are exactly the same. The position of the camshaft and valves is now in perfect relationship with the crankshaft.

25 Fit the Woodruff key to the crankshaft. Encircle both sprockets with the timing chain and fit the assembly, making sure that the timing marks are aligned as shown in **FIG 1 : 23,** keeping the chain taut on the driving side. Take care not to move the camshaft.

26 The camshaft timing sprocket is provided with four holes which are equally spaced but are offset from a toothed centre. A half-tooth adjustment is obtained by turning the sprocket 90 deg. from its position. A quarter-tooth adjustment is obtained by turning the sprocket 'back to front' and a threequarter-tooth variation by turning it on the bolt locations by 90 deg. in this reverse face position. If new unmarked sprockets are fitted, ensure that the bolt locations line up correctly by adjusting the camshaft sprocket as previously described and ensuring that the chain is taut on the drive side. Refer to **FIG 1 : 23** and lightly mark the timing marks on the sprockets in relation to line **C**. Make a punch mark **B** on the camshaft mounting flange, through the open locating hole, and a light corresponding mark on the camshaft sprocket. Remove the sprockets and make punch marks (**A** and **B**) in the appropriate places. Refit the sprockets as described in operation 25.

27 Fit new locking plates, tighten the two securing bolts and bend over the lock tabs. Refer to **FIG 1 : 31** and fit the oil thrower with the dished periphery facing the timing cover.

28 Fit a new gasket to the timing cover and lubricate the chain with clean engine oil. Refer to **FIG 1 : 32** and hold back the blades of the chain tensioner with an Allen key or a bent stiff piece of wire, slide the timing cover into position and remove the Allen key without damaging the gasket. Secure the cover lightly in position with the securing bolts, screws and the single nut.

29 Examine the sealing face of the crankshaft pulley ensuring that it is not damaged, worn or scored, otherwise oil will leak between the rubbing surface and the seal. Oil the rubbing surface of the pulley and refit it to the crankshaft. Tighten the securing nut to a torque of 120 to 150 lb ft (16.6 to 20.7 kg m). Tighten evenly the timing cover bolts, screws and nut.

Distributor drive shaft and gear:

Before the distributor is fitted the requisite amount of packing must be determined under the distributor pedestal to give the drive gear an end float of .003 to .007 inch. It is not possible to measure the end float directly therefore the following procedure must be adopted.

30 Refer to **FIG 1 : 33** and place a $\frac{1}{2}$ inch (12.7 mm) ID washer 3 under the drive gear. Fit the drive gear and washer and make sure the oil pump drive has mated with the gearshaft. Try the gear in another position and if necessary turn the oil pump drive shaft with a screwdriver.

31 Fit the distributor pedestal over the studs and measure the gap **A** with feeler gauges; between the pedestal and the crankcase flange. Lift out the pedestal and drive gear and measure the thickness of the washer with a micrometer. Subtract the measurement of gap **A** from the thickness of the washer and make a note of the difference.

32 The correct end float is .005 inch (.13 mm) and this is made up with gaskets at the gap **A.** Subtract the measured difference from .005 inch and this is the thickness of gaskets required.
Example:

Thickness of washer	..	..	.100 inch (2.54 mm)
Gap **A** ..	..	..	.098 inch (2.49 mm)
End float	..	..	.002 inch (.05 mm)
Add gasket	..	..	.003 inch (.08 mm)
Correct end float		..	.005 inch (.13 mm)

If the measured gap is greater than the washer thickness, **add** the difference to .005 inch to obtain the correct gasket thickness.

33 Turn the engine until No. 1 piston is at TDC on the **compression** stroke (both valves closed). Lower the drive gear into position, turning it slightly to allow it to mesh with the camshaft gear and the driving dogs of the oil pump drive shaft. The gear is correctly meshed when it is in the position shown in **FIG 1 : 34,** with the smallest crescent 1 of the offset nearest the cylinder block and the slot in line with the thread hole of the oil filter attachment 2.

34 Fit the gaskets and the pedestal, fit the washers and tighten the nuts. Refit the distributor. Engage the drive gear with the brass rotor arm in such a position, as to be adjacent to the No. 1 firing segment if the distributor cap was fitted.

Final assembly:

35 Refit all other parts in the reverse order of dismantling. Adjust the rocker gear clearances by referring to **Section 1 : 16.** Refill the system with coolant. Start the engine and examine for leaks. After about 500 miles, recheck the cylinder head nut torque and the rocker gear clearances.

1 : 6 Removing oil sump

1 Drain the cooling system (see **Chapter 4**) and disconnect the top and bottom hoses to the engine.

2 Position a jack under the gearbox, interspaced with a block of wood, and take the weight of the engine.

3 Refer to **FIG 1 : 6** and remove the four nuts and bolts securing the front engine mountings to the subframe.

4 Refer to **FIG 1 : 35,** remove the drain plug and drain off the sump oil.

5 Remove the sixteen bolts around the sump flange and raise the engine sufficiently so that the sump can be turned approximately 90 deg. and withdrawn.

Refitting:

6 Clean the crankcase and sump flange gasket faces. Smear the crankcase flange with grease and fit a new gasket, align the bolt holes to avoid tearing the gasket.

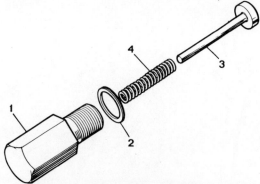

FIG 1 : 37   Components of oil pressure relief valve

Key to Fig 1 : 37   1 Body   2 Washer   3 Plunger
4 Spring

7 Refit the sump, locating the longer bolts at the rear. Tighten them all to a torque of 16 to 20 lb ft (2 to 3 kg m):

8 Replace the remaining parts, remove the jack and refill the engine with oil. Reconnect the hoses and fill with coolant.

1 : 7 Oil pressure relief valve

1 Refer to **FIG 1 : 36** and unscrew the relief valve body 1 from the cylinder block. Take out the plunger and spring and remove the washer. Refer to **FIG 1 : 37.**

2 The free length of the spring 4 should be 1.53 inch (38.8 mm), renew it if it does not measure up to this.

3 Clean the parts in petrol, air dry them and refit.

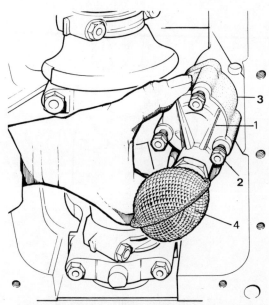

FIG 1 : 38   Removing the oil pump and strainer

Key to Fig 1 : 38   1 Coverplate   2 Securing bolts
3 Oil pump   4 Strainer

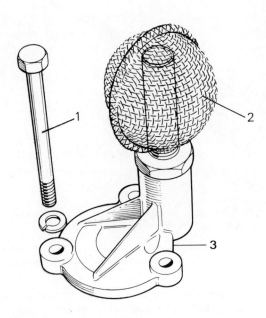

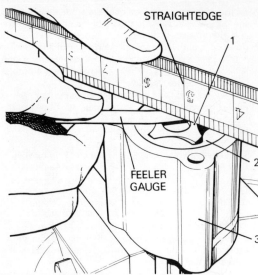

FIG 1:40 Checking the clearance between the rotors and a straightedge

Key to Fig 1:40   1 Inner lobe   2 Outer lobe   3 Body

1:8 Dismantling and reassembling oil pump

1 Remove the sump as described in **Section 1:6.**

2 Refer to **FIG 1:38** and remove the three bolts 2 complete with spring washers. Detach the oil pump and coverplate and unscrew the wire strainer.

3 Refer to **FIG 1:39**, wash all the parts in petrol and dry them off with an air-line.

4 Assemble the parts dry and measure with a feeler gauge the clearance between the inner and outer rotors, the clearance between the outer rotor and the body and the clearance between the rotors and the coverplate. To carry out the latter, place a straightedge across the pump body face as shown in **FIG 1:40**; the straightedge simulates the coverplate. The clearance should not exceed .004 inch (.10 mm). Refer to **FIG 1:41** to measure the clearance between the outer rotor and the inner rotor, this should not exceed .010 inch (.25 mm). Finally, measure the clearance between the outer rotor and the pump body as shown in **FIG 1:42**, this should not exceed .008 inch (.20 mm).

5 Check the coverplate 3 in **FIG 1:39** for wear, score marks or distortion and the drive spindle in the pump body 6 for excessive clearance.

6 Renew any part that does not come within the required specifications, this is important as worn parts will effect the oil pressure and may cause irrepairable damage to the engine. Renew the whole pump if a satisfactory test cannot be achieved.

7 Replace the parts, oiling them liberally with clean engine oil. Ensure that the drive shaft engages correctly in the drive pinion and that the securing bolts are evenly tightened.

8 If possible, get the oil pressure checked at the service garage. For information, the oil pressure warning light goes out when the pressure reaches 3 to 5 lb/sq inch (.21 to .35 kg/sq cm).

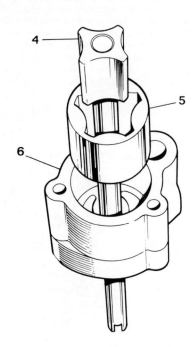

FIG 1:39   Components of oil pump

Key to Fig 1:39   1 Securing bolt   2 Strainer   3 Coverplate   4 Inner rotor and shaft assembly   5 Outer rotor   6 Body

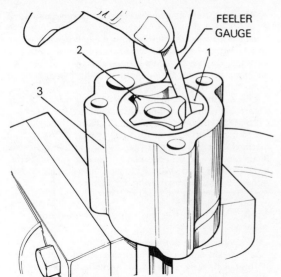

FIG 1:41 Checking the clearance between the inner lobe and outer lobe

Key to Fig 1:41   1 Outer lobe   2 Inner lobe   3 Body

1:9 The clutch and flywheel

Full details on servicing the clutch and its associated parts are given in **Chapter 5.** This Section will only deal with removing and replacing the clutch. If the clutch or flywheel are to be examined while the engine is still in the car then the gearbox will have to be removed, refer to **Chapter 6, Section 6:2.**

1 Turn the engine so that Nos. 1 and 4 pistons are at TDC. This will make it easier to replace the flywheel in the correct position. Progressively slacken the ring of bolts securing the clutch cover to the flywheel. Remove the clutch assembly and driven plate.

2 Remove the four bolts 3 securing the flywheel to the crankshaft (see **FIG 1:43**). Pull the flywheel back to

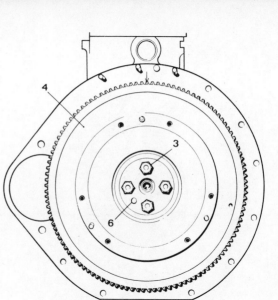

FIG 1:43   Removing flywheel

Key to Fig 1:43   3 Securing bolts   4 Flywheel face
6 Dowel

clear it from the dowel 6. Take care not to drop the flywheel when it comes free.

3 If the face of the flywheel is scored it may be rectified by skimming off in a lathe. No more than .030 inch (.762 mm) of metal may be removed and if the damage is greater than this the flywheel will have to be renewed.

4 If the spigot bush in **FIG 1:44** is worn or shows chatter or fret marks inside it, remove the old bush and press in a new one using zinc oxide grease as a lubricant.

5 The parts are replaced in the reverse order of removal. Before refitting the flywheel, clean off all dirt and particles from the mating faces of the flywheel and

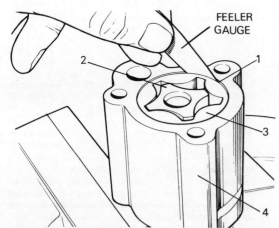

FIG 1:42   Measuring the clearance between the outer rotor and the pump body
Key to Fig 1:42   1 Clearance gap   2 Inner rotor   3 Outer rotor   4 Body

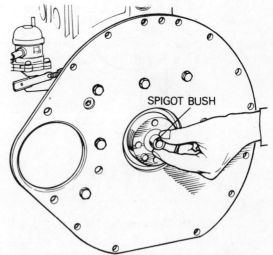

FIG 1:44   Renewing the spigot bush

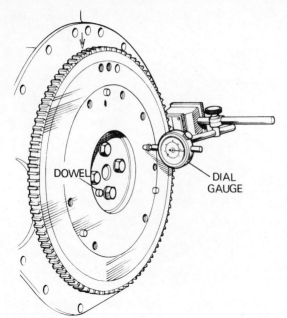

FIG 1 :45 Checking the flywheel runout with a dial gauge

crankshaft. Replace the flywheel and progressively tighten the bolts to pull the flywheel back onto the dowel. Mount a DTI (Dial Test Indicator) on the engine rear plate as shown in **FIG 1 :45** and measure the runout on the flywheel. Keep the crankshaft pressed firmly forwards so that crankshaft end float does not falsify the runout figures for the flywheel. The runout should not exceed .002 inch (.051 mm) at a radius of 3 inches (76.2 mm) from the centre of the spigot bush. Use a mandrel to centralize the driven plate while refitting the clutch.

Starter ring gear:

Because the engine, when switched off, will nearly always stop in the same position due to the compressions, there may be on the flywheel ring gear one place which shows considerable wear, caused by the constant meshing of the starter pinion. Worn ring gear teeth will cause the starter to jam or even spin ineffectually. Lay the

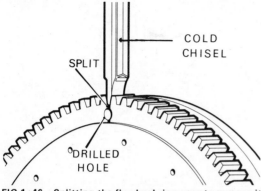

FIG 1 :46 Splitting the flywheel ring gear to remove it

flywheel, clutch face upwards, on three hardwood blocks. Use a drift to drive the ring gear evenly and in small stages from the flywheel. In difficult cases the ring may be weakened by drilling at the root of a tooth and then split open with a cold chisel as shown in **FIG 1 :46** but great care must be taken while using this method to avoid damaging or marking the flywheel.

Use a wire brush to remove all traces of dirt or rust from the flywheel periphery and then lay the flywheel, clutch face downwards, on the hardwood blocks. Heat the ring gear to expand it. It is most implrtant to heat the new ring evenly otherwise it may become distorted. Place the hot ring into position on the flywheel and drive it evenly into place with light taps from a copper drift. Allow it to cool before moving the flywheel.

1 :10 Splitting big-ends, removing rods and pistons

1 Disconnect the battery.
2 Place the car on a ramp or over a pit, if this is not practicable, raise the car on jacks but make sure the car is well supported on stands or blocks.
3 Refer to **Section 1 :3** and remove the cylinder head.
4 Remove the oil sump by referring to **Section 1 :6**.
5 Unscrew the oil strainer from the oil pump (see **FIG 1 :38**).
6 Turn the crankshaft to bring big-ends 1 and 4 into a suitable position for removing the securing bolts. Scrape the ring of carbon from the top of the cylinders, to avoid damaging the piston rings when the pistons are pushed out of the bores.
7 Refer to **FIG 1 :47** and check that the identifying marks 7 are shown on the bearing caps and rods, if not, mark them with light punch marks.
8 Unscrew and remove the connecting rod bolts 8. Take off the bearing caps 9 complete with bolt bushes and collect the bearing shells which may be stuck to the crankshaft.
9 Push the connecting rod and piston upwards and withdraw them, collect the upper bearing halfshell 2. Refit the bearing shells and cap to the connecting rod to ensure they are not mixed with similar parts from the other assemblies. Repeat these operations on the remaining pistons and connecting rods.

Checking crankpins:

10 Examine the crankpins and measure them with a micrometer. If the crankpins are excessively worn, scored, oval or tapered the crankshaft should be removed and reground (see **Section 1 :11**). The minimum permissible diameter is 1.875 inch (47.625 mm).

Cylinder bores:

11 Examine the bores. The maximum point of wear will be near the top of the bore and at right angles to the gudgeon pins. The thickness of the unworn ridge at the top of the bore will give a good guide to the amount of wear that has taken place (see **FIG 1 :48**). If the wear is excessive the liners will have to be rebored to take over-size pistons. If the wear is such that oversize pistons are too small then the cylinders will have to be bored oversize and new dry liners

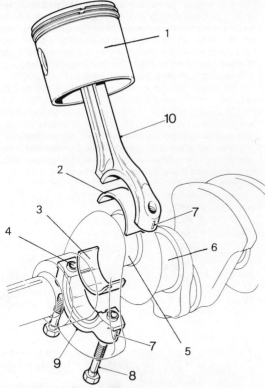

FIG 1:47   Removing piston and connecting rod

Key to Fig 1:47   1 Piston   2 Upper bearing halfshell
3 Lower bearing halfshell   4 Bolt bush   5 Crankpin
6 Main journal   7 Identifying marks   8 Securing bolts
9 Bearing cap   10 Connecting rod

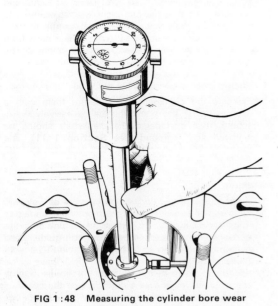

FIG 1:48   Measuring the cylinder bore wear

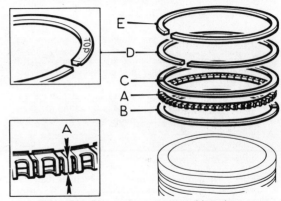

FIG 1:49   Separating piston from connecting rod
Key to Fig 1:49   1 Gudgeon pin bush   2 Circlip
3 Gudgeon pin   4 Halfshell bearings

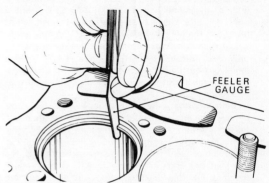

FIG 1:50   Piston rings, types and locations

Key to Fig 1:50   A Expander ring (inset). Make sure the
ends are butting and not overlapping when fitting   B Lower
expander rail   C Upper expander rail   D Scraper ring
E Compression ring

FIG 1:51   Checking the ring gaps in the cylinder bore

fitted. These liners can then be bored to accept standard pistons. This operation should be left to a qualified garage. Refer to **Technical Data** for information on the cylinder bore gradings and sizes.

12 If the wear is not sufficient to warrant reboring, but new piston rings are to be fitted, the unworn ridge around the top of the bore should be removed, using garage equipment. A new unworn top ring will hit this ridge, if it is left, and cause early failure of the ring. At the same time the glaze on the cylinder bore should be removed by light honing, or at least scuffed off with careful use of medium-grade carborundum paper. Removing the glaze will allow the new piston rings to bed in better and more quickly.

Bearing shells:

13 Bearing shells are renewable. If any are pitted, scored or worn, renew the complete set. **Do not file the bearing caps or the connecting rods in an attempt to take up wear,** otherwise the parts will then form an oval hole as well as being unfit for exchange. If new shell bearings are being fitted, they should only be cleaned to remove the protective coating. They do not require scraping or boring to make them fit. If the crankpins have been reground, bearing shells are available in the appropriate undersizes (see **Technical Data**).

Pistons and piston rings:

14 Gudgeon pins are fully floating and can be pushed out of their bores in the piston and connecting rods without much effort. To separate the piston from the connecting rod, refer to **FIG 1:49** and remove the circlip 2 with the special pliers. Push out the gudgeon pin 3, separate the connecting rod and piston and remove the second circlip.

Three rings are fitted to each piston; a plain compression ring at the top, a stepped compression ring in the middle and an oil control ring in the bottom groove. The bottom oil control ring is a three-part ring (see **FIG 1:50**). Lacquering on the sides of the piston indicates that gases are blowing past the piston rings.

A piston ring expanding tool will greatly facilitate removing and replacing the piston rings, but it is not essential. Remove the rings from the top of the piston by sliding a thin piece of metal, such as a discarded feeler gauge, under one end and passing it around the ring, at the same time pressing the raised portion onto the land above. Use three equi-spaced shims to protect the piston when sliding the rings on or off.

Clean carbon from the ring grooves using a piece of broken ring, but taking great care not to remove metal or else the oil consumption will be increased. Carefully clean out the oil drain holes behind the oil control ring.

Before fitting new rings check that the gaps between the ends are correct when the rings are fitted. Fit the ring into the cylinder bore and press it down, using a reversed piston, to about $\frac{1}{4}$ inch from the top of the bore. Use feeler gauges to measure the gap between the ends as shown in **FIG 1:51** and, if required, carefully file the ends until the gaps are correct. Ring gaps are given in **Technical Data**.

The corrugated spacer **A** of the oil control ring is fitted first then the expander ring **B** is slid up the piston and fitted between the bottom edge of the spacer and the bottom side of the ring groove. The other expander ring **C** is similarly fitted, but above the spacer. The second ring **D** is fitted with the narrowest diameter of the taper uppermost, and the marking T or Top also uppermost. The compression ring **E** fits in the top groove.

15 Pistons are graded to their respective bores during manufacture and are identified with a letter **F** or **G** stamped on the piston crown. These letters represent the different sizes of standard bores. The grading and respective sizes of the bores and the pistons are given in **Technical Data**. If new standard pistons are to be fitted it is essential that the correct grade is obtained.

Oversize pistons and rings to fit rebored cylinders are also available.

Connecting rods and gudgeon pins:

16 The gudgeon pin is a thumb push-fit through the small-end bush at 20°C (68°F) room temperature. If the gudgeon pin passes through the bush under its own weight it is too slack and the bush should be renewed. This operation should be carried out by the service garage as the bush must be jig-reamed after fitting. Check the gudgeon pin for wear with a micrometer and to the dimensions given in **Technical Data**.

17 Checking the connecting rods for bend or twist should also be carried out by the service garage. The rods are checked on special fixtures.

Assembling connecting rods and pistons:

18 If a new set of pistons is being fitted, select the lightest piston to fit the heaviest connecting rod, progressively select each piston and connecting rod in turn until finally the heaviest piston will be fitted to the lightest connecting rod. This selection is necessary to ensure that the maximum variation between the set of four assemblies does not exceed 4 drams.

19 The connecting rods are fitted to the pistons in such a way as to position the small arrow, on top of the piston crown, towards the front of the engine. The open face of the offset big-end will face the camshaft side.

20 If the gudgeon pins are tight to assemble, immerse the piston and small-end into a bucket of hot water. Dry off the pistons and fit the rings as described in operation 14. Oil the gudgeon pins and rings with clean engine oil. Stagger the piston ring gaps and avoid positioning a gap on the thrust side of the piston, that is, the camshaft side.

Refitting:

21 Compress the rings into their grooves using a piston ring clamp of the correct size. In an emergency a large jubilee type clip can be used, but it is not easy to manipulate the piston down the bore with this method and care should be taken to avoid damaging the rings.

22 Push the piston down the bore and fit the upper bearing shell, making sure the tag locates properly in its groove. Lubricate the crankpin with clean engine

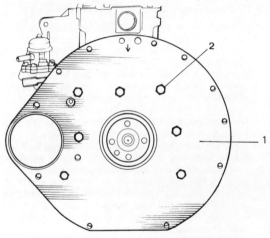

FIG 1 : 52   Removing gearbox adaptor plate

Key to Fig 1 : 52   1 Adaptor plate   2 Securing bolts

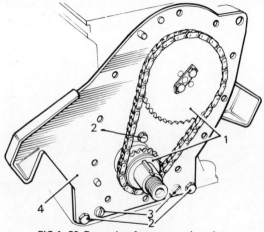

FIG 1 : 53 Removing front mounting plate

Key to Fig 1 : 53   1 Sprockets   2 Securing bolts
3 Securing screws   4 Mounting plate

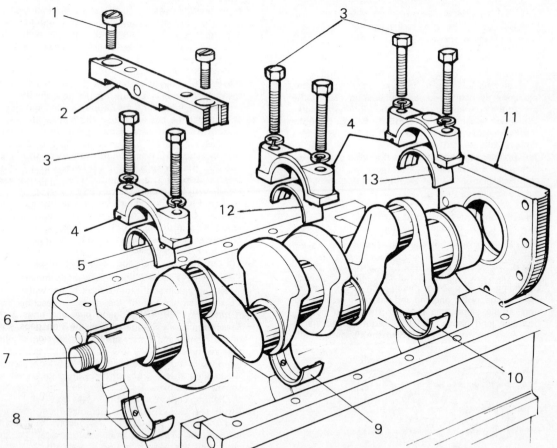

FIG 1 : 54   Crankshaft and main bearing details

Key to Fig 1 : 54   1 Sealing block retaining screws   2 Front sealing block   3 Securing bolts   4 Bearing caps   5 Lower main bearing halfshell (front)   6 Crankcase   7 Crankshaft   8 Upper main bearing halfshell (front)   9 Upper main bearing halfshell (centre)   10 Upper main bearing halfshell (rear)   11 Rear oil seal housing   12 Lower main bearing halfshell (centre)   13 Lower main bearing halfshell (rear)

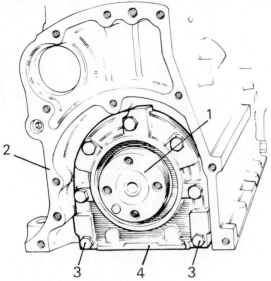

FIG 1:55   Removing rear oil seal housing

Key to Fig 1:55   1 Crankshaft   2 Crankcase
3 Securing bolts   4 Housing

oil and pull the connecting rod onto it. Fit the lower
bearing shell to the cap, make sure the bolt bushes
are correctly positioned, oil the bearing and fit the
cap to the connecting rod with the identifying marks
marks on the same side (see **FIG 1:47**). Fit the bolts
and tighten them to a torque of 38 to 45 lb ft (5 to 6
kg m).

23 Repeat the fitting operations on the other assemblies.
Complete the reassembly by reversing operations
1 to 5. Replenish the sump with clean engine oil and
fill the cooling system.

Renewing big-end bearing shells only:

This operation can be done without removing the
cylinder head. It must be emphasized that after having
uncoupled the big-end, the piston must not be pushed
higher than TDC, otherwise the top piston ring will be
released and spring out on top of the cylinder bore. This
will mean removing the cylinder head to correct it.

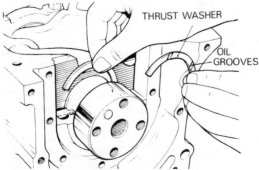

FIG 1:56   Fitting the thrust washers

1:11 Removing crankshaft and main bearings

1 Remove the engine from the car to the method
described in **Section 1:2**.
2 Take off the starter and detach the gearbox assembly,
refer to **Chapter 6** if necessary.
3 Remove the clutch and flywheel (see **Section 1:9**).
4 Refer to **FIG 1:52** to remove the gearbox adaptor
plate. Unscrew and remove the seven bolts 2.
5 Take off the alternator (see **Chapter 10**).
6 Refer to **Chapter 4** to remove the water pump and its
housing, the thermostat housing and the fan.
7 Carry out operations 8 to 12 in **Section 1:5**. It will
not be necessary to align the timing marks in operation 11. Collect the crankshaft sprocket shims.
8 Refer to **FIG 1:53** ignore items which have already
been removed, and remove the three bolts 2. Unscrew
and withdraw the two screws 3 and lift off the
mounting plate 4 complete with mounting rubbers.
Peel off the mounting plate gasket.
9 Lift out the dipstick and remove the sump (see
Section 1:6). Unscrew the oil pump strainer.
10 Refer to **FIG 1:54** and remove the front sealing
block 2.
11 Refer to **FIG 1:55** to remove the crankshaft rear oil
seal. Unscrew the seven bolts 3 and withdraw the
housing 4 complete with oil seal. Press the seal out
of its housing and scrap it, irrespective of its condition.
Clean the housing and press in a new oil seal. Smear
the outside of the seal with grease to assist its entry
into the housing and position it with the lip face
towards the main bearing. Put the housing and seal
on one side, ready for the subsequent reassembly.
12 Disconnect the big-ends from the crankshaft, taking
note of the markings and their position; do not mix
the bearing shells. **Do not push the pistons
beyond the TDC position in the bores otherwise
the top piston ring will be released and spring
out on top of the cylinder bore. The cylinder
heads will have to be removed to correct it.**
13 Refer to **FIG 1:54** and remove the three main bearing
caps 4. Check that the caps are marked for reassembling to the same positions. Remove the upper
and lower bearing shells ensuring that they do not mix
with their counterparts.
14 Lift out the crankshaft and collect the thrust washers
from the rear main bearing.

Cleaning and inspection:

15 Measure with a micrometer, and inspect, the journals
of the crankshaft. If they are excessively worn, oval,
tapered or scored the crankshaft will have to be
reground and undersize bearing shells fitted. Examine
the bearing shells. If any of these are pitted, worn or
scored the whole set should be renewed. Never file
the bearing caps in an attempt to take up wear.
16 Clean the crankshaft with paraffin under pressure
and then blow through all the oilways with compressed air. This is particularly important if the
crankshaft has been reground or a bearing has 'run',
otherwise particles may remain in the oilways and
later be forced into the bearings by the oil pressure.
Clean out the crankcase, and wash the bearing caps
in petrol.

17 Dimensions of the crankpins, main journals and undersize bearings are given in **Technical Data**. Examine the bearings for score marks and wear, renew the shells if either fault renders them suspect. The amount of undersize is marked on the back of the bearing shells. If a reground crankshaft is fitted, the amount of undersize is stamped on the crankshaft webs. Ensure that the bearing sizes correspond with crankpin and journal sizes.

18 During manufacture the bearing caps are assembled to the cylinder block and machine-bored to very fine limits. For this reason alone they must not be interchanged and neither must they be filed or altered in any way. Similarly, standard and undersize bearing shells are pre-finished to precise limits and must not be either filed or scraped.

Checking crankshaft runout:

19 This operation may be more suitable performed at the service garage. Mount the crankshaft end journals on V-blocks which are positioned on a metal platten table or face plate. Position a dial gauge with the stylus on the centre journal, zero the gauge and turn the shaft slowly. Runout should not exceed .003 inch (.076 mm).

Refitting the crankshaft:

20 Lubricate all bearing surfaces with clean engine oil before assembling.

21 Fit the upper bearing shells to the crankcase and the thrust washers to the rear main bearing, the oil grooves in the washers to bear against the crankshaft face, make sure the washers register correctly in the bearing bore (see **FIG 1:56**). Lower the crankshaft onto the bearing shells.

22 Fit the lower bearing shells to the caps, fit the caps and tighten the securing bolts and the rear main bearing nuts to a torque of 50 to 65 lb ft (7 to 9 kg m).

23 Refer to **FIG 1:57** to check the crankshaft end float. Mount a dial gauge to the crankcase so that the stylus rests, in a loaded condition, on a machined surface of the crankshaft throw. With a screwdriver between the centre main bearing cap and the adjacent throw, lever the shaft rearwards as far as it will go and against the dial gauge stylus. Zero the gauge.

24 Lever the crankshaft forwards and note the gauge reading. End float should be between .006 and .014 inch (.1524 and .3556 mm).

25 Adjust the end float, to bring it within these dimensions, by renewing with different thickness of thrust washers.

26 If necessary, instead of using a dial gauge, the end float can be checked with feeler gauges inserted between the thrust washer and crankshaft.

27 Refer to **FIG 1:58**. Smear the front sealing block gaskets with jointing compound, fit the block and secure it only lightly in position, with the two screws.

28 Drive new wedges into the slots and align the face of the sealing block with the crankcase as shown in **FIG 1:59**. Tighten the two screws fully and trim off the protruding edges of the wedges flush with the crankcase. Do not undercut.

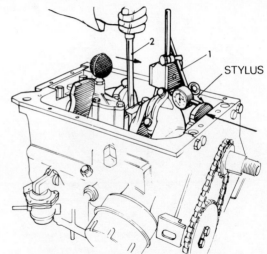

FIG 1:57   Checking the crankshaft end float

Key to Fig 1:57   1 Dial gauge   2 Screwdriver

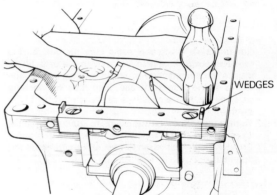

FIG 1:58   Fitting new sealing wedges between the crankcase and sealing block

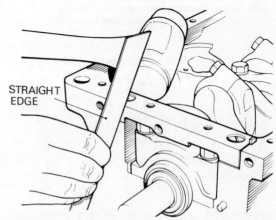

FIG 1:59   Aligning the face of the front sealing block

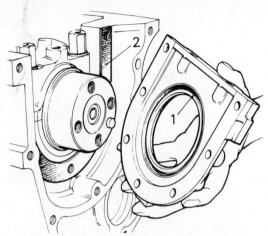

FIG 1:60   Refitting the rear oil seal and housing

Key to Fig 1:60   1 Rear oil seal   2 Gasket

29 Refer to **FIG 1:60** to fit the rear oil seal and housing. If the seal has not yet been renewed, refer to operation 11. Ensure that the crankcase joint face is clean, then apply a smear of jointing compound, fit a new gasket and smear a film of oil over the crankshaft and the edge of the seal.

30 Carefully slide the seal housing over the centralizing tool No. S335. It is essential that this tool is either borrowed or hired from the service garage. Push the tool over the crankshaft and slide the seal housing onto the crankcase joint face as shown in **FIG 1:61**.

31 Leave the tool in position and fit the securing bolts. Tighten them to a torque of 16 to 20 lb ft (2 to 3 kg m). Withdraw the centralizing tool.

32 Complete the final assembly operations by reversing operations 1 to 9 and referring to the relevant sections.

1:12 Renewing a main bearing set

It is possible to renew the main bearings without removing the engine providing the car is over a pit, or supported on ramps or stands sufficiently high enough to allow for a comfortable working area.

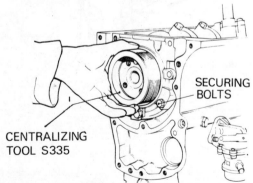

FIG 1:61   Aligning the rear oil seal and housing with special tool S335

The stands must be well placed and secure to afford maximum safety.

1 Refer to **Section 1:6** and remove the sump. Unscrew the oil pump strainer.

2 Complete operations 5 to 8 and operation 10 in **Section 1:11**.

3 The bearing shells can now be removed and renewed. Make sure the locating tags register correctly. Refer to **Section 1:11** for any relevant information and if necessary, to check the crankshaft end float.

1:13 Renewing a crankshaft rear oil seal

Although instructions on changing the rear oil seal were given in **Section 1:11** the whole operation can be done without removing the engine, however, the gearbox must be removed.

1 Refer to **Chapter 6** and take out the gearbox.

2 Remove the flywheel by referring to **Section 1:9**.

3 Refer to **FIG 1:52** and remove the gearbox adaptor plate.

4 Take out the two bolts securing the sump to the rear oil seal housing and then complete operations 11, 29, 30 and 31 in **Section 1:11**.

5 Reassemble the remaining parts and refer to the appropriate Chapters and Sections.

1:14 External oil filter

The external oil filter unit is a sealed assembly and therefore it cannot be dismantled for cleaning. The renewal of the oil filter should be carried out during alternate oil changes, that is, every 12,000 miles (20,000 kilometres).

1 Refer to **FIG 1:62**. Disconnect the battery. Grasp the filter with both hands and turn it anticlockwise until it is released from the crankcase.

2 Clean the crankcase joint face and smear a film of grease on the rubber O-ring gasket to prevent it 'picking up'. Refit the new filter.

3 Reconnect the battery. Fill the sump with oil, refer to **Technical Data** for capacities, start the engine and check for leaks.

1:15 Reassembling a stripped engine

The order for completely dismantling the engine has already been given in the previous section. All dismantling and reassembling operations have been given in detail in the various sections, so it is simply a matter of tackling the task in the correct sequence. **Always fit new gaskets,** which are available in complete kits. Make sure all parts are clean before reassembly, using petrol or paraffin and drying it off with air or non-fluffy rags. Blow through oilways with pressurized paraffin followed by compressed air. Lubricate all running surfaces with clean engine oil. **Cleanliness is essential. Dirt will cause rapid wear and premature failure of the parts.**

Start by refitting the crankshaft, followed by the pistons, connecting rods and big-end bearings. Replace the front and rear engine plates next. If the timing sprockets are marked, refit the camshaft and valve timing gear completely. The oil pump and sump can then be refitted to complete the bottom end of the engine so that it can then be turned the right way up for the remainder of the work. The flywheel and clutch can be fitted next, followed by the cylinder head. Leave accessories such as alternator, oil filter, distributor and carburetters until last as they will only make the engine cumbersome to handle and can easily be damaged if the engine accidentally rolls over. Refit the engine to the car after mating it up with the gearbox. Torque wrench loads for all important fixings are given in **Technical Data.**

Before refitting the engine to the car adjust the valve clearances as described in the following section. The clearances are normally adjusted with the engine in the car, but it will be found easier to turn the engine over by the flywheel. When the engine has been fitted to the car, fill the gearbox and engine with oil and the cooling system with water. Check for leaks as soon as the engine is started.

1:16 Adjusting the valve rocker clearances

As there is no starting handle fitted the engine will have to be turned over by some other method. Remove the sparking plugs and try turning the engine over by pulling the fan belt. If the engine is too stiff for this method, engage a gear and turn the engine either by pushing the car or rotating a jacked-up rear wheel.

1 Remove the rocker cover, **FIG 1 : 63** shows the method of adjusting the valve clearances. All the clearances should be set, with the engine cold, to .010 inch (.254 mm).
2 Check that the working faces of the rockers are not worn. If the face has a pit worn in it the feeler gauge will simply bridge the depression giving a false reading.
3 Each valve must be adjusted when its tappet is on the base of the cam, opposite to the peak. This is readily done by turning the engine and working to the following sequence:
Adjust No. 1 rocker with No. 8 valve fully open.
Adjust No. 3 rocker with No. 6 valve fully open.
Adjust No. 5 rocker with No. 4 valve fully open.
Adjust No. 2 rocker with No. 7 valve fully open.
Adjust No. 8 rocker with No. 1 valve fully open.
Adjust No. 6 rocker with No. 3 valve fully open.
Adjust No. 4 rocker with No. 5 valve fully open.
Adjust No. 7 rocker with No. 2 valve fully open.
Notice that the numbers in each line add up to 9. Remembering this and, as the table is laid out to turn the engine by the minimum amount between each adjustment, it is easy to go on checking without constant reference to the table. The rockers are numbered from the front of the engine. The valve is 'fully open' when its springs are fully compressed.
4 Hold the adjuster with a screwdriver and slacken the locknut with a spanner. Insert a .010 inch feeler gauge between the valve stem and the rocker. Tighten the adjuster with the screwdriver until the rocker lightly grips the feeler gauge. Hold the screwdriver still and tighten the locknut. Check, with the feeler gauge, to ensure that the adjuster has not been turned while tightening the locknut. Turn the engine and repeat this operation on the next valve in sequence.

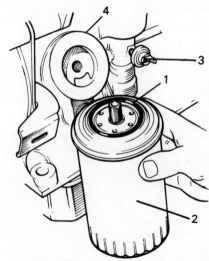

FIG 1 : 62   Renewing the oil filter

Key to Fig 1 : 62   1 Rubber O-ring   2 Filter body
3 Oil pressure sending unit   4 Crankcase joint face

5 Check the cork gasket on the rock cover before replacing the cover. If the gasket is damaged or partially flattened renew it, as if it is left oil leaks will quickly develop. Glue the new gasket to the rocker cover with jointing compound, after removing all traces of the old gasket, and lay the rocker cover on a flat surface with a weight on it while the jointing compound dries. Run the engine and check for oil leaks after fitting the rocker cover. The oil supply to the rocker gear is metered, so allow a few minutes' running before checking for leaks.

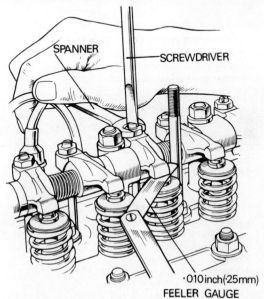

FIG 1 : 63   Adjusting the valve rocker clearances

1:17 Fault diagnosis

(a) Engine will not start

1 Defective coil
2 Faulty distributor capacitor (condenser)
3 Dirty, pitted or incorrectly set ignition contact breaker points
4 Ignition wires loose or insulation faulty
5 Water on sparking plug leads
6 Battery discharged, corrosion on terminals
7 Faulty or jammed starter
8 Sparking plug leads wrongly connected
9 Vapour lock in fuel pipes (hot weather only)
10 Defective fuel pump
11 Overchoking or underchoking
12 Blocked petrol filter (if fitted)
13 Leaking valves
14 Sticking valves
15 Valve timing incorrect
16 Ignition timing incorrect

(b) Engine stalls

1 Check 1, 2, 3, 4, 5, 10, 11, 12, 13 and 14 in (a)
2 Sparking plugs defective or gaps incorrect
3 Retarded ignition
4 Mixture too weak
5 Water in fuel system
6 Petrol tank vent blocked
7 Incorrect valve clearances

(c) Engine idles badly

1 Check 2 and 7 in (b)
2 Air leak at manifold joints
3 Carburetter jet wrongly set
4 Worn piston rings
5 Worn valve stems or guides
6 Weak exhaust valve springs

(d) Engine misfires

1 Check 1, 2, 3, 4, 5, 8, 10, 12, 13, 14, 15 and 16 in (a); and 2, 3, 4 and 7 in (b)
2 Weak or broken valve springs

(e) Engine overheats (see **Chapter 4**)

(f) Compression low

1 Check 14 and 15 in (a); 4 and 5 in (c) and 2 in (d)
2 Worn piston ring grooves
3 Scored or worn cylinder bores

(g) Engine lacks power

1 Check 3, 10, 11, 13, 14, 15, 16 in (a); 1, 2, 3 and 6 in (b); 4 and 5 in (c) and 2 in (d). Also check (e) and (f)
2 Leaking cylinder head gasket
3 Fouled sparking plugs
4 Automatic advance not operating
5 Piston sticking in carburetter

(h) Burnt valves or seats

1 Check 14 and 15 in (a); 6 in (b) and 2 in (d). Also check (f)
2 Excessive carbon around valve head or in cylinder head

(j) Sticking valves

1 Check 2 in (d)
2 Bent valve stem
3 Scored valve stem or guide
4 Incorrect valve clearance
5 Gummy deposits on valve stem

(k) Excessive cylinder wear

1 Check 11 in (a). Also check (f)
2 Lack of oil
3 Dirty oil
4 Piston rings gummed up or broken
5 Badly fitting piston rings
6 Bent connecting rod

(l) Excessive oil consumption

1 Check 4 and 5 in (c) and check (k)
2 Ring gaps too wide
3 Oil return holes in pistons choked with carbon
4 Scored cylinders
5 Oil level too high
6 External oil leaks

(m) Low oil pressure

1 Lack of oil
2 Dirty oil
3 Excessively worn engine
4 Weak relief valve springs
5 Faulty gauge or connections

(n) Crankshaft or connecting rod bearing failure

1 Check 2, 3 and 6 in (k), also check 1, 2, 3 and 4 in (m)
2 Restricted oilways
3 Worn journals or crankpins
4 Loose bearing caps

(o) Internal water leakage (see **Chapter 4**)

(p) Poor water circulation (see **Chapter 4**)

(q) Corrosion (see **Chapter 4**)

(r) High fuel consumption (see **Chapter 2**)

(s) 'Pinking'

1 Too low a grade of fuel
2 Ignition too far advanced
3 Excessive carbon in the cylinder head

(t) Engine 'knocks'

1 Worn big-end bearings
2 Worn main bearing
3 Piston knock (slap)
4 Worn small-ends
5 Incorrectly adjusted rocker clearances

CHAPTER 2

THE FUEL SYSTEM

2:1 Description

All Toledo models are equipped with a mechanically operated fuel pump of the diaphragm type. The 1300 models and the 1500 two-door export models are fitted with a single, sidedraught SU HS4 carburetter whereas the 1500 four-door export models incorporate two SU HS2 sidedraught carburetters.

A combined air cleaner and silencer is fitted over the carburetter intake bore and depending on the model, the replaceable paper filter elements will be either a single or twin. The elements should be cleaned every 6000 miles (10,000 kilometres) and renewed every 12,000 miles (20,000 kilometres). Servicing details are given in **Section 2:13**.

Instructions are given in the Chapter on how to service the fuel pump and carburetter(s). The actual details given relate to a complete strip-down of the carburetter(s), however, by following the instructions under the various headings, individual items can be removed from the carburetter and serviced. In most instances without removing the carburetter from the engine.

The instructions on tuning the carburetter(s) are given on the understanding that all other working parts of the engine are in good condition. It is almost impossible to obtain a fine tuning if the engine is badly worn and the ignition and valve timings are out of phase. These culminating defects result in a very erratic and 'lumpy' running engine. Even if the engine is worn, at least check and adjust the contact breaker points, sparking plugs, ignition timing and valve rocker clearances beforehand.

2:2 The mechanical fuel pump

The mechanical fuel pump is situated on the lefthand side of the engine, directly above the starter (see **FIG 1:9**). There are two types, and only one type may be dismantled, this type is illustrated in **FIG 2:1**, the other type, if defective, must be renewed. The filters on both types are cleaned in a similar manner.

At approximately every 12,000 miles (20,000 kilometres) the filter should be removed and cleaned. Referring to **FIG 2:1** access to the filter is gained by unscrewing the cover retaining screw 1 and lifting off the domed cover 2. Remove the sealing ring 3 and take off the filter 4. Soak up any excess fuel in the filter bowl with a **lint-free** cloth. Wash the filter in petrol and with a compressed air-line, a foot pump air-line is ideal, blow compressed air through the filter and into the filter bowl to clear any sediment. Take care not to damage the non-return valves during the process.

Reassemble the parts in the reverse order of removal. If the gasket 3 has hardened or it is broken, renew it. Fit the filter with the gauze face downwards; it is more easily removed from its location when fitted this way.

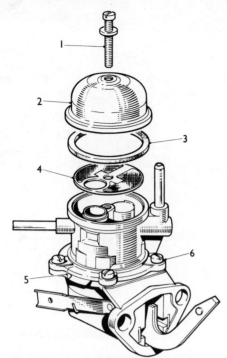

FIG 2:1   Petrol pump components

Key to Fig 2:1   1 Screw   **2** Cover   **3** Gasket   **4** Filter
5 Re-locating marks   **6** Body screws

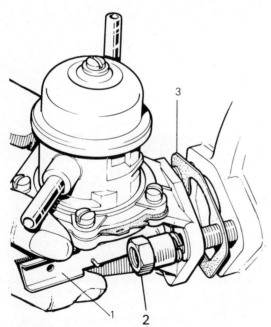

FIG 2:2   Removing petrol pump from engine

Key to Fig 2:2   1 Hand priming lever   **2** Special
mounting nut   **3** Gasket

Removing the fuel pump:

1 Pull the two flexible pipes off the pump and plug the pipes and pump openings to prevent dirt entering.
2 Refer to **FIG 2:2** and unscrew one plain and one special mounting nut 2 securing the pump to the cylinder block. Withdraw the pump and gasket off the mounting studs.

Dismantling:

3 Remove the filter, referring to **FIG 2:1** if necessary.
4 Scribe a line across the mating flange of the upper and lower pump bodies; this is to ensure they are refitted in the same position. Unscrew the five screws 6, collect the spring washers, then separate the body halves.
5 Similarly, mark the relative position of the pump diaphragm before removing it. Turn the diaphragm through 90 deg., either way, and lift it to unhook it from the pump lever operating fork. Take off the diaphragm spring.
6 Refer to **FIG 2:3** and prise the valves out of their seating with a screwdriver, bearing in mind that having done so the valves will have to be renewed, due to the inevitable mutilation.

Inspecting:

7 Examine the parts for wear or damage and particularly the diaphragm for deterioration, renew all gaskets. Clean the parts with petrol and blow through the passages with compressed air.

Reassembling:

8 Fit the new valves in the lower body by pressing them into their seatings with a utility tool made from a piece of tubing $\frac{3}{4}$ inch (19.05 mm) OD x $\frac{9}{16}$ inch (14.28 mm) ID. Refer to **FIG 2:4** and set the inlet valve with its raised side face towards the diaphragm, note its relative position to the induction pipe. Set the outlet valve with its concave face towards the diaphragm.
9 Using a centre punch, stake the valves in about six places to prevent them from coming out.
10 Reverse operations 1 to 5 to complete the reassembly but leave the outlet pipe to the carburetter disconnected.

Testing:

11 Use the hand priming lever and pump the fuel from the tank. A well defined spurt of fuel should be ejected from the pump outlet pipe.
12 A more positive test would be to connect a T-piece complete with flexible tubing between the outlet extension of the pump and the inlet extension of the carburetter. Install a pressure gauge, start the engine and note the reading. The pressure should be between 2.5 and 3.5 lb/sq inch (.176 and .246 kg/sq cm). If the pressure is too high, it may be reduced by fitting an extra gasket between the pump and the cylinder block.

2:3 Operation of SU carburetter

The bore through the body is fitted with the usual butterfly valve. On the air intake side of this valve is a variable choke aperture formed by a piston rising and

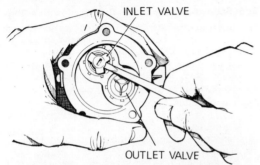

FIG 2:3   Removing the one-way valves

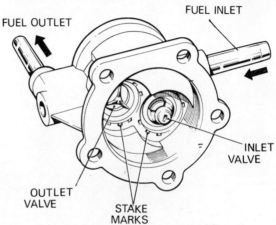

FIG 2:4   Fitting the one-way valves

falling inside a top chamber. This action is automatic, depending on the depression in the intake system arising from the amount of throttle opening and the load on the engine. The varying volume of air will need a varying flow of fuel to give the correct mixture throughout. This is done by using a tapered needle attached to the piston and the needle rises and falls in a fixed size of jet aperture. The smallest diameter of the needle is in the jet aperture when the piston is at the top of its travel and the flow of fuel is then at its greatest. Rapid fluctuations of the piston are damped out by a hydraulic damper, the fluid being contained in oil well. Rich mixture for starting is obtained by pulling down the jet to a smaller diameter of the needle. A spring is fitted to assist gravity to return the piston.

2:4 Removing and refitting carburetter(s)

Single carburetter:

1 Remove the air cleaner as described in **Section 2:13**.
2 Refer to **FIG 2:5** and pull off the engine breather pipe 1, the vacuum advance pipe 2 and the fuel feed pipe 3.
3 Disconnect the throttle link rod 4 at its lower connection. Disconnect the choke cable 5 and take off the throttle return spring.
4 Unscrew the two nuts 6 which secure the carburetter to the inlet manifold; the lower nut also secures the return-spring bracket. Collect the spring washers.
5 Lift the carburetter off the manifold and remove the gasket 7.

Refitting:

6 Fit a new gasket and reverse operations 1 to 5.

Twin carburetters:

1 Remove the air cleaners as described in **Section 2:13**.
2 Refer to **FIG 2:6** and pull the flexible hoses from the breather pipes 1 on the carburetters. Disconnect the choke cable at the trunnion 2 and the link rod 3 between the cable linkage 4 and the interconnection shaft 5. Unhook the throttle return springs 6.
3 Disconnect the vacuum advance pipe and the fuel feed pipe at the connection 7.

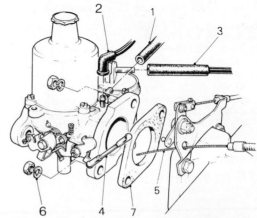

FIG 2:5   Removing single carburetter from engine
Key to Fig 2:5   1 Breather pipe   2 Vacuum advance pipe   3 Fuel feed pipe   4 Link rod   5 Choke cable   6 Mounting nuts   7 Gasket

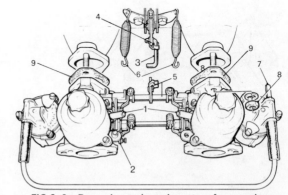

FIG 2:6   Removing twin carburetters from engine
Key to Fig 2:6   1 Breather pipe ducts   2 Trunnion and screw   3 Link rod   4 Fulcrum plate   5 Link and interconnection shaft   6 Springs   7 Fuel pipe connector   8 Mounting nuts   9 Gasket

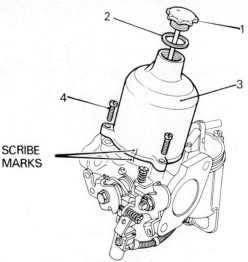

SCRIBE MARKS

FIG 2:7   Removing suction chamber

Key to Fig 2:7   1 Damper rod   2 Washer   3 Suction chamber   4 Securing screws

4 Unscrew the four nuts 8 (two for each mounting flange) which secure the carburetters to the inlet manifold.

5 Carefully lift the carburetters off the manifold without twisting or straining the interconnecting shafts. Remove the gaskets 9.

Refitting:

6 Fit new gaskets and reverse operations 1 to 5.

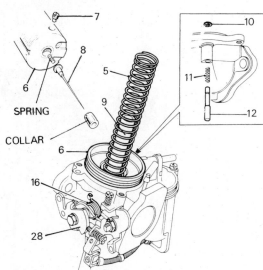

SPRING

COLLAR

FIG 2:8   Removing piston assembly and lifting pin

Key to Fig 2:8   5 Spring   6 Piston   7 Locking screw
8 Jet needle   9 Piston rod   10 Circlip   11 Spring
12 Lifting pin   16 Return spring   28 Fast idle cam

2:5   SU carburetter dismantling and reassembling

(a)   Suction chamber (see **FIGS 2:7** and **2:8**):

1 Remove the carburetter(s) from the engine and clean the outside of the carburetter(s).

2 Mark the relative positions of the suction chamber and the carburetter body to facilitate reassembly.

3 Remove the damper 1 and its washer 2. Empty the damper oil from the piston.

4 Unscrew retaining screws 4 and lift off the chamber 3 without tilting it.

5 Remove the piston spring 5 and carefully lift out the piston assembly 6.

6 Remove the needle locking screw 7 and withdraw the needle 8. If it cannot be easily removed, tap the needle inwards first and then pull outwards. Do not bend or scratch the needle.

7 Remove the retaining circlip 10 and spring 11, then push the lifting pin 12 upwards to remove it from its guide.

(b)   Jet linkage and assembly (see **FiGS 2:9** and **2:10**):

8 Support the moulded base of the jet assembly 13 and slacken the screw 14 retaining the jet pickup link 15.

9 Relieve the tension of the pickup lever return spring 16 from its retaining lug and remove the screw 14.

10 Unscrew the brass sleeve nut 17 retaining the flexible jet tube 18 to the float chamber and withdraw the jet assembly from the carburetter body. Note the gland 19, washer 20 and ferrule 21 at the end of the jet tube.

11 Remove the jet adjusting nut 22 and spring 23. Unscrew the jet locking nut 24 and detach the nut and jet bearing 25. Withdraw the bearing from the nut.

12 Observe the location points of the two ends of the pickup lever return springs 16 and 29, unscrew the lever pivot bolt 26 together with its spacer 27. Detach the lever assembly 28 and return springs 16 and 29, but note the positions of the pivot bolt tubes 30 and and skid washer 31.

(c)   Float chamber assembly (see **FIG 2:11**):

13 Slacken and remove the bolt 32 retaining the float chamber to the carburetter body.

14 Mark the location of the float chamber lid 33. Detach the lid 34 and its gasket 35 complete with float assembly.

15 Push out the float hinge pin 36 from the end opposite its serrations and detach the float 37.

16 Extract the float needle 38 from its seating and unscrew the seating 39 from the lid, using a box spanner. Do not distort the seating.

(d)   Throttle disc assembly (see **FIG 2:12**):

17 Close the throttle and mark the relative positions of the throttle disc 40 and the carburetter flange (see marks in inset). Do not mark the disc near the limit valve 41 (twin carburetters only).

18 Unscrew the two disc retaining screws 42. Open the throttle and ease out the disc 40 from its slot in the throttle spindle 44.

19 Tap back the tabwasher 45 securing the spindle nut 46. Note the location of the lever arm 47 in relation to the spindle and carburetter body. Remove the nut 46, detach the tabwasher 45, lever 47 and washer 48, withdraw the spindle 44.

Inspecting:

20 Examine the components for general wear and possible damage. Check the throttle spindle in the body for excessive play and renew if necessary. Examine the float needle for small ridges or grooves in the seat, these defects may be difficult to see with the naked eye, so use a magnifying glass. Check that the spring-loaded plunger in the needle operates freely. Renew the needle and valve as an assembly not as individual items. Renew the throttle disc retaining screws and all gaskets and seals whatever the condition. Renew also the jet needle retaining screw 7.

Reassembling:

(a) Throttle disc assembly (see FIG 2:12):

21 Refit the spindle 44 to the body and align it so that the countersunk holes face outwards. Assemble the washer 48, lever 47, tabwasher 45 and nut 46. Align the spindle in what would be the closed position if the valve were fitted, ensure the idling stop on the lever is against the idling screw abutment on the body. Tighten the spindle nut and lock it with the tabwasher.

22 Fit the throttle disc 40 into the spindle, to the previously made location marks. The limit valve 41 on the twin carburetters is positioned at the bottom half of the disc with the head of the valve towards the engine. Centralize the disc and snap the throttle open and closed to align it in the bore. Fit the new screws 42, but do not tighten them fully until another check has been made on the disc alignment. If this is satisfactory tighten the screws and open the split ends very slightly, just enough to prevent them turning.

(b) Float chamber assembly (see FIG 2:11):

23 Fit the float needle valve seating 39 into the cover and avoid overtightening. Insert the needle 38 cone-end first. Locate the float 37 insert the hinge pin 36. To check the position of the float refer to **FIG 2:13**. Hold the lid assembly upside down and place a $\frac{1}{8}$ inch round bar across the centre of the lid as shown. Keep it parallel with the float lever hinge pin. The face of the float lever should just rest on the bar when the needle is on its seating. If this is not so, carefully set the lever at point C. Do not curve the lever itself.

24 Fit the new gasket 35 to the cover 34 and refit the cover to the previous markings. Tighten the screws evenly.

25 Fit the chamber to the carburetter body, fit the distance piece between them and secure with the bolt 32 and washers.

(c) Suction chamber (see FIGS 2:7 and 2:8):

26 Refit the piston lifting pin 12, spring 11 and circlip 10. Clean with petrol and examine the surfaces of the piston rod for damage. Lightly oil the outside of the piston rod.

PISTON KEY

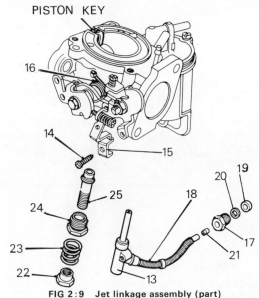

FIG 2:9   Jet linkage assembly (part)

Key to Fig 2:9   13 Jet assembly   14 Retaining screw
15 Pickup link   16 Return spring   17 Sleeve nut   18 Jet tube   19 Gland   20 Washer   21 Ferrule   22 Adjusting nut
23 Spring   24 Locking nut   25 Jet bearing

Similarly clean the inside of the suction chamber and piston rod guide. Refit the damper assembly 1 and washer 2. Seal the transfer holes in the piston assembly with rubber plugs or corks and fit the piston to the suction chamber as shown in **FIG 2:14**. Turn the assembly upside down, hold the piston and check the time, in seconds, for the suction chamber to fall the full extent of its travel. This should take 5 to 7 seconds. If it takes longer, the cause is likely to be

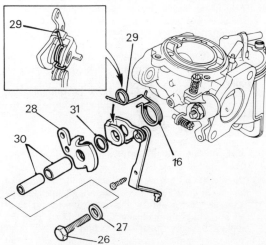

FIG 2:10   Jet linkage assembly (part)

Key to Fig 2:10   16 Return spring   26 Pivot bolt
27 Washer   28 Fast idling cam   29 Return spring
30 Pivot bolt tubes   31 Skid washer

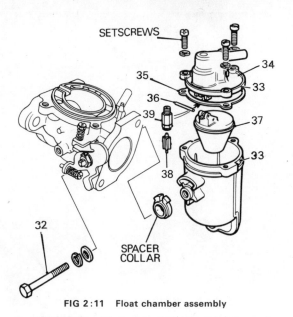

FIG 2:11 Float chamber assembly

SETSCREWS

34
35
36
39
37
33
38
32
SPACER COLLAR
33

Key to Fig 2:11 32 Retaining bolt 33 Relocating marks
34 Cover 35 Gasket 36 Hinge pin 37 Float 38 Float
needle 39 Seating

FIG 2:12 Throttle disc assembly

44
48
47
45 43
42
40
46

LOCATION MARKS
44
41

Key to Fig 2:12 40 Throttle disc 41 Limit valve
42 Split-end screws 43 Idling screw 44 Spindle
45 Tabwasher 46 Nut 47 Fast idling cam 48 Washer

thick oil on the piston rod, or an oil film on the piston or inside the suction chamber. Remove the oil and recheck.

If the time is still not within limits, renew the suction chamber and piston assembly.

27 Refer to **FIG 2:15** and fit the spring and guide to the needle and insert the assembly into the piston. Make sure the lower face of the guide is flush with the face of the piston and the etched locating mark is adjacent to and in line with the centre line between the two piston transfer holes. Fit and tighten the new locking screw 7.

Alternative needle guides may be fitted which have a flat machined on the guide. These guides must be positioned so that the screw tightens down on the flat. Incorrect positioning will allow the guide face to remain proud of the piston, resulting in damage to the piston bore.

(d) Jet linkage and assembly (see **FIGS 2:9** and **2:10**):

28 Check that the piston key is secure in the body of the carburetter. Fit the jet bearing 25 and loosely fit the jet locking nut 24. Do not fit the spring 23 at this stage but fit the adjusting nut 22. Make sure the bearing 25 can be turned with the fingers.

29 Pick up the suction chamber, fit the spring and piston assembly and remove the damper rod 1 if it is fitted.

30 Fit the suction chamber and piston assembly on the carburetter body to the original location marks, and tighten the four screws evenly and securely.

Jet centralizing:

31 Press down on the piston and push the jet tube up as far as it will go. Ensure that the piston is bearing on the jet bridge, check this by looking through the air intake bore. Continue to press the piston down and the jet tube up and tighten the jet bearing locking nut 24.

32 To check the jet needle centralizing, lift the piston and let it fall back freely onto the jet bridge. Confirm this by looking through the air intake bore and listening for a soft metallic click as the piston contacts the bridge. Lower the jet assembly 13 and repeat the test. If the sound of the impact is sharper this will mean the needle was probably catching the jet tube before it was lowered. Repeat the centring operation until the tests are successful, then refit the spring 23.

33 When refitting the jet adjusting nut 22, screw it down two complete turns only (12 flats). This is to provide a jet setting so that the engine can be started and a finer adjustment can then be accomplished.

34 Refer to operation 12 and fit the operation levers, springs and tubes. Make sure the two ends of the return springs are positioned correctly.

35 Fit the brass sleeve nut 17, ferrule 21, washer 20 and gland 19 to the flexible tube 13. Note, when assembling, the end of the tube must protrude a minimum of $\frac{3}{16}$ inch (4.8 mm) beyond the gland 19. Tighten the sleeve nut until the gland is compressed. Do not overtighten.

36 Hold up the choke lever to relieve the pressure on the jet pick-up link 15, refit the link bracket (if used), support the moulded base of the jet and tighten the securing screw 14.

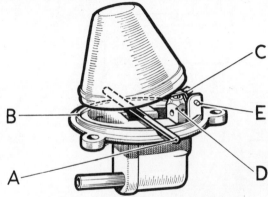

FIG 2:13 Checking and adjusting float lever

Key to Fig 2:13   A $\frac{1}{8}$ to $\frac{3}{16}$ inch (3 to 5 mm) diameter bar
B Machined lip   **C** Float lever resetting point   **D** Needle
valve assembly   **E** Hinge pin

37 Refit the carburetter(s) to the manifold (see **Section 2:4**). Allow $\frac{1}{16}$ inch (1.6 mm) free movement in the choke cable before the linkage moves the cam. Tune the carburetter(s) as described in the next section.

2:6 Tuning the carburetter(s)

1 Check and top up the piston damper(s) with 20W50 engine oil until the level is $\frac{1}{2}$ inch (13 mm) above the top of the hollow piston rod.
2 Check the throttle linkages for any signs of sticking and ensure that the choke cable has $\frac{1}{16}$ inch (1.6 mm) free movement.
3 Remove the air cleaner (twin carburetters only).
4 Connect a tachometer to the engine.
5 Start the engine and run it until it has reached a normal working temperature, then run it for a full minute at 2500 rev/min. It will be necessary to run the engine at this speed, for the same period, as often as possible during the tuning up process.

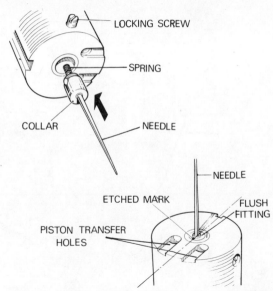

FIG 2:15 Fitting the jet needle, guide and spring

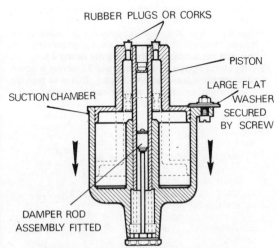

FIG 2:14 Checking the rate of piston drop

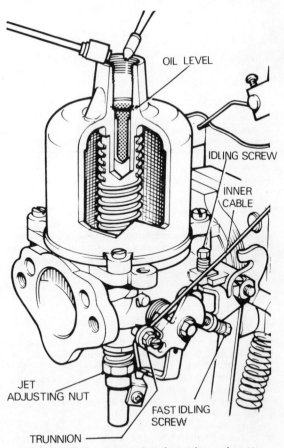

FIG 2:16 Adjustment points for tuning carburetter

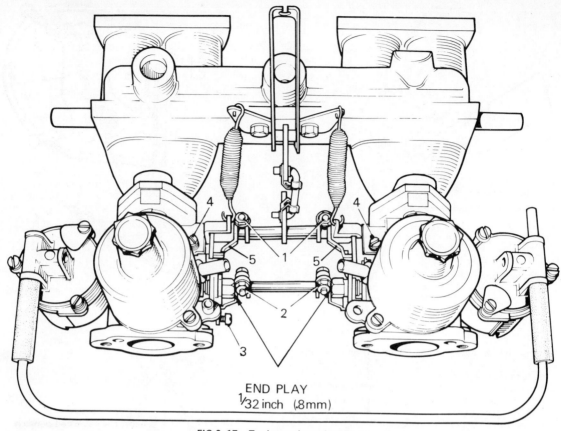

END PLAY
1/32 inch (.8mm)

FIG 2:17 Tuning twin carburetters

Key to Fig 2:17   1 Throttle shaft clamping nuts   2 Jet control shaft clamping nuts   3 Choke cable trunnion and screw
4 Idling screw   5 Clamp lever forks

Single carburetter:

6 Check the idling speed with the tachometer, which should be between 700 and 750 rev/min. If this is incorrect adjust the idling screw (refer to **FIG 2:16**) clockwise to increase the speed and anticlockwise to decrease it. Should the engine not run smoothly at this speed, switch off and make sure the piston is not sticking in the suction chamber, by raising the lifting pin and allowing the piston to fall freely. A free and uninterrupted fall should be discerned by a soft metallic click, as the piston contacts the jet bridge. If it does not fall freely, rectify the fault by referring to the previous section.

7 Restart the engine and turn the jet adjusting nut up or down, one flat at a time, until the fastest engine speed is achieved. Keep a constant watch on the tachometer whilst doing this and ensure that the highest speed is consistent with a smooth running.

8 Recheck the idling speed and adjust, if necessary, to between 700 and 750 rev/min.

9 Stop the engine. Pull the choke knob out approximately ½ inch (13 mm). At this point the control cable and linkage will have all the slack taken up and just about to lower the jet tube. Get a second operator to help with this check, to ensure the cable tension is correct and the jet tube is not moved too far into the enriching position.

10 Restart the engine and adjust the fast idling screw to obtain a fast-idle speed of between 1100 and 1300 rev/min. Push in the choke knob and recheck the normal idle speed.

11 Disconnect the tachometer.

Twin carburetters:

6a Stop the engine and check that each piston falls freely in the jet bridge as described for the single carburetter. Restart the engine and check the idling speed, which should be between 700 and 800 rev/min. If this is not correct, or even if it is correct but the engine does not run smoothly refer to **FIG 2:17** and proceed as follows:

7a Slacken both clamp nuts 1 on the throttle interconnection shaft and the clamp nuts 2 on the jet control shaft. Slacken also, the trunnion screw 3 which secures the choke control cable.

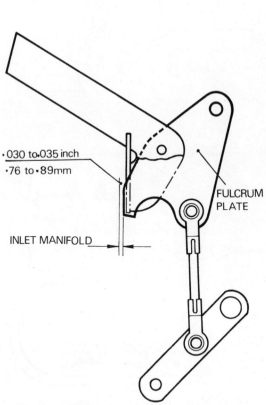

·030 to·035 inch
·76 to·89mm

INLET MANIFOLD

FULCRUM PLATE

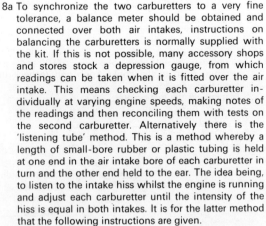

FIG 2:18   Adjusting the throttle clearance (twin carburetters)

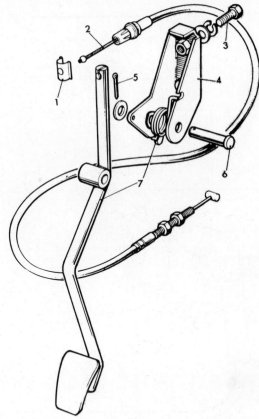

FIG 2:19   Throttle pedal and cable components

Key to Fig 2:19   1 Retaining clip   2 Inner cable
3 Securing bolt   4 Pedal bracket   5 Splitpin   6 Clevis pin
7 Return spring

8a To synchronize the two carburetters to a very fine tolerance, a balance meter should be obtained and connected over both air intakes, instructions on balancing the carburetters is normally supplied with the kit. If this is not possible, many accessory shops and stores stock a depression gauge, from which readings can be taken when it is fitted over the air intake. This means checking each carburetter individually at varying engine speeds, making notes of the readings and then reconciling them with tests on the second carburetter. Alternatively there is the 'listening tube' method. This is a method whereby a length of small-bore rubber or plastic tubing is held at one end in the air intake bore of each carburetter in turn and the other end held to the ear. The idea being, to listen to the intake hiss whilst the engine is running and adjust each carburetter until the intensity of the hiss is equal in both intakes. It is for the latter method that the following instructions are given.

9a Start the engine, ensure it is at normal working temperature and hold the tube as described. Turn the throttle adjusting screw 4 on each carburetter, alternating with the listening tube, until the intensity of

the hiss is equal in both carburetters with a correct idling speed of between 700 and 800 rev/min. If the correct idling speed is obtained and it is constant and smooth go to operation 12a. If the idling is still erratic, stop the engine and refer to FIG 2:16.

10a Screw up fully the jet adjusting nuts then turn each of them down two complete turns (12 flats). Restart the engine and working each adjusting nut exactly the same amount, turn them one flat at a time, up or down until the fastest engine speed is obtained and

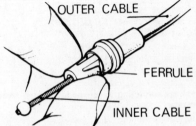

OUTER CABLE

FERRULE

INNER CABLE

FIG 2:20   Squeeze the ears of the ferrule to push the cable through the bulkhead grommet

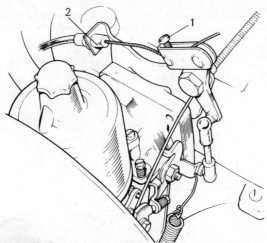

FIG 2:21 Removing the throttle cable from the single carburetter

Key to Fig 2:21   1 Pinch screw   2 Ferrule

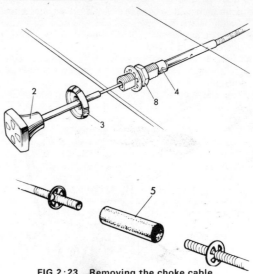

FIG 2:23   Removing the choke cable

Key to Fig 2:23   2 Choke knob   3 Ferrule   4 Outer cable   5 Connector   8 Locknut

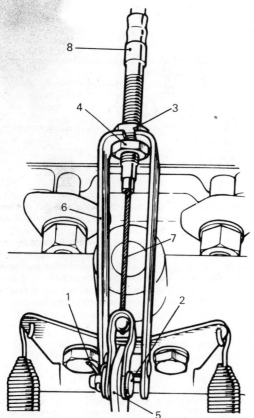

FIG 2:22 Removing the throttle cable from twin carburetters

Key to Fig 2:22   1 Splitpin   2 Clevis pin   3 Locknut
4 Locknut   5 Fulcrum plate   6 Cable yoke   7 Inner cable
8 Outer cable

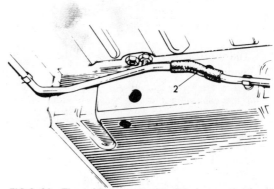

FIG 2:24   The rubber connection 2 between the front and intermediate fuel pipes

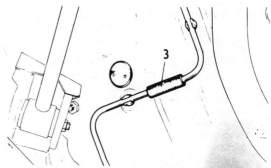

FIG 2:25   The rubber connection 3 between the intermediate and rear fuel pipes

consistent with a smooth running. Keep a constant watch on the tachometer. Then turn each one down one flat at a time until the engine speed starts to decrease, at this point turn each nut up one flat.

11a Recheck the idling speed and, if necessary, adjust the throttle screws to obtain between 700 and 800 rev/min.

12a Stop the engine. Position the throttle interconnection clamp lever forks 5 so that the lever pin in the fork aperture rests on the top edge of the lower arm, make sure the position is identical on both forks. Hold this position whilst carrying out the next operation.

13a Refer to **FIG 2 : 18** and insert a feeler gauge of .030 to .035 inch (.76 to .89 mm) between the heel of the fulcrum plate and the machined surface of the inlet manifold; then tighten the clamping nuts. A clearance should now exist between the lever pin and the top edge of the lower fork, the size of the clearance is not important providing it is the same at both forks.

14a Check that there is approximately $\frac{1}{32}$ inch (8 mm) end play between the jet control shaft clamp levers and the adjacent nuts (see **FIG 2 : 17**). Tighten the clamp nuts. Secure the choke control cable with the trunnion screw 3 making sure there is approximately $\frac{1}{16}$ inch (1.6 mm) free movement in the cable.

15a Pull out the choke knob approximately $\frac{1}{2}$ inch (13 mm) start the engine and adjust evenly the fast idle screws (see **FIG 2 : 16**) to obtain an engine speed of 1100 to 1300 rev/min.

16a Refit the air cleaner and disconnect the tachometer.

2 : 7 The throttle pedal

Removing :

1 Refer to **FIG 2 : 19** and remove the retaining clip 1, lift the cable 2 out of the fork end. Remove the bracket securing bolts 3 with plain and spring washers; work on the bolts from the engine compartment bulkhead.

2 Lift off the bracket and pedal assembly, take out the splitpin 5, collect the washers and withdraw the clevis pin 6.

3 Separate the pedal and return spring from the bracket.

Refitting :

4 Reverse the instructions 1 to 3 but ensure that the return spring is positioned correctly, a new splitpin is fitted and the cable clip is fitted so that it grips the inner cable securely.

2 : 8 The throttle cable

Removing, single carburetter :

1 Refer to **FIG 2 : 19** and spring off the retaining clip 1; lift the cable out of the pedal fork end.

2 Refer to **FIG 2 : 20**, squeeze the ears of the ferrule between thumb and forefinger and push the cable through the bulkhead. A second operator would simplify the withdrawal of the cable, by pulling from the engine compartment.

3 Refer to **FIG 2 : 21**, slacken the screw 1 and squeeze the ears of the ferrule 2 to separate the cable from the bracket.

Refitting :

4 Reverse operations 1 to 3 but ensure the cable is not kinked and the cable clip is fitted so that it has a secure grip on the inner cable at the pedal.

Removing twin carburetter :

1 Complete operations 1 and 2 which relate to the single carburetter.

2 Refer to **FIG 2 : 22** and remove the splitpin 1 from the linkage clevis pin 2. Withdraw the clevis pin and collect the washer.

3 Slacken the cable adjuster locknut 3 and screw the locknut 4 off the end of the cable.

4 Separate the cable from the slot in the bracket.

Refitting :

5 Reverse operations 1 to 4 ensuring the same conditions apply as in operation 4 relating to the single carburetter. The cable tension is adjusted so that the heel of the fulcrum plate is just touching the machined face of the manifold.

2 : 9 The choke cable

Removing :

1 Refer to **FIG 2 : 16** and disconnect the inner cable from the carburetter. To remove the inner cable from the outer cable, pull on the choke control knob until the inner cable is extracted.

2 Refer to **FIG 2 : 23**, unscrew the ferrule 3 from the outer cable and control panel, separate the ends of the cables from the connector 5 in the engine compartment. From inside the car, withdraw the cable from the control panel and pull it through the bulkhead grommets.

Refitting :

3 Feed the rear half of the cable through the bulkhead grommet into the engine compartment and secure the end to the control panel with the ferrule and locknut.

4 Feed the inner cable into the rear half of the outer cable at the control panel.

5 In the engine compartment, thread the exposed end of the inner cable through the front half of the outer cable and join the outer cables with the connector 5. Connect the inner cable to the carburetter.

6 Allow $\frac{1}{16}$ inch (1.6 mm) free movement of the cable before the linkage starts to move the cam.

2 : 10 Petrol pipes

Removing, engine end :

1 Disconnect the battery and extinguish all naked lights, unscrew the drain plug from the tank and drain off the petrol into a clean container.

2 Refer to **FIG 2 : 24** and at the rubber connector disconnect the front section. Disconnect the other end at the fuel pump. Pull the pipe away from the spring clips and remove it.

3 Renew the rubber connections if they are cracked or damaged.

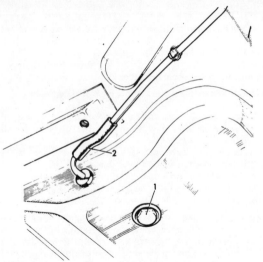

FIG 2:26 The rubber connection 2 between the rear fuel pipe and the tank outlet pipe

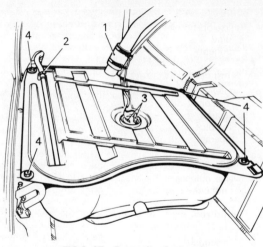

FIG 2:27 Removing fuel tank

Key to Fig 2:27   1 Filler hose   2 Breather hose
3 Tank gauge connections   4 Supporting bolts

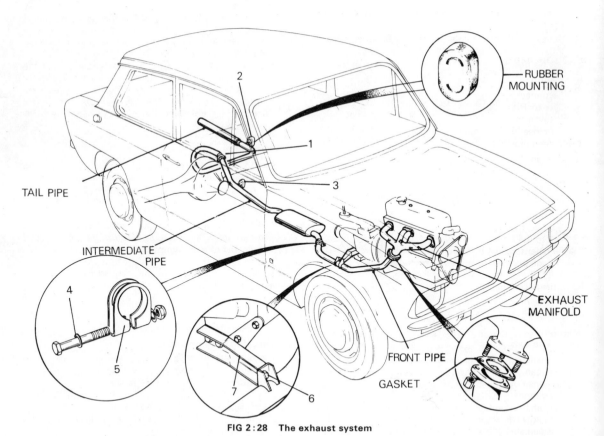

FIG 2:28 The exhaust system

Key to Fig 2:28   1 Intermediate pipe to tailpipe clip   2 Rubber mounting   3 Rubber mounting   4 Clamp bolt   5 Clamp
6 Bracket bolt   7 Support bracket

Refitting:

4 Reverse operations 1 to 3 but ensure when fitting that the pipe is not chafing against the body or other components.

Removing centre section:

5 Complete operation 1. Refer to **FIGS 2 : 24** and **2 : 25** and disconnect the centre section from the rubber connections where it joins the front and rear sections.
6 Pull the pipe away from the spring clips.
7 See operation 3.

Refitting:

8 Reverse operations 5 and 6 and make sure the pipe does not chafe against the body at any point.

Removing rear section:

9 Complete operation 1. Refer to **FIGS 2 : 25** and **2 : 26** and disconnect the rear section at the rubber connections where it joins the centre section and the fuel tank outlet pipe.
10 Pull the pipe away from the spring clips.
11 See operation 3.

Refitting:

12 Reverse operation 9 and 10 and observe the warnings against chafing in 4 and 8.

2 : 11 The petrol tank

Removing:

1 Disconnect the battery and extinguish all naked lights. Refer to **FIG 2 : 26**, remove the drain plug and drain the fuel into a clean container. Store the drained off fuel in a closed container. Disconnect the rear section of the feed pipe from the rubber connector.
2 Open up the luggage boot, remove the carpet, spare wheel cover and spare wheel.
3 Refer to **FIG 2 : 27**, disconnect the filler hose 1 from the filler pipe and the breather hose 2 from the breather pipe.
4 Disconnect the leads from the fuel tank gauge unit 3.
5 Remove the four bolts 4 and washers securing the tank to the body.
6 Lift the tank out of the boot taking care not to damage the tank outlet pipe.

Refitting:

8 Reverse operations 1 to 6.

2 : 12 The exhaust system

The exhaust system is in three sections and each section can be renewed individually. The following instructions cover the complete removal, but by omitting the operations that are not applicable each separate section can be removed from the vehicle.
1 Refer to **FIG 2 : 28** and release the clip 1 joining the intermediate pipe to the tail pipe. Remove the rubber mounting holding the tail pipe to the bracket. Detach and withdraw the tail pipe.

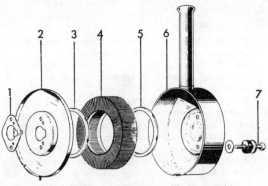

FIG 2 : 29   Single carburetter filter assembly

Key to Fig 2 : 29   1 Gasket   2 Coverplate   3 Seal
4 Element   5 Seal   6 Cover   7 Retaining bolt

2 Remove the flexible mounting 3 on the intermediate pipe. Unscrew the clamp bolt 4 and release the clip 5 Detach and withdraw the intermediate pipe and silencer.
3 Remove the bolt 6 on the front pipe support bracket 7. Unscrew and remove the three nuts securing the front pipe to the manifold. Withdraw the front exhaust pipe.

Refitting:

4 Refitting is the reverse of operations 1 to 3. Make sure the pipes are correctly aligned before bolting them to their retaining points. There must be no strain on any of the three sections. Clean the bolt and nut threads before refitting with an appropriate tap or die nut. Use an exhaust pipe sealant at the exhaust pipe joints.

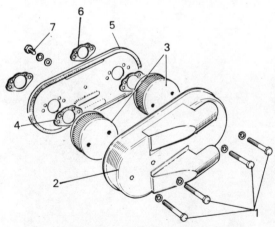

FIG 2 : 30   Twin carburetter filter assembly

Key to Fig 2 : 30   1 Retaining bolts   2 Cover   3 Elements
4 Gaskets   5 Coverplate and seal   6 Gasket   7 Coverplate bolt

2:13 The air cleaners

Single carburetter:

1 Refer to **FIG 2:29** and remove the bolts securing the air cleaner assembly to the carburetter.

2 Lift off the assembly complete with gaskets and bolts and place them in a clean working area.

3 Separate all the parts.

4 Use a compressed air-line to blow dirt and dust off the filter element. If it is extremely dirty or punctured, renew it. Check the gaskets and sealing rings for deterioration and renew them as necessary.

5 Refit the assembly to the carburetter but make sure the seals are correctly located and the mounting gasket is the right way up. Do not overtighten the securing bolts.

Twin carburetters:

1 Refer to **FIG 2:30** and remove the four bolts securing the air cleaner assembly to the carburetter. The two centre bolts also retain support brackets for the fuel link pipe.

2 Disconnect the fuel link pipe from the carburetters.

3 Lift off the air cleaner assembly.

4 To separate the coverplate from the container, remove the bolt 7.

5 Carry out operation 4 relating to the single carburetter.

6 Refit in the reverse order of removal. Do not overtighten the securing bolts.

2:14 Fault diagnosis

(a) Leakage or insufficient fuel delivered

1 Air vent in tank restricted
2 Petrol pipes blocked
3 Air leaks at pipe connections
4 Pump or carburetter filters blocked

5 Pump gaskets faulty
6 Pump diaphragm defective
7 Pump valves sticking or seating badly
8 Fuel vaporizing in pipelines due to heat

(b) Excessive fuel consumption

1 Carburetters need adjusting
2 Fuel leakage
3 Sticking controls or choke device
4 Dirty air cleaners
5 Excessive engine temperature
6 Brakes binding
7 Tyres under-inflated
8 Idling speed too high
9 Car overloaded

(c) Idling speed too high

1 Rich fuel mixture
2 Carburetter controls sticking
3 Slow-running screws incorrectly adjusted
4 Worn carburetter butterfly valve

(d) Noisy fuel pump

1 Loose mountings
2 Air leaks on suction side and at diaphragm
3 Obstruction in fuel pipe
4 Clogged pump filter

(e) No fuel delivery

1 Float needle stuck
2 Vent in tank blocked
3 Pipeline obstructed
4 Pump diaphragm stiff or damaged
5 Inlet valve in pump stuck open
6 Bad air leak on suction side of pump

CHAPTER 3

THE IGNITION SYSTEM

3:1 Description

The 'Toledo' model range is equipped with a Lucas 25D4 distributor fitted with a 'Quickafit' one-piece contact breaker set. Later models have a 45D4 type. Because of the variations in engine power and subsequent modifications since the concept of the design, the centrifugal and vacuum advance characteristics have been varied to match each power unit. Before ordering spares or renewing the distributor as a complete unit, refer to **Technical Data** for the part number of the distributor applicable to the type of power unit fitted.

The distributor is mounted on the engine and driven by the camshaft at half engine speed (each cylinder only fires once for every two revolutions of the engine). The distributor consists of a shaft, keyed to the engine, which has a cam at the top opening and closing contacts in the body. A rotor arm on top of the cam and a distributor cap mounted on the body feed the HT voltage to the firing cylinder. When the contacts are closed an LT current flows through the ignition coil primary circuit and contact points. There are four lobes on the rotating cam and the distributor position is so set that a lobe is just opening the contacts when the appropriate cylinder is in the exact firing position. As the contacts open the current is sharply cut off, assisted by the action of the capacitor, and the

magnetic field in the coil collapses rapidly inducing a high voltage in the secondary turns of the coil. This high voltage is taken by an HT lead to the carbon brush in the centre of the distributor cap and from that directly to the rotor arm. The rotor arm directs the high voltage, through the appropriate contact in the distributor cap and HT lead, to the sparking plug where the spark fires the mixture.

A centrifugal advance mechanism is fitted to the distributor shaft. As the engine speed increases, two weights are flung out by centrifugal force against the restraint of the springs. The movement of the weights turns the cam further in relation to the shaft in the direction of rotation, thus advancing the ignition point as the engine speed rises.

A vacuum unit is connected to the inlet manifold by a small-bore pipe and to the base plate of the contact breakers, rotating them about the fixed position and so adjusting the ignition timing for the engine load and throttle opening.

The distributor, type 25D4, is fitted with a micrometer adjustment so the ignition point can be accurately set for different grades of fuel or adjusted to suit the engine condition.

The various components of the distributor are shown in **FIG 3:1**.

3:2 Routine maintenance

Ensure that the outside of the distributor, the HT leads and the top of the ignition coil are always kept clean and dry. Wipe away moisture or oil with a clean, dry cloth, paying particular attention to the crevices between the HT leads on the distributor cap.

Remove the distributor cap and refer to **FIG 3:2.** Lift off the rotor arm and pour a few drops of engine oil over the screw 2. A clearance is provided around the screw, so it should not be removed. Put a single drop of oil on the contact pivot 5. Work the moving contact to ensure that it is free on the pivot and to allow the oil to spread evenly. If the contact sticks, the points will have to be removed and the pivot lightly polished with a piece of fine emerycloth. Lightly grease the surface of the cam 4. Inject a few drops of oil between the contact breaker base plate and the side of the housing 3. Wipe away any surplus oil. Wipe the inside of the distributor cap and the rotor arm with soft, dry cloth and replace them on the distributor.

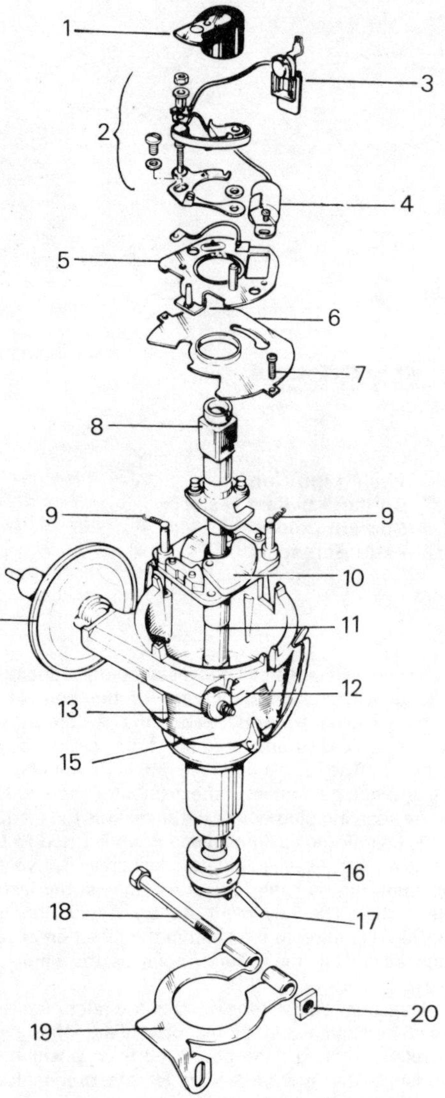

Adjusting the contact breaker points:

Before adjusting the points make sure that they are clean. With the distributor cap and rotor arm removed, slacken the fixed contact securing screw 3 in **FIG 3:3.** Insert a screwdriver between the slot in the fixed contact and the slotted hole in the base plate 5. Turn the engine so that a lobe of the cam 2 is under the foot of the moving contact and the contact points gap is widest. Measure the gap with feeler gauges and turn the screwdriver until the gap measures .015 inch (.38 mm). Tighten the securing screw and recheck the points gap.

Cleaning the contact breaker points:

If the points are dirty they should be cleaned using a small piece of carborundum paper, but if they are pitted it is best to remove them and clean them using a fine carborundum stone or file. Remove the distributor cap and rotor arm. Unscrew the nut 1 shown in **FIG 3:4,** and lift off the wires for the capacitor and LT terminal. Remove the securing screw 2, spring washer and flat washer and lift out the assembly. **Clean the points, carefully removing metal so that the points are flat and meet squarely when assembled.**

Refit the points in the reverse order of dismantling. If the points are excessively worn a new set should be fitted. Use a spring balance to check that the tension on the moving contact spring is 18 to 24 oz. Lubricate and then adjust the points as described earlier. **Make sure the rotor arm is replaced before refitting the distributor cap.**

3:3 Ignition faults

If the engine runs unevenly, and the carburetter is correctly adjusted, set the engine to idle at a fast speed. Taking care not to touch the metal parts, short out or disconnect each plug in turn. Use an insulated handle screwdriver between the sparking plug top and the cylinder head to short the plug. Shorting, or disconnecting a plug that is not firing will make no difference to the running but doing the same to a plug that is firing properly will make the uneven running more pronounced.

Having located the faulty cylinder, stop the engine and remove any insulator or shroud fitted to that plug lead. Start the engine and using insulated tongs, or taking other precautions to avoid shocks, hold the metal end of the HT lead about $\frac{3}{16}$ inch from an earthed clean bit of metal (not near the carburetter). A strong regular spark shows that the fault may lie with the sparking plug. Remember that the fault may be in the engine and not in the ignition circuit, as a sticking valve can cause similar

FIG 3:1   Components of distributor

Key to Fig 3:1   1 Rotor   2 Contact breaker set 3 Terminal block   4 Capacitor   5 Contact plate   6 Base plate   7 Screws   8 Cam spindle   9 Control springs 10 Weights   11 Drive shaft   12 Ratchet spring 13 Adjusting nut   14 Vacuum control   15 Body   16 Drive coupling   17 Pin   18 Clamp bolt   19 Clamp   20 Nut

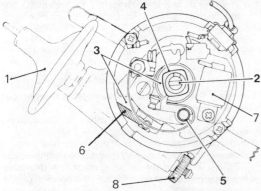

FIG 3:2 The distributor with cap removed

Key to Fig 3:2 1 Vacuum control 2 Cam spindle retaining screw 3 Lubricating points 4 Cam 5 Pivot post 6 Vacuum control link and spring 7 Capacitor 8 Adjusting screw

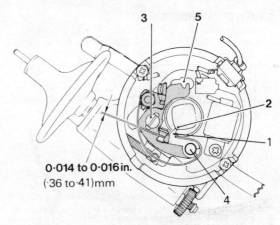

0·014 to 0·016 in.
(·36 to ·41) mm

FIG 3:3 Adjusting the contact breaker points

Key to Fig 3:3 1 Moving contact foot 2 Cam lobe 3 Securing screw 4 Pivot post 5 Adjusting slots

symptoms. Stop the engine, remove the sparking plug and either clean it, as described in **Section 3:8,** or else substitute it with a new sparking plug.

If the spark is weak or irregular check that the HT lead is not cracked or perished. If the lead is found to be faulty, renew it and repeat the test. If there is no improvement, remove the distributor cap and wipe the inside with a clean soft cloth. Check that the carbon brush protrudes from the moulding and moves freely against the internal spring. Examine the inside surface of the cap for cracks or 'tracking'. 'Tracking' can be seen as a thin black line between the electrodes or to some metal part in contact with the cap. Scraping away tracking with a sharp knife may effect a temporary cure. Renew the cap if it is cracked or shows signs of 'tracking'. Use a sharp knife to clean away deposits from the distributor cap contacts. Check the rotor arm, though if this is split or faulty all the cylinders will be affected.

Testing the low-tension circuit:

Before carrying out any electrical tests, confirm that the contact points are clean and correctly set.

1 Disconnect the LT cable from the CB terminal of the ignition coil. Connect a low-wattage 12-volt test bulb between the terminal and the cable end. Switch on the ignition and turn the engine slowly over by hand. To turn the engine over by hand first remove the sparking plugs and try turning it by pulling the fan belt. If the engine is too stiff to be turned by this method engage a gear and turn it either by pushing the car or by rotating a jacked up rear wheel. The test lamp should light when the points are closed and go out when the points open. Either staying continuously on, or failing to light at all indicates a fault. The lamp staying on continuously indicates a shortcircuit in the distributor, or a faulty capacitor.

2 If the lamp does not light, remove it and reconnect the cable to the CB terminal on the coil. Disconnect the other cable from the SW terminal on the coil and connect the test bulb between this cable and a good earth. The lamp should now be on continuously with the ignition switched on. If it now lights but did not light

previously then the ignition coil is at fault and must be renewed. If the lamp still fails to light, reconnect the cable to the SW terminal and turn the engine until the contact points are open. Using the wiring diagram in **Technical Data** as a guide, trace through the wiring with either a test lamp or 0–20 voltmeter until the fault is found.

Capacitor:

The capacitor (condenser) is made up of metal foil insulated with paper. If the insulation breaks down the spark tends to erode away the metal foil in the area, preventing a shortcircuit. However, with the ignition switched on, if a voltmeter connected across the points shows no reading then the capacitor is suspect.

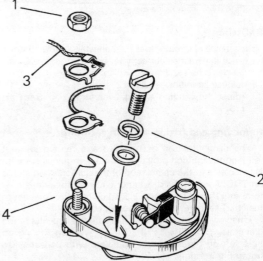

FIG 3:4 Components of 'Quickafit' contact breaker set

Key to Fig 3:4 1 Retaining nut 2 Retaining screw 3 Low-tension and capacitor terminals 4 Terminal post

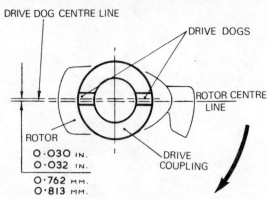

DRIVE DOG CENTRE LINE

DRIVE DOGS

ROTOR CENTRE LINE

ROTOR

0·030 IN.
0·032 IN.
0·762 MM.
0·813 MM.

DRIVE COUPLING

FIG 3:5 Ensure that the centre line of the offset drive dogs is positioned to a dimension of .031 inch (.79 mm) from the centre line of the rotor

A open circuit capacitor is more difficult to diagnose, but it may be suspected if either the points are badly burnt or 'blued' and starting is difficult.

Specialized equipment is necessary for testing a capacitor so the best method readily available is to substitute it with a known satisfactory one. The capacitor is held to the base plate by a single screw and the wire is held on by nut 1 (see **FIG 3:4**).

3:4 Removing and refitting distributor

1 Pull off the high tension lead connection to the ignition coil and the high-tension leads to the sparking plugs.
2 Remove the distributor cover.
3 Disconnect the low-tension Lucar connector from the distributor and pull off the vacuum pipe.
4 Unscrew the clamp nut 20 in **FIG 3:1**, collect the washer and withdraw the clamp bolt 18. Withdraw the distributor from its pedestal.

Refitting:

5 Insert the distributor into the pedestal. Ensure that the offset key locates correctly in the drive gear slot, refit the clamp bolt and nut but do not tighten.
6 Reverse operations 1, 2 and 3.
7 Adjust the ignition timing by referring to **Section 3:6.**

Removing and fitting without retiming:

The distributor can be removed and refitted without retiming the ignition providing that the engine is set with No. 1 piston at the completion of the compression stroke on TDC. Remove the distributor cover to check this. The rotor arm should be in such a position as to be adjacent to the No. 1 segment in the distributor cover.

Unscrew the two nuts which secure the pedestal to the crankcase (see **FIG 1:19**). Do not slacken the clamp bolt. Lift off the distributor complete with pedestal. Do not turn the engine.

When refitting (providing the clamp bolt has not been slackened) turn the rotor until the arm is in the No. 1 firing position and re-engage the driving dogs into the drive gear. Reassemble the relevant parts.

It is worth noting that using this method may upset the end float dimensions for the distributor drive gear. The end float is determined by the thickness of the pedestal gasket. This should be checked by referring to **Chapter 1, Section 1:5** under the appropriate heading.

3:5 Dismantling and reassembling distributor

1 Remove the distributor as described in the previous section, operations 1 to 4.
2 Refer to **FIG 3:1**, pull off the rotor 1 and remove the contact breaker set 2 (see **Sections 3:2**).
3 Remove the screw and lift out the capacitor 4.
4 Remove the two screws 7 and collect the spring washers. Remove the terminal block 3 and unhook the vacuum control link, lift out the contact plate 5 and base plate 6.
5 Prise off the circlip at the face of the adjusting nut 13, unscrew the nut, remove the spring and withdraw the vacuum control 14. Remove the ratchet spring 12.
6 With a drift, tap out the pin 17 and pull off the drive coupling 16 and thrust washer. Make sure the shaft is free of burrs, particularly around the pin hole, then withdraw it from the body of the distributor.
7 Remove the control springs 9, taking care not to distort them in any way, remove the screw from the cam spindle 8, withdraw the spindle and take off the weights 10.

Servicing:

8 Check all the component parts for wear including the bush bearing inside the distributor body, renew any suspect or worn parts. Renew the thrust washer.
9 Lubricate the cam surface, the action plate sliding surface, the cam spindle bearing, the weight supporting pillars and the drive shaft with Rocal 'moly pad'.

Reassembling:

10 Position the weights on the action plate, fit the cam spindle and secure it with the screw. Hook up the control springs, without distorting them, and check the action and movement of the weights.
11 Fit the new thrust washer, after inserting the drive shaft into the body, followed by the drive coupling. Refer to **FIG 3:5** when fitting the drive coupling and ensure that the offset drive dogs are positioned correctly in relation to the rotor.
12 Fit the ratchet spring and the vacuum control. Do not forget to fit the circlip when the adjusting nut has been fitted. Fit the contact breaker plate and base plate and hook on the vacuum control link. Fit the terminal block and secure the plates with the two screws. Reconnect the earth lead tag to the appropriate screw.
13 Fit the capacitor and the contact breaker set, lubricate the moving parts as described in **Section 3:2**.
14 Refit the distributor as instructed in **Section 3:4**, operations 5, 6 and 7.

3:6 Timing the ignition

1 Adjust the contact breaker gap (see **Section 3:2**).
2 Remove the rocker gear cover and, if necessary, the sparking plugs so that the engine can be turned easily.

3 Turn the engine to bring No. 1 piston on the compression stroke, the valves on No. 4 cylinder should be on a point of balance, that is, the exhaust just about to close and the inlet about to open. Both valves on No. 1 should be fully closed.

4 Refer to **FIG 3:6** and reset the engine so that the notch on the pulley is aligned to the pointer on the scale, which reads 24 deg. **before** TDC.

5 Disconnect the distributor low-tension lead at the coil and connect it to a 12-volt test lamp, which is wired as shown in **FIG 3:7.**

6 Switch on the ignition. The test lamp should be illuminated. If not refer to operation 8.

7 Turn the engine slowly, in the direction shown by the arrow in **FIG 3:6,** and stop immediately the lamp goes out. The pulley notch should now be aligned with the pointer to the reading given in **Technical Data.** If only a small adjustment is required on the distributor, correct it by turning the micrometer adjusting nut, 13 in **FIG 3:1.** If a large adjustment is required refer to operation 8.

8 Turn the micrometer adjusting nut in the required direction to centralize the distributor within the range. Slacken the distributor clamp bolt (see 18 and 20 in **FIG 3:1**). Align the pulley notch to the pointer as given in **Technical Data.** Rotate the distributor body anticlockwise until the lamp lights then carefully rotate it clockwise until it just goes out. Tighten the clamp bolt with the distributor in this position, and repeat operations 4 and 7.

3:7 Ignition coil and ballast resistor

A ballast resistor is positioned in series into the current supply to the coil, which causes a voltage drop in the circuit so that the 12-volt supply is reduced to the nominally rated 6-volt coil.

During engine start the resistor is bypassed and the battery voltage, which is greatly reduced by the starter motor load, is applied to the coil direct from the starter solenoid. This means in effect that the coil is receiving a slight voltage overload during starting, to provide an increased high-tension voltage at the sparking plugs. The system is designed to assist engine starting under adverse conditions. Under normal running the ballast resistor is reconnected to the circuit to reduce the voltage to the coil.

The circuit is shown in **FIG 3:8.**

Removing and refitting coil:

1 Disconnect the two low-tension Lucar connectors at the coil and pull off the high-tension lead.

2 Remove the two retaining screws and washers and lift off the coil.

Refitting:

3 Position the coil and secure it with the retaining screws and washers. In the rear screw, include the lug from the ballast resistor.

4 Push on the high-tension lead and connect the two low-tension leads; white/yellow to positive and white/black to negative.

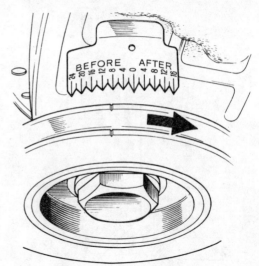

FIG 3:6   Timing scale—O=TDC

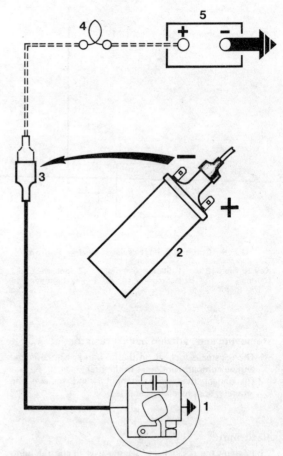

FIG 3:7   Wiring diagram for connecting a test lamp

Key to Fig 3:7   1 Distributor   2 Coil   3 Terminal disconnected from coil   4 Test lamp   5 Battery

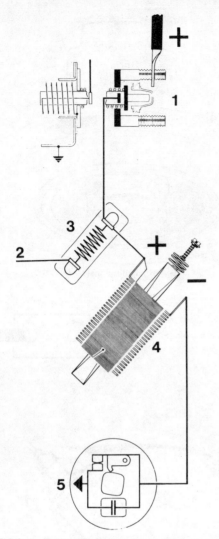

FIG 3:8   Coil and ballast resistor wiring diagram

Key to Fig 3:8   1 Starter solenoid   2 Ignition supply
(normal)   3 Ballast resistor   4 6-volt ignition coil
5 Distributor

Removing and refitting ballast resistor

1 The resistor is located on the lefthand valance in the
engine compartment, next to the coil.
2 Disconnect the Lucar connector and remove the
retaining springs and washers.

Refitting:

1 Position the resistor and secure it with the retaining
screws and washers.
2 Connect the leads; white to the lower terminal and
white/yellow to the upper terminal.

3:8 Sparking plugs

Inspect, clean and adjust sparking plugs regularly. The
inspection of the deposits on the electrodes is particularly
useful because the type and colour of the deposit gives a
clue to the conditions inside the combustion chamber,
and is therefore most useful when tuning the engine.

Remove the sparking plugs by loosening them a couple
of turns and blowing away loose dirt from the plug
recesses with compressed air or a tyre pump before
removing them completely. Store the sparking plugs in the
order of removal. Examine the gaskets and renew them if
they are less than half their original thickness.

Examine the firing end of the sparking plug to note
the type of deposit. Normally the deposit should be
powdery and range in colour from brown to greyish tan.
There will also be light wear on the electrodes and the
general effect is one which comes from mixed periods of
high-speed and low-speed driving. Cleaning and resetting the gaps is all that will be required. If the deposits are
white or yellowish they indicate long periods of constant-
speed or much low-speed city driving. Again the treatment is straightforward.

Black, wet deposits are caused by oil entering the
combustion chamber past worn pistons, rings or worn
down valve guides or worn valve stems. Hotter running
sparking plugs may help to alleviate the problem, but
the only cure is an engine overhaul.

Overheated electrodes have a white, blistered look
about the centre electrode and the side electrode may be
badly eroded. This may be caused by poor cooling, incorrect ignition, running with too weak a mixture,
incorrect grade of sparking plugs or sustained high-
speeds with heavy loads.

Dry, black, fluffy deposits are usually the result of
running with a rich mixture. Incomplete combustion may
also be a cause and this might be traced to defective
ignition or excessive idling.

Have the sparking plugs cleaned on an abrasive-
blasting machine and then tested under pressure after
attention to the electrodes. File these until they are clean,
bright and parallel. Set the electrode gap to .025 inch.
(.64 mm). **Do not bend the centre electrode.**
Sparking plugs should be renewed every 12,000 miles.

Before replacing the sparking plugs clean the threads
with a wire brush and smear the threads with a little
graphite grease to prevent them binding in the cylinder
head. Never use ordinary grease or oil as it will bake hard
and jam the plug. If it is found that the sparking plugs
cannot be screwed into place by hand, run a tap down the
threads in the cylinder head. Failing a tap, use an old
sparking plug with crosscuts down the threads. Grease
the tool well so that chips and dirt stick to the grease
instead of falling down the cylinder bore. Clean the
insulator on the sparking plug with a petrol-moistened
cloth to remove all dirt and grease. Screw the sparking
plug in hand tight, by hand only, and finally tighten it to a
torque of 15 to 20 lb ft. If a torque wrench is not available,
tighten with a normal box spanner through half a turn.

HT cables:

These are 7 mm neoprene covered and are of the
resistive type for suppression of radio and television
interference. They should not be replaced by ordinary tinned copper HT cables as the conductor consists of a

special nylon or cotton thread impregnated with carbon Their resistance is approximately 420 ohms per inch so a serviceable cable should give a reading between 3000 and 12,000 ohms. In some cases a short length of tinned copper is inserted in the end of the cable to provide a suitable pick-up point so do not be misled by this into thinking that the conductor is all tinned copper.

The HT cables are held in the distributor cap by spiked screws in the individual contact points. The positions of the HT leads, in the correct firing order of 1-3-4-2 are set in an anticlockwise direction when viewed from the top of the cap.

3:9 Fault diagnosis

(a) Engine will not fire

1 Battery discharged
2 Distributor points dirty, pitted or out of adjustment
3 Distributor cap dirty, cracked or 'tracking'
4 Carbon brush inside distributor cap not in contact with rotor arm
5 Faulty cable or loose connection in low-tension circuit
6 Distributor rotor arm cracked
7 Faulty ignition coil
8 Broken contact breaker spring
9 Contact points stuck open
10 Faulty capacitor
11 Water on HT leads, distributor cap or ignition coil
12 Faulty HT lead between ignition coil and distributor

(b) Engine misfires

1 Check 2, 3, 5 and 7 in (a)
2 Weak contact spring
3 HT leads cracked or perished
4 Sparking plug loose
5 Sparking plug insulation cracked
6 Sparking plug gap incorrect
7 Ignition timing too far advanced

NOTES

CHAPTER 4

THE COOLING SYSTEM

4:1 Principle of the system

The system is of the pressurized 'no loss' type, comprising a radiator where the thermo-syphon action of the coolant is assisted by a water pump driven by a fan belt. A thermostat is fitted to prevent water circulation until engine operating temperature has been reached. Cooling is assisted by fan blades fitted to the water pump pulley.

An overflow reservoir collects excess coolant from the radiator as the coolant in the system expands with heat. The depression created as the system cools, causes the coolant to flow back from the reservoir into the radiator. The fluid level in the reservoir should be maintained at half-full when cold.

4:2 Routine maintenance

Keep the coolant to the correct level in the reservoir. From time to time check the tightness of the hose clips and inspect the hoses for hardening or cracking and renew if necessary (see **FIG 4:1**).

Antifreeze of a suitable brand should be put into the system and changed each autumn for fresh solution. The capacity of the system, with heater, is $8\frac{1}{2}$ pints and a 25 per cent solution of antifreeze is adequate for normal climatic conditions. If this procedure is regularly carried out there should be no need to flush the system. However if due to neglect, the system has to be flushed, then a hose should be placed in the filler neck of the radiator, the drain taps, shown in **FIG 4:2,** opened and the water kept running until it flows clear from them.

Never put cold water into a hot engine and during emptying, refilling or flushing keep the heater controls to 'HOT'. In extreme conditions of corrosion or neglect which might cause a blockage in the radiator core, the radiator should be removed, a hose inserted into the bottom outlet and the water turned on. This is known as back flushing.

The appearance of oil in the coolant may be indicative of an internal water leak and either this or the opposite occurence of water in the sump oil should be immediately rectified (see **Section 4:6**).

On early models a blanking plug is fitted to the water pump. Later models are not fitted with this plug. On the earlier type the plug should be removed and a grease nipple fitted. Apply a grease gun and pump grease into the housing until it exudes from the pressure release hole. Replace the plug.

This operation should be carried out every 12,000 miles (20,000 kilometres).

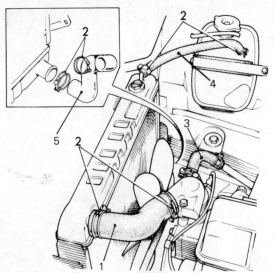

FIG 4:1   Water hose details

Key to Fig 4:1   1 Upper hose   2 Hose clips   3 Inlet manifold heater hose   4 Radiator to expansion tank hose   5 Bottom hose

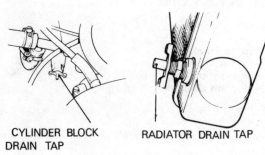

CYLINDER BLOCK DRAIN TAP   RADIATOR DRAIN TAP

FIG 4:2   Cooling system drain taps where fitted

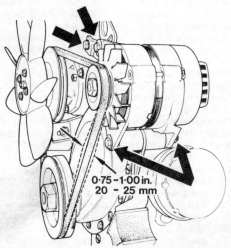

0.75 – 1.00 in.
20 – 25 mm

FIG 4:3   Adjusting the fan belt tension

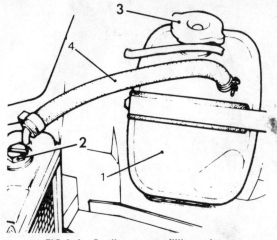

FIG 4:4   Cooling system filling points

Key to Fig 4:4   1 Expansion tank   2 Radiator filler plug   3 Expansion tank cap   4 Radiator to expansion tank hose

The fan belt should be tightened sufficiently to drive the water pump and alternator without unduly loading the bearings. To check the tension refer to **FIG 4:3**.

Adjust the belt by slackening the adjusting bolts and the pivot bolt (arrowed). Pivot the alternator until the belt can be moved $\frac{3}{4}$ to 1 inch sideways at the mid-point of its longest run. Maintaining the alternator in this position, securely tighten the adjusting bolts and the pivot bolt.

4:3   Draining and refilling

1 Under no circumstances should the radiator filler plug or the expansion tank cap be removed when the engine is hot, otherwise severe scalding to the hand or face may be the unfortunate result.
2 Move the heater control knob to the 'HOT' position.
3 Refer to **FIG 4:4** and remove the radiator filler plug 2 and the expansion filler cap 3.
4 Refer to **FIG 4:2** and open the drain taps, if fitted, at the cylinder block and at the base of the radiator, or remove bottom radiator hose.

Refilling:

5 Close the drain taps or refit the hose and half fill the expansion tank with water.
6 Fill the system through the radiator filler orifice. Replace the expansion tank cap and the filler plug.
7 Start the engine and run it for about three minutes.
8 Top up the system through the radiator filler orifice.

4:4   Removing and refitting expansion tank

1 Refer to **FIG 4:5**. Disconnect the hoses 1 and 2, remove the two bolts 3 to release the securing strap 4.
2 Lift off the tank and drain the coolant.

Refitting:

3 Reverse the removal instructions and top up the tank to the half-full mark.

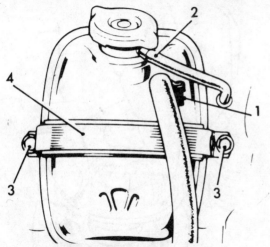

FIG 4:5   Removing expansion tank

Key to Fig 4:5   1 Hose connection   2 Overflow hose
3 Strap securing bolts   4 Supporting strap and rubber
packing

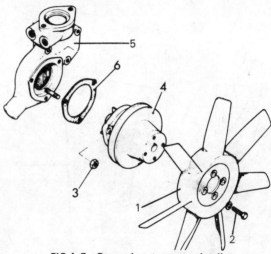

FIG 4:7   Fan and water pump details

Key to Fig 4:7   1 Fan   2 Retaining bolts   3 Pump
securing nuts   4 Water pump and pulley   5 Water pump
and thermostat housing   6 Gasket

4:5   Removing and refitting water pump

1 The water pump and pulley assembly fitted to
vehicles from engine number DG 1605 is serviced only
as a complete assembly and no separate parts are
provided.

2 Refer to **FIG 4:6** and take out the four bolts 1 which
secure the fan blades to the pulley.

3 Drain the coolant (see **Section 4:3**) and referring
to **FIG 4:7** remove the three nuts 3 which secure the
water pump to its housing.

4 On earlier models, up to engine number DG 1604,
extract the pulley by referring to **FIG 4:8**, remove the

nut 3 and washer and detach the pulley with a
suitable puller.

5 In all cases, a defective pump should be renewed
complete as a service item, the earlier type can be
stripped down for overhaul but it is far easier to
obtain replacement units rather than component parts.
Special tools also would be required to reface the
carbon bearing and reset the impeller clearance.

Refitting:

6 To assemble the dismantled items, reverse the
operations. Fit new gaskets where applicable and
smear them with a film of grease.

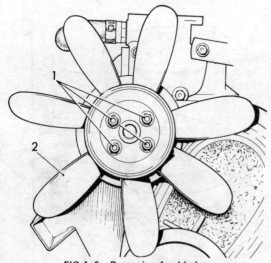

FIG 4:6   Removing fan blades

Key to Fig 4:6   1 Retaining bolts   2 Fan blades

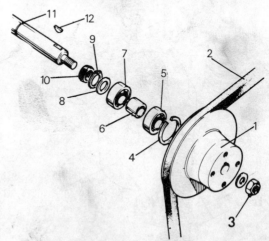

FIG 4:8   Water pump details (early type)

Key to Fig 4:8   1 Pulley   2 Fan belt   3 Securing nut
4 Circlip   5 Ballrace   6 Distance piece   7 Ballrace
8 Washer   9 Circlip   10 Spinner   11 Shaft   12 Drive key

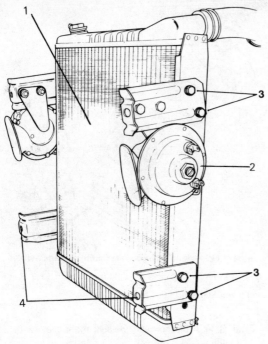

FIG 4 : 9   Removing radiator

Key to Fig 4 : 9   1 Radiator   2 Horn   3 Securing point, radiator to mounting brackets   4 Securing point, mounting bracket to body

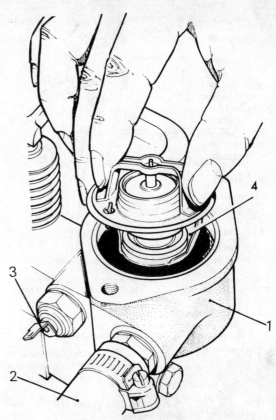

FIG 4 : 11   Removing thermostat

Key to Fig 4 : 11   1 Housing   2 Heater hose to inlet manifold   3 Coolant temperature sending unit   4 Thermostat

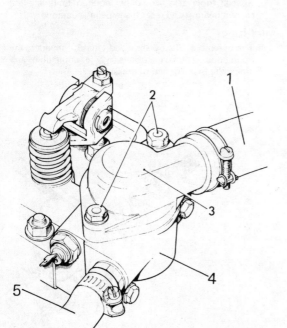

FIG 4 : 10   Removing thermostat housing cover

Key to Fig 4 : 10   1 Upper hose   2 Thermostat housing cover securing bolts   3 Cover   4 Housing   5 Heater hose to inlet manifold

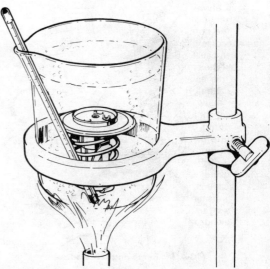

FIG 4 : 12   Testing thermostat opening temperature

4:6 Removing and refitting radiator

1 Drain the cooling system as described in **Section 4:3**.
2 Disconnect and remove all connecting hoses (see **FIG 4:1**).
3 Refer to **FIG 4:9**. Note the positions of the wire connectors to the horns, pull off the connectors and unscrew the four bolts which secure the radiator mounting brackets to the body.

If it is more convenient, the eight bolts 3 can be removed so that the horns and brackets are left in position.

Refitting:

4 Reverse the operations 1 to 3. Fill up with coolant as described in **Section 4:3**.

4:7 Removing and refitting thermostat

1 Refer to **Section 4:3** and partially drain the radiator.
2 Refer to **FIG 4:10** and remove the two bolts 2 which secure the water elbow to the pump housing.
3 Lift out the thermostat (see **FIG 4:11**).

Inspecting:

4 A known faulty thermostat should be renewed with one having the same opening temperatures. These temperatures are stamped on the base of the thermostat or on its flange. If the thermostat is merely suspected of causing a fault in the cooling system, it can be tested by immersing it in a container of water, which is heated and tested with a thermometer to the opening temperatures (see **FIG 4:12**).

Refitting:

5 Replace the parts in the reverse order of dismantling and renew the housing gasket. Refill the system with coolant as described in **Section 4:3**.

4:8 Frost precautions

It is always advisable to use antifreeze in cold weather. If it is very cold and no antifreeze has been used, the bottom half of the radiator is liable to freeze and become blocked, even when the engine is running. This can cause further damage because with the radiator blocked the engine will boil. In very cold weather therefore if the engine boils, stop the engine and wrap the engine and radiator to allow the heat from the engine to slowly thaw out the ice in the radiator. The use of sufficient antifreeze will prevent this trouble.

Draining the cooling system overnight is not an adequate precaution against frost as some water will remain in the heater

Most of the branded names of antifreeze are suitable, but ensure that they meet BSI.3152 or BSI.3151 specifications. The total cooling system capacity (including heater) is 8.5 Imperial pints (10.2 US pints, 4.8 litres) and the quantity of antifreeze should be as recommended by the following.

Degrees of protection:

A 25 per cent solution of antifreeze, 2.25 pints (1.28 litres or 2.71 US pints) will give protection up to minus 13°C and freeze solid at minus 26°C.

A 33 per cent solution of antifreeze, 3 pints (1.70 litres or 3.6 US pints) will give protection up to minus 19°C and freeze solid at minus 36°C.

A 50 per cent solution of antifreeze, 4.25 pints (2.42 litres or 5.1 US pints) will give protection up to minus 36°C and freeze solid at minus 48°C.

The cooling system should be flushed out before adding antifreeze. It should also be checked for leaks and loose connections before the antifreeze is added, as antifreeze will penetrate through cracks which hold back pure water. **Close the drain taps after flushing.** Pour in the correct quantity of antifreeze first and then add soft clean water to fill the system to the correct normal cold level. Add a little antifreeze to the expansion tank. Run the engine until it is hot to allow the antifreeze to mix with the water, and again check for leaks. If topping up is required use a mixture of antifreeze and water to prevent dilution of the antifreeze already in the system.

Never use antifreeze in the windscreen washers. A mixture of one part of methylated spirits to two parts of water should be used instead.

4:9 Fault diagnosis

(a) Internal water leakage

1 Cracked cylinder wall
2 Cracked cylinder head
3 Loose cylinder head nuts
4 Faulty head gasket

(b) Poor circulation

1 Radiator core blocked
2 Engine water passages restricted by deposits
3 Low water level
4 Loose fan belt
5 Defective fan belt
6 Perished or collapsed water hoses

(c) Corrosion

1 Impurities in the water
2 Infrequent draining and flushing

(d) Overheating

1 Check (b)
2 Sludge in crankcase
3 Incorrect ignition timing
4 Weak mixture
5 Low oil level in sump
6 Tight engine
7 Choked exhaust system
8 Binding brakes
9 Slipping clutch
10 Incorrect valve timing

NOTES

CHAPTER 5

THE CLUTCH

5 : 1 Description

The 1300 model is fitted with a 6½ inch (165 mm) diaphragm, single dry plate clutch, the 1500 export model is fitted with a 7¼ inch (184 mm) type. Both work on exactly the same principle, being hydraulically operated through a master cylinder and slave cylinder.

The assembly consists of a pressed steel cover 6 (see **FIG 5:1**) and a cast iron pressure plate 2 which are linked together by three flat steel straps 7 and a steel diaphragm spring 4. The diaphragm spring is pinched between two fulcrum rings 3 and 5 which are secured to the cover by special rivets. A release plate assembly is attached to the cover by three spring steel straps, each riveted at one end of the cover and at the other end to the release plate.

Finally, three retractor clips 9 bolted to the pressure plate, clip over the rim of the diaphragm spring to ensure that the pressure plate retracts during clutch disengagement.

This type of clutch unit should never be dismantled or serviced.

In the event of a fault the unit should be renewed as a complete assembly. Never disturb the cover strap drive bolts. Under no circumstances must the clutch be lifted or pulled by means of the thrust plate or the straps will be bent and the alignment of the thrust plate destroyed.

When the clutch is fully engaged, the diaphragm spring exerts a powerful pull on the pressure plate.

This pressure nips the driven plate by means of its friction linings between the faces of the flywheel and the pressure plate.

When the engine is running, the driven plate is therefore revolving with the flywheel and carries round with it the transmission drive shaft to which it is splined.

To disengage the clutch, a hinged lever hydraulically connected to the clutch pedal causes the release bearing to bear upon the diaphragm release plate which in turn moves the pressure plate away from the driven plate and so disconnects the drive. The driven plate and the transmission shaft are then free to revolve or come to a stop without transmitting any drive even though the engine is still rotating.

The hydraulic withdrawal mechanism consists of a master cylinder directly connected to the clutch pedal and a hydraulic fluid pipe running to the slave cylinder which operates through a pushrod, to the clutch withdrawal hinge lever.

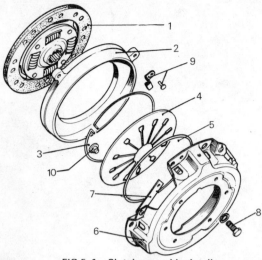

FIG 5:1 Clutch assembly details

Key to Fig 5:1

	1 Driven plate	2 Pressure plate
3 Fulcrum ring	4 Diaphragm spring	5 Fulcrum ring
6 Cover pressing	7 Drive strap	8 Securing bolts
9 Retractor clip and rivet	10 Rivet	

5:2 Routine maintenance

This consists of occasionally checking firstly the fluid level in the master cylinder reservoir. The correct level is $\frac{1}{4}$ inch from the top using only recommended Girling-Castrol fluid for this purpose (see **FIG 5:2**).

Never use any other fluid as this may damage the rubber seals both in the master cylinder and slave cylinder.

If the master cylinder needs constant topping up or the level suddenly falls, the system should be inspected for leaks.

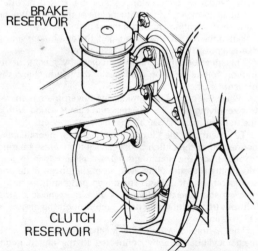

BRAKE
RESERVOIR

CLUTCH
RESERVOIR

FIG 5:2 The clutch reservoir is easily distinguished from the brake reservoir as the smaller of the two. The correct fluid is $\frac{1}{4}$ inch (6 mm) from the top

It is strongly recommended that the system be dismantled at three-yearly intervals and old seals and fluid discarded. Before dismantling the system pump the old fluid out through the bleed nipple on the slave cylinder and pump at least a pint of methylated spirits through to remove any dirt or old gummy fluid from the pipes.

5:3 Removing and refitting clutch

1 Refer to **Chapter 6** and remove the gearbox.
2 Working from inside the car, remove the six bolts 8 (see **FIG 5:1**) which secure the clutch assembly to the flywheel.
3 Remove the assembly and the driven plate 1.

Inspecting:

When the clutch-flywheel cover pressing is removed, place clean rags around the lower portion of the clutch unit to prevent loose nuts, bolts, etc., from falling into the well on top of the transmission casing. Before refitting the cover ensure that nothing is lodged on the transmission casing beneath the clutch unit, as irreparable damage may be caused to the clutch unit and transmission casing when the engine is started.

Upon separating the component parts, the driven plate should be examined and if the linings are worn nearly to the retaining rivets or they are oil stained, then the plate should be renewed on an exchange basis. Never attempt to reline a clutch driven plate yourself. Check the flywheel for scoring (see **Chapter 1, Section 1:9**).

The clutch cover, pressure plate and spring assembly should never be dismantled, as already explained earlier in this Chapter, but if necessary renew it completely on an exchange basis.

The linings should appear an even shade of medium brown all over. Extreme glazing or dark brown colouring may indicate that the clutch has been slipping.

The appearance of oil staining on the driven plate may be due to failure of oil seals or too high an oil level in the transmission unit.

Refitting:

1 Before reassembling the clutch assembly and refitting the gearbox, check the condition of the clutch release bearing and mechanism inside the clutch housing attached to the gearbox (see **Section 5:4**).
2 Refer to **FIG 5:1** and position the driven plate so that when it is assembled, the longer boss of the splined hub will be towards the gearbox.
3 Offer up the driven plate and pressure plate assembly, centralize the driven plate with a mandrel, which will be a sliding fit through the driven plate hub splines and stepped down to enter the bush at the end of the crankshaft.
4 Ensure that the pressure plate locates correctly on the dowels of the flywheel.
5 Insert the six bolts and secure them evenly and progressively. Tighten the $\frac{5}{16}$ inch UNF bolts in the 1300 model to a torque of 16 to 20 lb ft (2 to 3 kg m) and the $\frac{1}{4}$ inch UNF bolts in the 1500 model to a torque of 8 to 11 lb ft (1 to $1\frac{1}{2}$ kg m).
6 Refix the gearbox as described in **Chapter 6**.

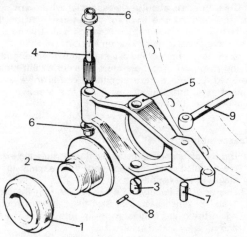

FIG 5:3   Details of clutch release mechanism

Key to Fig 5:3   1 Release bearing   **2** Sleeve   **3** Plug
4 Pivot   **5** Operating lever   **6** Trunnion   **7** Pushrod
pivot pin   **8** Retaining pin   **9** Pushrod

5:4 Clutch release mechanism

The components shown in **FIG 5:3** are mounted in the
bellhousing. To gain access, the gearbox must first be
removed (see **Chapter 6, Section 6:2**). Drive the pin 4
out of the bellhousing to free the assembly. Drive out the
pins 8 with a suitable punch and extract the plugs 3 to
free the bearing sleeve 2 and bearing 1.

The bearing 1 is a press fit on the sleeve 2, it is a sealed
unit and must be renewed if worn or noisy. The parts are
replaced in the reverse order of removal, making sure that
the trunnions 6 are in place and that the pushrod 9 seats
correctly on the piston of the slave cylinder.

5:5 Removing and replacing master cylinder

1 Drain the hydraulic system, either by pumping the
   hydraulic fluid out through a small bore hose connected to the bleed screw on the slave cylinder, or by
   syphoning the fluid out of the reservoir. If the latter
   method is used take precautions with regard to the
   paintwork otherwise the fluid will soften and lift the
   paint.
2 Refer to **FIG 5:4** and disconnect the fluid pipe 2.
3 From inside the car, extract the splitpin and withdraw
   the clevis pin, which connects the fork end of the
   master cylinder pushrod to the clutch pedal.
4 Remove the two nuts 3 which secure the master
   cylinder to the bulkhead and clutch pedal bracket.
   Lift out the master cylinder.

Refitting:

5 Complete operations 2 to 4 in the reverse order and
   bleed the hydraulic system as described in **Section
   5:9**.

5:6 Overhauling master cylinder

1 Remove the master cylinder as described in the
   previous section. Refer to **FIG 5:5**.

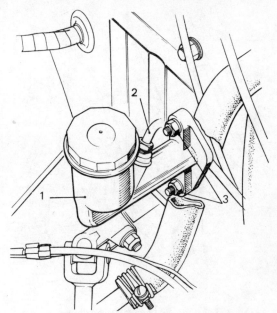

FIG 5:4   Removing master cylinder

Key to Fig 5:4   1 Reservoir   **2** Fluid pipe   **3** Securing
nuts

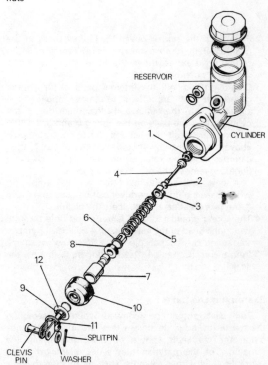

FIG 5:5   Component parts of master cylinder

Key to Fig 5:5   1 Seal   **2** Spring washer   **3** Distance
piece   **4** Valve shank   **5** Spring   **6** Spring retainer
7 Piston   **8** Seal   **9** Pushrod   **10** Dust cover   **11** Circlip
12 Pushrod stop

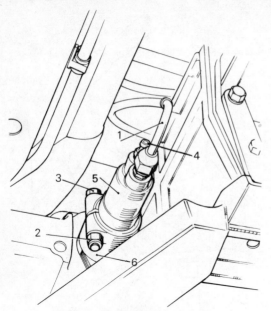

FIG 5:6   Removing slave cylinder

Key to Fig 5:6   1 Fluid pipe   2 Clamp nut   3 Clamp bolt
4 Bleed connection   5 Slave cylinder   6 Housing

2 Push back the rubber cover 10. Lightly press in the pushrod 9 to remove the pressure from the return spring 5 and extract the circlip 11. Remove the pushrod 9 and pushrod stop 12.

3 Carefully shake out the internal parts of the master cylinder. If these are difficult to remove, apply gentle air pressure to the outlet and blow them out of the cylinder. Part the coils on the spring 5 and use a thin screwdriver to lift the leaf on the spring retainer 6 above the level of the shoulder on the piston 7, then carefully pull the retainer off the piston. Use the fingers to remove the seal from the piston.

   A new seal should be fitted on reassembly, in which case a blunt screwdriver can be used to remove it, but take great care not to score the piston.

4 The spring retainer 6 has a larger offset hole through which the head of the valve shank 4 will pass. Remove the spring 5, distance piece 3 and spring washer 2 from the valve shank 4. Use the fingers to remove the seal 1.

Examining the parts:

   Both seals should be renewed when reassembling the master cylinder, so unless they are in perfect condition the old seals should be discarded. Clean the remainder of the parts in methylated spirits or clean hydraulic fluid. Other solvents, such as trichlorethylene, can be used on the metal parts but these must be absolutely dry and free from any traces of solvent before reassembly. Solvents other than methylated spirits will attack the material of the seals if it comes in contact with them.

Cleanliness is absolutely essential when working on any part of the hydraulic system so when the parts have been cleaned lay them on a clean sheet of paper to prevent them picking up any dirt.

   Examine the bore of the cylinder and the working face of the plunger 7. The bore must be smooth and highly polished, without a trace of pitting, corrosion or wear. Any of these three defects will mean that a new master cylinder assembly must be fitted.

Reassembling:

1 Dip the parts in clean hydraulic fluid as they are being reassembled, and fit them wet. This applies to all stages of reassembly.

2 Use only the fingers, no other tool, to refit the seals 1 and 8. When each seal is in place work it round, again using the fingers, to make sure that it is fully and squarely seated in its recess.

3 Replace the spring washer 2 so that its convex side is facing the flange on the valve shank 4. Replace the distance piece 3 so that its legs will face into the cylinder bore, and then the return spring 5 on top of this. Fit the head of the valve shank 4 through the larger offset hole in the spring retainer 6 and slide the retainer into position in the spring. Make sure that the stem of the valve shank is central in the spring retainer to prevent the spring retainer from coming off again.

4 Press the spring retainer 6 back onto the plunger 7 so that the leaf on the retainer seats squarely behind the shoulder on the plunger. Use a thin screwdriver between the coils of the spring to press the leaf gently into place if it will not seat on its own.

5 Though the individual parts should have been wetted as they were replaced, dip the complete internal assembly into clean hydraulic fluid and insert it wet into the bore of the cylinder. When the seal 8 starts to enter the bore take great care not to bend back or damage its lips, which should be facing into the bore. Use the fingers to press the edges into the bore and, when satisfied that all the edges of the lips are properly in the bore, press the plunger in further.

6 Refit the pushrod 9 and its stop 12, using the pushrod to press the plunger down the bore while refitting the circlip 11. Press the plunger fully down the bore and make sure that it returns under the action of the return spring before refitting the dust cover 10. Check that the breathing hole in the filler cap is clear.

7 Refit the master cylinder as described in **Section 5:5**.

5:7   Removing and refitting slave cylinder

1 Removing the slave cylinder will entail working under the car. Jack up the front end or drive it onto a raised ramp. If it is jacked up, make sure it is safely secured with stands.

2 Drain the hydraulic system as described in **Section 5:5** then refer to **FIG 5:6**.

3 Uncouple the hydraulic pipe and push it clear. Unscrew the clamp nut and withdraw the clamp bolt.

4 Pull the slave cylinder clear of the housing.

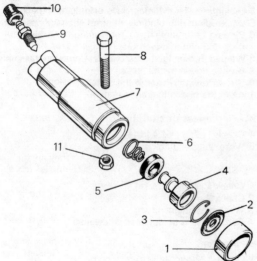

FIG 5:7   Component parts of slave cylinder

Key to Fig 5:7   1 Dust cover   2 Retainer   3 Circlip
4 Piston   5 Seal   6 Spring   7 Slave cylinder   8 Clamp
bolt   9 Bleed screw   10 Cap   11 Clamp nut

Refitting:

5 Centralize the pushrod on the clutch release mechanism so that it will enter the slave cylinder. Push the cylinder into the housing, link up the clamp **bolt** groove, insert the clamp **bolt** and tighten the nut securely.

6 Reconnect the hydraulic pipe and bleed the system as described in **Section 5:9.**

5:8 Overhauling slave cylinder

1 Remove the slave cylinder as described in the previous section.

2 Refer to **FIG 5:7,** remove the dust cover 1 and retainer 2.

3 Spring the circlip 3 out of its groove but be most careful not to scratch or damage the cylinder bore whilst doing so.

4 Remove the piston 4 by either shaking it out of the cylinder or applying a light air pressure with a foot pump through the bleed screws. Do not try and extract the piston with a metal tool.

5 Remove the spring 6.

Examing the parts:

6 The same conditions apply with regard to cleaning and general cleanliness as those described for the master cylinder. Also examine the piston and cylinder bore for similar defects. Renew the seal 5 and dust cover 1 whatever the condition. Renew the circlip 3 if the tension is weak.

Reassembling:

7 Dip all the parts in clean brake fluid whilst assembling them and thoroughly wet the cylinder bore. Replace the parts in the reverse order of dismantling and check the positions by referring to **FIG 5:7.**

8 Refit the slave cylinder to the car (see **Section 5:7).**

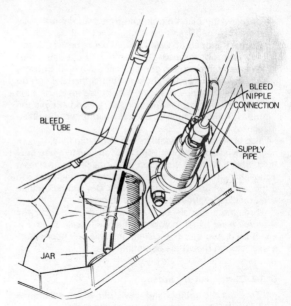

FIG 5:8   Bleeding the clutch system

5:9 Bleeding the hydraulic system

This operation will only normally be required when component parts of the clutch hydraulic system have been dismantled.

1 Ensure that the clutch reservoir is topped to within $\frac{1}{4}$ inch from the top. The clutch master cylinder reservoir is smaller than the brake reservoir which is located on the engine bulkhead.

2 Wipe the slave cylinder bleed nipple clean (see **FIG 5:8**) and attach a length of rubber tubing. Place the end of the tubing in a jar containing hydraulic fluid and ensure that its end is kept below the fluid level in the jar.

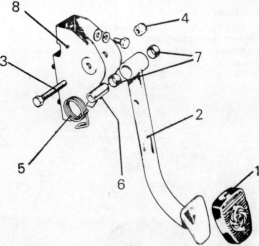

FIG 5:9   Removing clutch pedal return spring

Key to Fig 5:9   1 Rubber pad   2 Pedal   3 Pivot bolt
4 Nut   5 Spring   6 Sleeve   7 Pedal bushes   8 Bracket

3 Unscrew the bleed nipple one turn then depress fully the clutch pedal and let it return without assistance. Repeat this operation with a slight pause between each depression of the pedal. Observe the fluid being discharged into the glass container and when all bubbles have ceased to appear, hold the clutch pedal down on the following down stroke. Whilst the pedal is thus held, securely tighten the bleed screw and remove the tubing from the nipple. Do not overtighten the bleed screw.

4 Top up the master cylinder with hydraulic fluid.

For bleeding or replenishment of the system use only fluid that has been stored in a container sealed from atmosphere. Use only authorized Castrol-Girling fluid and if the expelled fluid in the jar is retained it should only be used for bleeder tube immersion purposes.

Throughout the bleeding operation, do not allow the reservoir level to fall below the half-full mark or air will again be drawn into the system and this will necessitate a fresh start to the whole operation.

5:10 Clutch return spring

1 Take out the splitpin and clevis pin which secure the master cylinder pushrod to the clutch pedal.

2 Unscrew and remove the clutch pedal pivot bolt (see **FIG 5:9**).

3 Disconnect the pedal return spring.

If during the operation it becomes necessary to remove the parcel shelf, and in some cases this might be a possibility, refer to **Chapter 12.**

Refitting:

4 Position the new spring on the pedal and align the pivot sleeve to the holes in the bracket.

5 Lubricate the pivot bolt and insert it in the bush, fit a new locking nut and tighten.

6 Refit the pushrod fork end. Use a new splitpin.

5:11 Fault diagnosis

(a) Drag or spin

1 Oil or grease on driven plate linings
2 Bent engine backplate
3 Misalignment between the engine and transmission unit

4 Leaking master cylinder, slave cylinder or pipeline
5 Driven plate hub binding on input shaft splines
6 Binding of input shaft spigot bearing
7 Distorted clutch driven plate
8 Warped or damaged pressure plate or cover assembly
9 Broken driven plate linings
10 Dirt or foreign matter in the clutch
11 Air in the clutch hydraulic system

(b) Fierceness or snatch

1 Check 1, 2, 3 and 4 in (a)
2 Worn clutch linings

(c) Slip

1 Check 1, 2 and 3 in (a)
2 Check 2 in (b)
3 Weak diaphragm spring
4 Seized piston in clutch slave cylinder

(d) Judder

1 Check 1, 2 and 3 in (a)
2 Pressure plate not parallel with flywheel
3 Contact area of driven plate linings not evenly distributed
4 Bent input shaft
5 Buckled driven plate
6 Faulty engine transmission unit rubber mountings

(e) Rattle

1 Check 3 in (c)
2 Broken springs in driven plate
3 Worn release mechanism
4 Excessive backlash in transmission and final drive unit
5 Wear in transmission bearings
6 Release bearing loose in its throwout lever

(f) Tick or knock

1 Worn input shaft spigot or bearings
2 Badly worn splines in driven plate hub
3 Throwout lever out of line or bent
4 Faulty starter motor drive
5 Loose flywheel

(g) Driven plate fracture

1 Check 2 and 3 in (a)

CHAPTER 6

THE GEARBOX

6 : 1 Description

The gearbox is fitted with four forward speeds and one reverse. All four forward speeds are fitted with synchromesh engagement and reverse is obtained by sliding into mesh an idler which reverses the direction of rotation of the mainshaft. The gearlever is mounted on a separate extension which brings it within easy reach of the driver's hand. Gear selection is by three selector shafts and forks mounted in the gearbox top cover. The three selector shafts are fitted with an interlock mechanism which allows only one shaft to be moved at a time and so prevents the inadvertent selection of two gears at the same time. Spring-operated plungers engage in detents in the selector shafts to prevent them moving from the selected position.

The mainshaft rotates in two ballbearings, the rear bearing being held in the removable rear extension. The input shaft also rotates in a ballbearing mounted in the front of the gearbox casing. A spigot on the mainshaft fits into a roller bearing in the input shaft and the countershaft gear cluster rotates about similar roller bearings on the countershaft. Thrust washers are fitted to take the end thrusts and to control the end float.

A drain plug is fitted underneath the gearbox casing and a combined level and filler plug is fitted to the right-hand side of the gearbox casing as shown in **FIG 6 : 1**. The gearbox is filled with the correct grade of Hypoid oil so that the level is just at the bottom of the filler hole.

The gearchange extension, top cover, rear extension and speedometer drive pinion parts can be removed without fully taking the gearbox out of the car.

6 : 2 Removing the gearbox

The gearbox can be removed from the car without removing the engine. During the process the car must be raised on stands or a ramp to gain access to the underside. It must be stressed, that if the car is raised on jacks and supported with stands, the supports must be firmly based and rigid enough to afford complete safety for the operator.

1 Disconnect the battery.
2 Refer to **Chapter 12** to remove the front seats and the parcel shelf.
3 Refer to **FIG 6 : 2** to take out the gearbox tunnel. To remove the reinforcement tube (inset) unscrew the

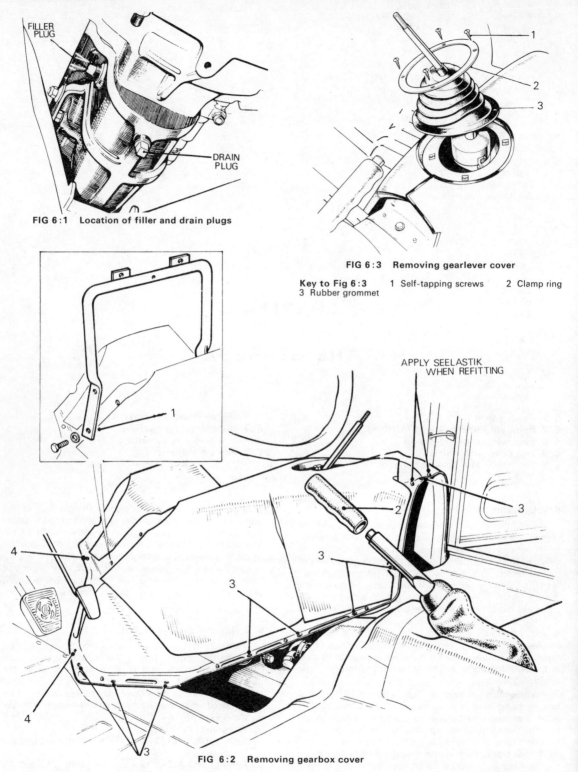

FIG 6 : 1   Location of filler and drain plugs

FILLER PLUG

DRAIN PLUG

FIG 6 : 3   Removing gearlever cover

Key to Fig 6 : 3   1 Self-tapping screws   2 Clamp ring
3 Rubber grommet

APPLY SEELASTIK
WHEN REFITTING

FIG 6 : 2   Removing gearbox cover

Key to Fig 6 : 2   1 Reinforcement tube   2 Handbrake grip   3 Securing bolts   4 Securing nuts

two setscrews and collect the washers. Unscrew the gearlever knob and locknut, take up the cover carpet and remove the four self-tapping screws which secure a clamp ring over the rubber grommet (see **FIG 6:3**). Lift off the rubber grommet. Pull off the handbrake lever grip 2. Unscrew and remove the fifteen surround bolts 3, the four nuts 4 (setscrews on early cars) and break the seal between the tunnel and the floor. Carefully lift the gearbox tunnel cover over the gearlever and out of the car.

4 Refer to **FIG 6:1** and drain the gearbox oil.
5 Working below the car, disconnect the propeller shaft universal coupling from the gearbox rear flange (see **Chapter 7**).
6 Disconnect the speedometer cable. Refer to **Chapter 5, Section 5:7** and remove the clutch slave cylinder.
7 Support the engine by placing a jack under the sump, position a block of wood between the jack pad and the sump casing before taking the weight. Disconnect the exhaust pipe from its support bracket.
8 Refer to **FIG 6:4** and take off the mounting nut and washer 2. Remove all the bellhousing bolts which are only accessible from underneath the car including the lower mounting bolt for the starter. From the engine compartment remove the starter upper mounting bolt and take note of any shims that may be fitted between the starter motor and its packing. Remove the remaining bolts from inside the car and detach the gearbox rear mounting assembly.
9 Lift and manoeuvre the gearbox clear of the car. It is of paramount importance that the gearbox constant pinion shaft, or input shaft, is not at any time allowed to support the gearbox by hanging onto the clutch plate splines.
10 If any work is to be carried out on the clutch, refer to **Chapter 5.**

Refitting:

11 Check that the clutch driven plate is perfectly aligned (see **Chapter 5, Section 5:3** under the heading 'Refitting').
12 Manoeuvre the gearbox into position, align the splines and heed the warning given in operation 9. Refer to **FIG 6:4** and fit the dowel bolt and nut 5, but do not fully tighten at this stage.
13 Fit the bellhousing bolts and nuts and assembly the gearbox mounting brackets. Fit the starter and then fully tighten the mounting and bellhousing bolts.
14 Refit the remaining parts in the reverse order of dismantling, operations 1 to 7.
15 Fill the gearbox with the correct grade of hypoid oil (SAE.90.EP).

6:3 Removing rear extension

The rear extension can be removed from the gearbox, without removing the gearbox, to renew any malfunctioning part that is housed within it; such as the roller bearing or the speedometer drive gear. It will be necessary to work under the vehicle to complete the operation so take precautions when raising the car and make sure it is supported safely with stands.

1 Refer to **Chapter 7** and disconnect the propeller shaft.

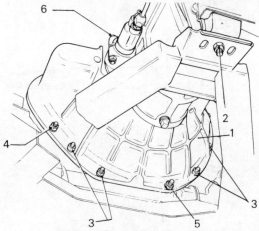

FIG 6:4   Removing bellhousing

Key to Fig 6:4   1 Bellhousing   2 Mounting nut
3 Securing bolts   4 Starter lower mounting bolt
5 Aligning bolt   6 Clamp bolt

2 Select 1st gear, refer to **FIG 6:5**, unscrew the flange nut 1, collect the washer 2 and carefully remove the drive flange 3.
3 Support the engine by placing a jack under the sump and spread the load by interspacing with a block of wood between the jack pad and the sump casing.
4 Disconnect the exhaust pipe support bracket 4 and remove the gearbox mounting assembly 5.
5 Uncouple the speedometer cable and remove the speedometer pinion (see operation 9), take out the retaining bolts 6 and collect the spring washers.
6 Withdraw the extension, the joint washer 7 and the mainshaft washer 8.

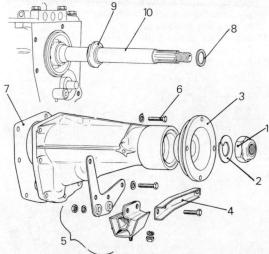

FIG 6:5   Dismantling rear extension

Key to Fig 6:5   1 Flange nut   2 Washer   3 Drive flange
4 Exhaust pipe support bracket   5 Gearbox mounting
brackets   6 Securing bolts   7 Gasket   8 Washer
9 Speedometer drive gear   10 Mainshaft

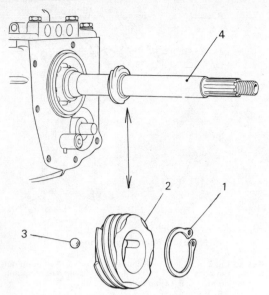

FIG 6:6   Removing speedometer drive gear

Key to Fig 6:6   1 Circlip   2 Drive gear   3 Detent ball
4 Mainshaft

Removing speedometer drive gear:

7 Refer to **FIG 6:6,** remove the circlip and slide the
drive gear off the mainshaft. Take care not to lose the
detent ball.

8 Fit the detent ball before sliding the gear over the
mainshaft and secure with a new circlip.

Removing speedometer drive gear pinion:

9 The pinion can be removed without taking off the
extension. Refer to **FIG 6:7,** unscrew and remove the
peg bolt 1 and washer, withdraw the pinion 2 and
housing 3 as an assembly.

10 Extract the pinion from its housing and renew the
O-rings 4 if necessary and the seal 5.

11 Replace the parts in the reverse order of removal.

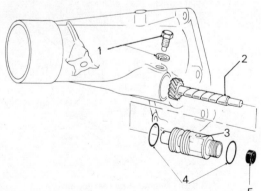

FIG 6:7   Removing speedometer drive pinion

Key to Fig 6:7   1 Peg bolt   2 Pinion   3 Housing
4 O-rings   5 Seal

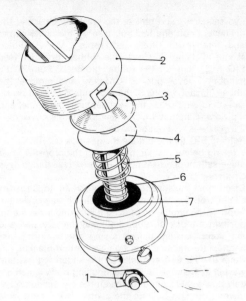

FIG 6:8   Removing gearlever

Key to Fig 6:8   1 Nut   2 Cap   3 Steel cap   4 Nylon
cap   5 Spring   6 Spring   7 Nylon sphere

Removing mainshaft rear bearing and seal:

12 Extract the seal and drive out the roller bearing with
a drift.

13 Press in a new bearing and a new seal.

Refitting rear extension:

14 Refer to **FIG 6:5,** fit the mainshaft washer 8 and the
gasket 7. Locate the extension and fit and tighten the
securing bolts 6.

15 Fit the remaining parts in the reverse order of dismantling and refer to the appropriate illustrations and
sections.

6:4 Top cover extension

Removing:

1 Refer to **FIG 6:3** and take up the gearbox cover
carpet. Remove the four self-tapping screws, unscrew
the gearlever knob and locknut, lift off the clamp ring
and the rubber grommet. Remove the fabric washer if
fitted.

2 Raise the car onto secure stands or a ramp. Working
underneath the vehicle, refer to **FIG 6:8,** unscrew the
nut 1 and withdraw the bolt and washer. From inside
the car, release the cap 2 and lift off the cap, the steel
and nylon cups and the spring. Withdraw the gearlever.

3 Open the bonnet and working in the engine compartment, unscrew the four nuts and pick up the spring
washers which secure the top cover extension (see
FIG 6:9).

4 Remove the extension from inside the car and lift off
the joint washer. Cover the opening over the gearbox
to prevent any carelessly dropped nuts and bolts, or
any other alien matter, from entering.

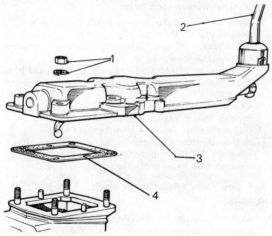

FIG 6 : 9   Top cover extension

Key to Fig 6 : 9   1 Retaining nut and washer   **2** Gearlever
3 Cover   **4** Gasket

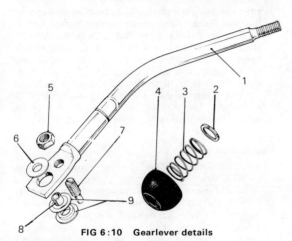

FIG 6 : 10   Gearlever details

Key to Fig 6 : 10   1 Gearlever   **2** Snap ring
3 Spring   **4** Nylon sphere   **5** Nut   **6** Washer   **7** Stop-bolt
8 Pinch sleeve   **9** Bush and washer

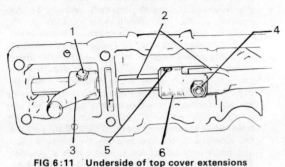

FIG 6 : 11   Underside of top cover extensions

Key to Fig 6 : 11   1 Taper locking pin   **2** Shaft assembly
3 Actuator   **4** Nut   **5** Locating pin   **6** Fork ends

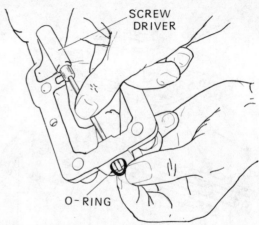

**FIG 6 : 12   Removing the O-rings from top cover exten-
sion**

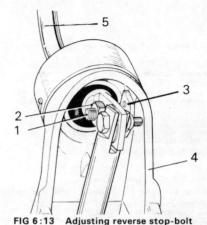

FIG 6 : 13   Adjusting reverse stop-bolt

Key to Fig 6 : 13   1 Stop-bolt   **2** Locknut   **3** Stop-plate
4 Cover extension   **5** Gearlever

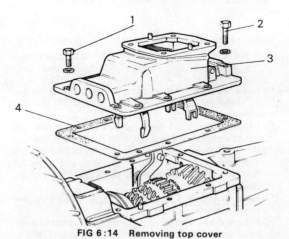

FIG 6 : 14   Removing top cover

Key to Fig 6 : 14   1 Securing bolt (front)   **2** Securing bolt
(rear)   **3** Cover   **4** Gasket

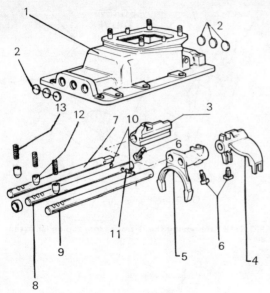

FIG 6:15   Top cover and selector details

Key to Fig 6:15   1 Cover   2 Welch plugs   3 Reverse selector   4 1st/2nd selector   5 3rd/4th selector   6 Taper locking pins   7 Reverse selector shaft   8 1st/2nd selector shaft   9 3rd/4th selector shaft   10 Interlock balls   11 Interlock plunger   12 Plungers   13 Springs

Overhauling gearlever:

5 Refer to **FIG 6:10** and remove the snap ring 2, spring 3 and the nylon sphere 4.

6 Take out the pinch sleeve 8 and the bushes and washers 9. Slacken the locknut 5 and unscrew the stop bolt 7.

7 Inspect the bushes, nylon sphere and stop bolt for wear. Renew the snap ring 2, the spring 3 and any other part that shows the least sign of wear.

8 Refer to the illustration to fit the new parts.

Overhauling cover extension:

9 If the reverse stop plate is severely scored, drill out the two rivets and renew it. Re-secure with pop rivets.

10 Refer to **FIG 6:11** and unscrew the taper locking pin 1, withdraw the shaft assembly 2 and lift out the actuator 3.

11 Unscrew the nut 4, take out the bolt, separate the shafts and collect the washers. If the bush is worn at the fork end connection, press or drift out the old bush and press in a new one. If the fork end is to be removed, drive out the pin 5 to separate it from the shaft.

12 Refer to **FIG 6:12** to remove the O-rings from the housing bores.

13 Renew the parts where necessary and reassemble the cover extension. Tighten the nut 4 to a torque of 8 to 10 lb ft (1 to $1\frac{1}{4}$ kg m). Fit a new gasket when refitting the cover and adjust the reverse stop bolt.

Adjusting reverse stop bolt:

14 Refer to **FIG 6:13** and position the gearlever in neutral, but at the side of the gate ready to select either 1st or 2nd gear. Adjust the stop bolt 1 with the lever in this position, the stop bolt should have a clearance of .010 to .050 inch (.26 to 1.27 mm) from the plate 3 to prevent the inadvertant selection of reverse.

15 Check the 1st and 2nd gear selections and then the reverse; tighten the locknut.

16 Smear the stop plate with a little grease.

17 If the adjustment cannot be obtained satisfactorily, wear in the plate and stop bolt will be the only logical cause, these should have been renewed.

6:5 Top cover and selector shafts

Removing:

1 Remove the top cover extension as described in the previous section. From the engine compartment and referring to **FIG 6:14** remove the top cover and selector shafts. Lift off the gasket.

2 Tap out the Welch plugs 2 using a $\frac{1}{8}$ inch (3.17 mm) diameter pin punch (see **FIG 6:15**). **Take care that the selector shafts are clear when removing the plugs.** Remove the tapered locking pins 6 to free the three selector forks. Press the selector shaft 8 out of the cover with the sleeve (early models only), followed by the other two selector shafts 7 and 9, taking out each selector fork as it is freed. Collect the interlock balls 10 as well as the interlock plunger 11. Shake out the three plungers 12 and springs 13. A packing disc may be fitted between the centre detent plunger and spring. Refit in the same position on reassembly.

Reassembling:

3 Thoroughly clean all the parts and examine them for wear. Check that the detents in the shafts are not worn and renew any parts that are worn or damaged.

   Fit the springs 13 into the recesses in the plungers 12 and slide them, springs first, into their bores in the cover. Slide the third/top selector shaft 9 into position from the front of the cover. Depress the appropriate plunger until the shaft has passed over it, also pick up the selector fork 5 on the shaft. Set the shaft so that the detent plunger registers in the middle notch on the shaft and the shaft is in the neutral position. Similarly refit the reverse selector shaft 7 and the selector 3. Place the interlock plunger 11 into position in the first/second selector shaft 8 and similarly, slide the shaft into position in the cover. Do not yet press the shaft fully home and note that the shaft also passes through the top/third selector fork 4. Before the shaft is fully in position replace the two interlock balls 10 as shown in **FIG 6:16**. With the balls in position press the selector shaft fully home so that it comes into the neutral position and the interlock balls are held in place. Secure the selector forks in place using the tapered pins 6. Make sure that the recesses for the Welch plugs are perfectly clean and press new plugs into position with a smear of jointing compound around the edges as a sealant. Slightly flatten the Welch plugs with a soft drift in order to lock them into position.

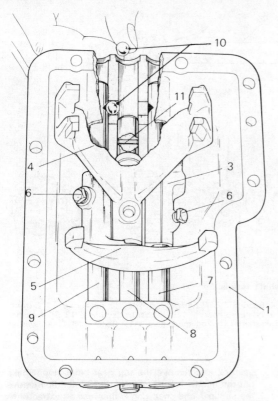

FIG 6:16 Replace the interlock balls before the shaft is in position

Key to Fig 6:16   1 Cover   2 Welch plugs   3 Reverse selector   4 1st/2nd selector   5 3rd/4th selector   6 Taper locking pins   7 Reverse selector shaft   8 1st/2nd selector shaft .   9 3rd/4th selector shaft   10 Interlock balls 11 Interlock plunger

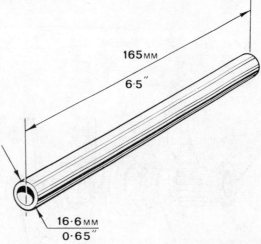

FIG 6:18   Countershaft gear cluster support tube (tool only)

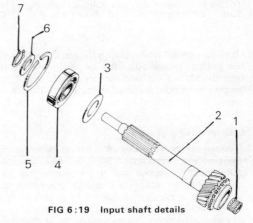

FIG 6:19   Input shaft details

Key to Fig 6:19   1 Needle roller bearing   2 Input shaft 3 Oil thrower   4 Bearing   5 Snap ring   6 Washer 7 Circlip

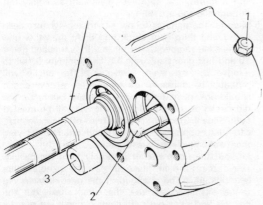

FIG 6:17   Removing countershaft

Key to Fig 6:17   1 Reverse spindle securing bolt 2 Reverse spindle   3 Distance piece

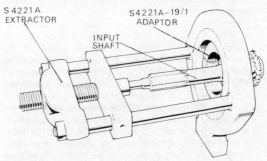

FIG 6:20   Extracting the bearing from the input shaft

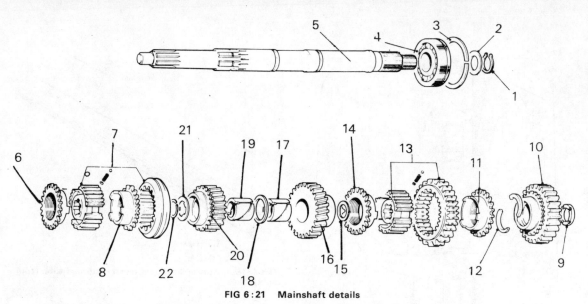

FIG 6:21 Mainshaft details

Key to Fig 6:21 1 Circlip 2 Distance washer 3 Snap ring 4 Bearing 5 Mainshaft 6 Top gear baulk ring 7 3rd/4th synchromesh unit 8 3rd gear baulk ring 9 Thrust washer 10 1st speed gear 11 1st gear baulk ring 12 Split washer 13 1st/2nd synchromesh unit 14 2nd gear baulk ring 15 Thrust washer 16 2nd speed gear 17 Bush 18 Thrust washer 19 Bush 20 3rd speed gear 21 Circlip washer 22 Circlip

4 Use a new gasket when refitting the top cover back to the gearbox. Make sure that all the gears are in neutral and that the selectors locate correctly. The longer pair of bolts are fitted at the rear of the cover.

6:6 Dismantling gearbox

1 Remove the gearbox from the car as described in **Section 6:2.** Some special tools will be required to dismantle the gearbox and if the owner has any doubts as to his ability to strip and reassemble the gearbox he is strongly advised to take the unit to a suitably equipped agent for expert attention.

Remove the clutch release mechanism as described in **Chapter 5, Section 5:4.** Take off the rear extension to the appropriate operations given in **Section 6:3** and the top cover and selector shafts to the operations given in **Section 6:5.** Unscrew and remove the four bolts which secure the bellhousing to the gearbox, including the single bolt with a copper washer.

2 Remove the reverse spindle securing bolt 1, as shown in **FIG 6:17,** and withdraw the spindle 2 and distance piece 3. Press out the countershaft, by inserting a piece of tubing .655 inch (16.64 mm) in diameter and 6.5 inch (165 mm) long as shown in **FIG 6:18,** from the front of the gearbox. Leave the tubing in place in the countershaft gear cluster so as to retain the roller bearings in position, allowing the countershaft gears to fall clear of the mainshaft gears.

3 Attach the special tool No. S.4235A-2 to the front end of the input shaft, and, by sliding the moving weight smartly along the shaft so that it impacts on the handle, draw the input shaft assembly out of the

gearbox and remove the top gear baulk ring. Shake out the needle roller bearing 1 in **FIG 6:19.** Remove the circlip 7 and snap ring 5 then use an extractor to remove the bearing 4 thus also freeing the oil thrower 3 (see **FIG 6:20**).

4 Refer to **FIG 6:21** to dismantle the mainshaft. Remove the circlip 1 distance washer 2 and snap ring 3. Use adaptor No. S.4221A-19/1 (which fits into the annular groove in the bearing 4 as shown in **FIG 6:22**) and the hand press to withdraw the bearing while supporting the front end of the mainshaft with the abutment plate No. S.4221A-19, as shown in **FIG 6:23.** Remove the abutment plate, tilt the front end of the mainshaft assembly upwards and withdraw the complete mainshaft assembly out through the top aperture.

5 Slide off the parts as follows: third/top synchromesh unit 7 and third gear baulk ring 8. At the other end of the shaft remove thrust washer 9, first speed geear 10 and first gear baulk ring 11. Use tool No. S.144 to remove the mainshaft circlip 22. The circlip will probably be damaged on removal so a new circlip should always be fitted on reassembly, but retain the old circlip as, despite damage, it will still be needed later. Slide the remainder of the parts off the mainshaft, carefully noting their position and order and laying them out on a clean sheet of paper.

6 Lift out the countershaft assembly from the casing. Leave the tube in place unless the needle roller bearings are to be changed. If the needle rollers are to be examined, remove the tube, shake out the needles and prise out the retaining rings. Lift out the reverse idler gear with its bush. Undo the nut to remove the parts of the reverse gear actuator (see **FIG 6:30**).

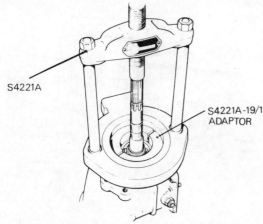

FIG 6:22 Removing bearing from mainshaft

S4221A

S4221A-19/1 ADAPTOR

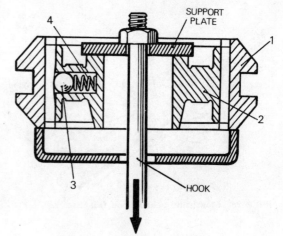

SUPPORT PLATE

4

1

2

3

HOOK

FIG 6:25 Testing synchromesh unit

Key to Fig 6:25 1 Outer member 2 Inner member
3 Ball 4 Spring

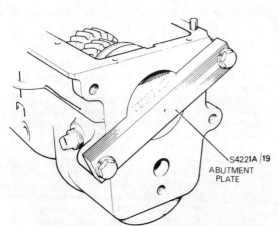

FIG 6:23 Supporting the front end of the mainshaft with an abutment plate

S4221A/19 ABUTMENT PLATE

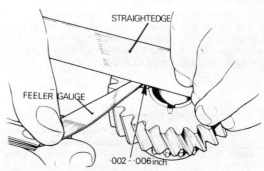

STRAIGHTEDGE

FEELER GAUGE

·002 - ·006 inch

FIG 6:26 Measuring the end float of the gear on its bush

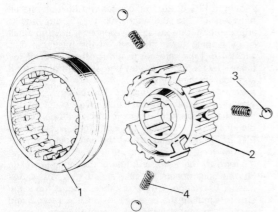

FIG 6:24 Synchromesh unit details

3

2

1

4

Key to Fig 6:24 1 Outer member 2 Inner member
3 Ball 4 Spring

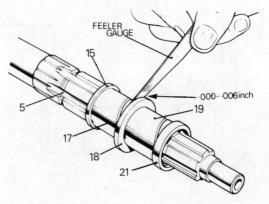

FEELER GAUGE

15

5

·000 - ·006 inch

19

17

18

21

FIG 6:27 Measuring end float of bushes (see Key to FIG 6:21)

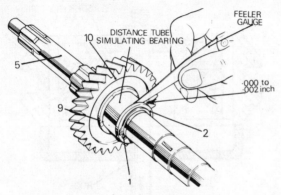

FIG 6:28 Measuring bearing end float (see Key to FIG 6:21)

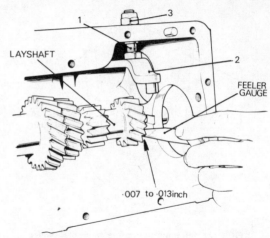

FIG 6:30 Measuring end float between countershaft gears and thrust washer

Key to Fig 6:30 1 Pivot bolt 2 Actuator 3 Securing nut

Synchromesh units:

These are easily dismantled by pressing the outer sleeve off the unit. Before dismantling them wrap them completely in a clean cloth and press the parts apart while still in the cloth in order to catch and keep the balls 3, springs 4 and shims (see **FIG 6:24**).

6:7 Reassembling the gearbox

Thoroughly clean all the parts, washing them at least twice, the second wash being in clean solvent. Carefully examine the parts and renew any that are worn or seem doubtful. Check all shafts and bearing surfaces for fret or chatter marks. Check the gears to make sure that there are no broken, worn or missing teeth. Renew all the oil

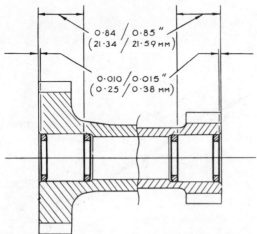

FIG 6:29 Fit the needle rollers and retaining rings to the dimensions shown

seals and fit new gaskets so as to ensure against oil leaks after the gearbox has been reassembled and refitted to the car.

1 Refit the balls and springs to the hubs of the synchromesh units, holding them in place with grease. Compress the balls back into the hubs using a hose clip tightened around the hub. Insert the hub into the outer sleeve and tap it into place, allowing the hose clip to slide off, until the balls click into the detent grooves in the sleeve. Test each synchromesh unit in a jig as shown in **FIG 6:25**. Apply a gradually increasing pull to the hook, using a spring balance, and note the load required to move the balls out of the detent position. If the load is incorrect, either adjust it by fitting new springs or reset it by fitting shims under the springs. The correct release load for both synchromesh units should be 19 to 21 lb (8.6 to 9.5 kg).

2 Measure the end float of each gear on its bush as shown in **FIG 6:26**. The correct end float should lie between .002 to .006 inch (.05 to .15 mm) and is adjusted either by fitting new bushes if it is too small or by lapping down the ends of the bushes if it is excessive. Take care not to reduce the length of the bushes by too much, as they partially control the total end float on the mainshaft.

3 Assemble the thrust washer 15, bush 17, thrust washer 18, bush 19, and circlip washer 21 to the mainshaft, securing the parts in place with part of the old circlip 22. Measure the end float as shown in **FIG 6:27**. If required, adjust the end float so that it lies between the correct limits 0 to .006 inch (0 to .15 mm) by the selective fitting of the thrust washers.

4 Fit the split collars 12 first speed gear 10, thrust washer 9, bearing 4 (or a distance tube of the same size to simulate the bearing) distance washer 2 and circlip 1 to the mainshaft. Measure the end float as shown in **FIG 6:28** and adjust it to the correct limits of 0 to .002 inch (0 to .05 mm) by selectively fitting the right width washer 2.

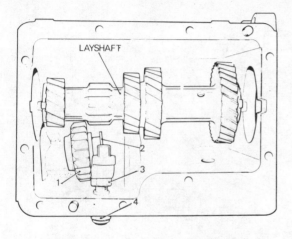

FIG 6:31   Refitting the reverse idler gear

Key to Fig 6:31   1 Reverse idler gear   2 Bush
3 Locknut   4 Securing nut

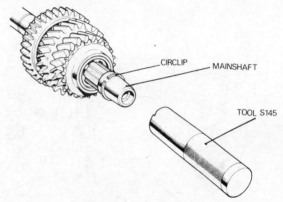

FIG 6:32   Fitting the circlip 22 to the mainshaft

5 If the needle roller bearings have been removed from the countershaft fit new retaining rings to the dimensions shown in **FIG 6:29**. Replace the needle rollers, holding them in with thick grease and finally retaining them in position using a tube of the dimensions given earlier. Fit the front thrust washer into place in the casing so that .its tag locates in the recess provided. Hold it in place with thick grease and centralize it by partially entering the countershaft. Lower the countershaft gear cluster assembly into position and press in the countershaft so that it ejects the tube and supports the gear cluster (see **FIG 6:34**). Fit the rear thrust washer correctly into place and pass the countershaft through it. Measure the end float of the gears between them and a thrust washer as shown in **FIG 6:30**. Adjust to the correct end float of .007 to .013 inch (.178 to .330 mm) by the selective fitting of the thrust washers. End float may be increased by lapping down the steel faces of the thrust washers but never the bronze faces. Once the end float is satisfactory, press back the bearing retaining tube and allow the cluster to slide to the bottom of the casing.

6 Refer to **FIG 6:30** and screw the pivot 1 back into the actuator 2 so that one thread protrudes through the boss. Secure the assembly back in place in the casing using the plain washer and nut 3. Refit the reverse idler gear and its bush so that they lie as shown in **FIG 6:31**.

7 Refit the parts to the mainshaft in the reverse order of removal. Refit the circlip 22 using special tool No. S145 as shown in **FIG 6:32** before refitting the remainder of the parts. Replace the mainshaft assembly in the gearbox and support the front end with the abutment plate tool as shown in **FIG 6:23**. Set the gearbox on end and support it by clamping the abutment plate in a vice. Slide in the thrust washer 9. Refit the snap ring 3 to the rear bearing

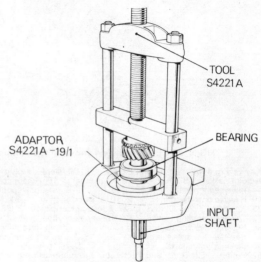

FIG 6:33   Fitting bearing to input shaft

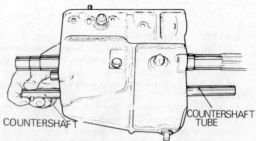

FIG 6:34   Press out the locating tube by inserting the countershaft from the rear of the gearbox

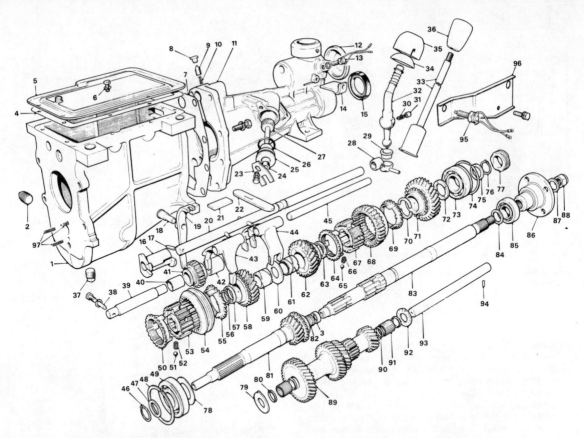

FIG 6:35 Exploded view showing the components of the later type gearbox fitted to the Toledo

Key to Fig 6:35   1 Gearbox case   2 Oil filler level plug   3 Spacer   4 Joint gaskets   5 Top cover   6 Top cover bolt
7 Joint gasket   8 Plug   9 Detent plunger   10 Detent spring   11 Rear extension   12 End cover   13 Reverse light switch
14 Reverse lift plate   15 Oil seal   16 Interlock spool   17 Selector shaft roll-pin   18 Reverse operating lever pin
19 Reverse operating lever   20 Gear selector shaft   21 Magnet   22 Interlock spool plate   23 Retaining clip   24 Seal
25 Housing   26 'O' ring   27 Speedometer pinion   28 Gearlever yoke   29 Seat   30 Spring   31 Anti-rattle plunger
32 Lower gearchange lever   33 Upper gearchange lever   34 Dust cover washer   35 Dust cover   36 Knob   37 Drain plug
38 Reverse idler spindle locating screw   39 Reverse idler spindle   40 Reverse idler gear bush   41 Reverse idler gear
42 Reverse idler distance piece   43 Third- and fourth-speed selector forks   44 First- and second-speed selector forks
45 Selector fork shaft   46 Circlip   47 Backing washer   48 Snap ring   49 Ballbearing   50 Synchromesh cup   51 Ball
52 Spring   53 Third- and fourth-speed synchromesh hub   54 Third- and fourth-speed operating sleeve   55 Synchromesh cup
56 Mainshaft circlip   57 Third-speed gear thrust washer   58 Third-speed gear   59 Gear bush   60 Selective washer
61 Gear bush   62 Second-speed gear   63 Thrust washer   64 Synchromesh cup   65 Ball   66 Spring   67 First- and
second-speed operating sleeve   68 Mainshaft reverse gear   69 Synchromesh cup   70 Split collar   71 First-speed gear
72 Thrust washer   73 Mainshaft centre bearing   74 Snap ring   75 Selective washer   76 Circlip   77 Speedometer wheel
78 Oil flinger   79 Front thrust washer   80 Bearing outer retaining ring   81 First-motion shaft   82 Needle-roller bearing
83 Mainshaft   84 Washer   85 Ballbearing   86 Drive flange   87 Washer   88 Self-locking nut   89 Laygear gear cluster
90 Bearing inner retaining ring   91 Needle-rollers   92 Thrust washer   93 Layshaft   94 Layshaft dowel   95 Seat belt
switch (if fitted)   96 Bracket (if fitted)   97 Laygear pre-load springs

4 and drive the bearing back into the casing so that
the snap ring is tight against the face of the casing.
Refit the distance washer 2 and the circlip 1. Press
into place the speedometer drive gear. Lay the gearbox back onto the bench and remove the abutment
plate.

8 Reassemble the parts of the input shaft assembly,
making sure that the oil thrower 3, in **FIG 6:19** is kept
squarely in position until the bearing 4 has been fully
pressed back into position (see **FIG 6:33**). Fit the
baulk ring back onto the mainshaft and drive the

input shaft assembly back into position, making sure
that the lugs on the baulk ring fit into the slots in the
synchromesh hub.

9 Turn the gearbox over, align the countershaft gear
cluster and thrust washers. Press out the locating tube
by inserting the countershaft from the rear of the
gearbox as shown in **FIG 6:34.** Keep the tube and
countershaft in firm contact throughout this operation to prevent either the thrust washers or needle
rollers from becoming misaligned. Make sure that the
reverse gear is in the correct position and slide into

place the reverse idler spindle 2 followed by the distance tube 3 (see **FIG 6:17**). Hold the spindle in place using the peg bolt 1 and washer.

10 Drive the bearing and oil seal into place in the rear extension. Refit the rear extension, using a new gasket and securing it in place with the bolts. Refer to **Section 6:3** if necessary. Replace the driving flange securing it with the washer and nut. Refit the speedometer driven gear parts, securing them with with the peg bolt (see **FIG 6:7**).

11 Refit the clutch cover using a new gasket. Use a new copper washer under the bolt if the old washer is damaged or distorted. Refit the parts of the clutch release mechanism.

12 Refit the top cover, referring to **Section 6:5** and refit the gearbox to the car as described in **Section 6:2**.

6:8 The single rail gearbox

This, like the earlier gearbox, has four forward speeds with full synchromesh and a reverse gear, the components being shown in the exploded view of **FIG 6:35**.

The gearlever is mounted on the rear extension housing and is connected by a shaft to the selector mechanism in the gearbox top extension. Moving the gearlever sideways rotates the shaft so that pins on the shaft fit into the appropriate selector fork. Pushing the gearlever forwards or backwards moves the selector fork to shift the outer sleeve of the appropriate synchromesh unit so that gear is selected. For reverse gear a pin on the selector shaft engages with a lever and movement of the gearlever then operates the reverse lever to slide an idler gear into mesh between the countershaft and mainshaft and so reversing the direction of drive.

Dismantling the single rail gearbox

Rear extension (see **FIG 6:36**):

1 Remove the speedometer drive assembly. Remove the screw and retaining clip, 23 in **FIG 6:35**, and pull out the speedometer cable from the drive pinion, then withdraw the pinion assembly, items 24 to 27.

2 Mount the gearbox in a vice, clamping the drain plug and using a piece of wood as a spacer.

3 Referring to **FIG 6:36**, remove the five bolts 1, noting the sealing washer fitted to the bottom bolt, and remove the clutch housing 2 and gasket. Remove the three laygear preload springs 3.

4 Use a tool 4, to hold the gearbox flange 5, unscrew the locking nut and remove the flange.

5 Remove the pin 6 from the end of the gear selector rod.

6 Remove the remaining eight bolts and spring washers 7, the ninth was holding the fuel pipe, and lift off the top cover and gasket.

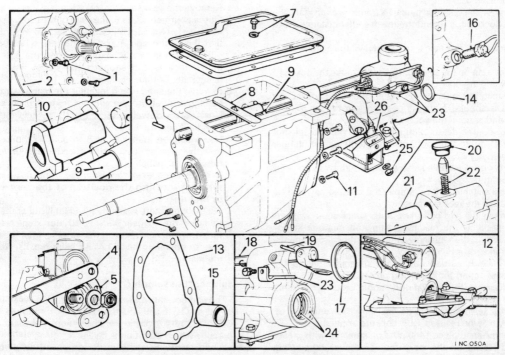

FIG 6:36 Sequence of operation in the removal of the rear extension

Key to Fig 6:36   1 Securing bolts   2 Clutch housing   3 Laygear preload springs   4 Tool 18G 1205   5 Drive flange   6 Roll pin   7 Top cover bolts   8 Interlock spool plate   9 Selector fork shaft   10 Interlock spool   11 Extension bolts   12 Tool 18G 2   13 Gasket   14 Distance piece   15 Distance piece   16 Reverse light switch   17 Cover   18 Selector rod   19 Roll pin   20 Detent plunger plug   21 Selector rod   22 Detent plunger and spring   23 Reverse gear lift plate   24 Oil seal and bearing   25 Rear mounting bolts and nuts   26 Rear mounting

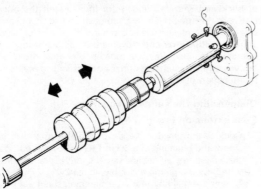

FIG 6:37 Using the impact hammer 18G 284 to remove the first motion shaft

7 Remove the interlock spool plate 8 and withdraw the selector fork shaft 9 to the front.

8 Rotate the gear selector rod until the pin engages in the reverse operating lever, slide the interlock spool 10 forwards on the selector rod and then rotate the rod out of engagement with the reverse lever.

9 Remove the bolts and spring washers 11 and pull off the rear extension from the main casing using an extractor as shown at 12, making sure that the selector rod does not foul as it is withdrawn. Remove the rear extension gasket 13.

10 Remove the distance piece 14 from the mainshaft, the interlock spool 10 and the reverse idler distance piece 15.

11 Disconnect the leads and unscrew the reverse light switch 16.

12 Gently tap on the selector rod and remove the cover 17 towards the rear.

13 Pushing the selector rod 18, to the rear exposes the gearlever yoke. Note the position, tap out the roll-pin 19 and remove the yoke.

14 Take out the detent plunger plug 20, pull the selector rod 21 out to the front and remove the detent plunger and spring 22.

15 Remove the retaining screw and withdraw the reverse gear lift plate 23.

16 Use a suitable drift to remove the bearing and oil seal 24 from the rear extension.

17 Remove the two bolts, two nuts, spacers and washers 25 securing the rear mounting and gearbox steady assembly, then unscrew the mounting 26 from the rear extension.

18 Refitting is carried out in the reverse order to the above, noting the following points.

If available, the special drift should be used for fitting the new oil seal.

If the selector shaft pins are slack but undamaged, they may be re-used with Locktite applied.

The distance piece 14 should be smeared with grease and placed on the inner face of the bearing before fitting the rear extension. Make sure that the roll-pin 6 is centrally located, otherwise difficulty will be experienced when fitting the clutch housing. Always use new gaskets and seals.

The torque specified for the bolts securing the rear extension to the gearbox is 18 to 20 lb ft (2.4 to

2.7 kgm) and for the drive flange nut 90 to 100 lb ft (12.4 to 13.8 kgm).

First motion (input) shaft:

1 Having removed the rear extension, tap out the dowel 94 (see **FIG 6:35**) from the layshaft (countershaft) and use a dummy layshaft to press the layshaft 93 out of the gearbox towards the rear. Make sure that the tool remains in contact with the layshaft until the lay-gear cluster is fully engaged and then lower it to the bottom of the case.

2 Use an impact hammer as shown in **FIG 6:37**, to extract the input shaft assembly from the box.

3 Remove the mainshaft spigot roller bearing 82 and spacer 3, the fourth-gear synchromesh cup and the bearing snap ring 48. The bearing circlip 46 and backing washer and the bearing 49 are then removed using a press and suitable tools. Remove the oil flinger 78.

4 Refitting is carried out in the reverse order. Make sure that the laygear thrust washers are correctly positioned. Stick the oil flinger on the face of the gear to prevent its displacement when fitting the bearing.

Main case components:

The dismantling of the remaining components in the gearbox will be assisted by reference to **FIG 6:38**.

1 Remove the two selector forks 1.

2 Fit the abutment plate to the front of the box, as shown at 2, using two clutch housing bolts and making sure that the centre bolt 3 and locknut are screwed right out. When the tool is in place screw the bolt in so that it locates and supports the spigot end of the mainshaft. Tighten the locknut.

3 Remove the snap ring 4 locating the mainshaft centre bearing and release the circlip 5 from its groove.

4 Unscrew the dowel bolt 6 so that the reverse idler gear spindle 7 can be removed.

5 Use a suitable puller as at 8 to pull off the bearing, selective washer, circlip and speedometer drive gear from the mainshaft.

6 Remove the special tool from the front of the casing **without altering the position of the centre bolt or locknut.**

7 Tilt the mainshaft assembly 9 and lift it out of the case. Remove the laygear cluster 10 not forgetting the thrust washers. Remove the reverse idler gear 11, reverse operating lever 12 and pivot pin 13. Remove the magnet 14.

Mainshaft assembly:

The components making up the mainshaft assembly are shown in **FIG 6:39** and they should be removed in the numerical order given in the illustration. There are a few points to which attention is called.

When removing the third/fourth-speed synchro hub and sleeve 23, note that the grooved face is towards the front of the mainshaft.

The third-gear circlip 25 is removed with a tool with three long prongs inserted in the splines between the tabs of the thrust washer. Use a new circlip when reassembling.

Before removing the second-gear washer 31 note the position of the oil grooved face.

The synchro units 23 and 32 should each be removed as an assembly. Certain components are very much alike and must not be interchanged, but must be stored for reassembly in their original positions.

If the synchromesh units are to be dismantled, they should be suitably identified for later assembly. It is advisable to wrap a unit in a clean cloth before pushing the inner hub out of the outer sleeve. In this way the small parts which will be freed will not shoot out and be lost.

Reassembling the gearbox:

Before commencing to rebuild the gearbox all parts should be thoroughly washed and inspected for wear or damage. Check the splines for wear and gear teeth for wear or chipping. Check the cones on the synchromesh cups (baulk rings) and gears for excessive wear or scoring. The bearings should be washed separately in

clean fuel to make sure that they do not pick up any dirt and then checked for smooth rotation.

Discard all the original seals and gaskets and use new ones when reassembling, which is carried out in the reverse order of dismantling, observing carefully the dimensions given for the various components and using selected bushes and washers as appropriate.

Mainshaft assembly:

Measure the end float of the second and third gears on their respective bushes, items 27 and 29, and fit a new bush if this is beyond the limits .002 to .006 inch (.050 to .152 mm).

Fit the second-gear washer as shown at 31 with the oil groove away from the shoulder on the mainshaft, then assemble on the mainshaft the following items in order: third-gear bush, selective washer 28, second-gear bush, third-gear thrust washer 26 (the oil grooved face being toward the bush). Fit the circlip 25 and then measure the

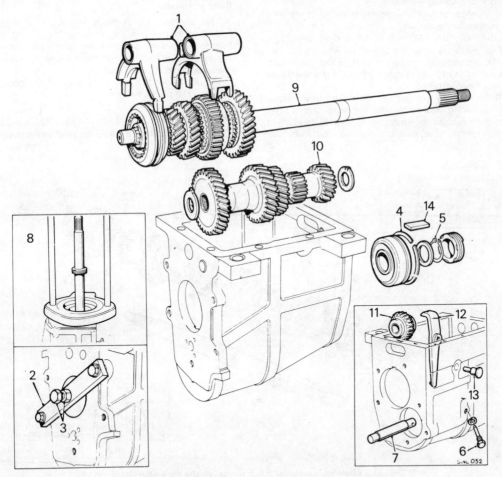

FIG 6:38 Exploded view of the main case components

Key to Fig 6:38 1 Selector forks 2 Tool 18G 47BP 3 Centre screw and locknut 4 Centre bearing snap ring 5 Circlip 6 Dowel bolt 7 Reverse idler gear spindle 8 Tool 47BP (3), C, CZ, and BF 9 Mainshaft 10 Laygear cluster 11 Reverse idler gear 12 Reverse operating lever 13 Pivot pin 14 Magnet

end float of the bushes on the mainshaft. This must be between .004 and .006 inch (.101 to .152 mm) and the correct selective washer must be chosen from the following range to obtain this dimension.

.152 to .154 inch (3.860 to 3.911 mm)
.156 to .158 inch (3.962 to 4.013 mm)
.161 to .163 inch (4.089 to 4.140 mm)
.165 to .167 inch (4.191 to 4.241 mm)
.169 to .171 inch (4.293 to 4.343 mm)

Main case components:

Fit the bush to the reverse idler gear so that it is flush at one end and to .010 inch (.254 mm) below the gear face.

Fit the laygear needle roller retaining rings, using tool 18G 1209 if available, to the specified fitted depth: Inner ring .840 to .850 inch (21.336 to 21.590 mm), outer ring .010 to .015 inch (.254 to .381 mm). Fit tool 18G 1208 to the layshaft to retain the needle rollers.

Fit the reverse idler spindle, 7 in **FIG 6:38**, to the reverse gear, locate it in the casing and secure with the dowel bolt and spring washer 6.

Fit the laygear assembly complete with thrust washers in the bottom of the casing.

Tilt the mainshaft and fit it in the casing, using tool 18G 47BP screwed on to the casing, as when removing, to locate and support the spigot end of the mainshaft. **Make sure that the settings noted on dismantling have not been altered.**

Refit the locating snap ring to the centre bearing and press the bearing into place until the snap ring is tight against the case. Fit the selective washer and secure it with the circlip, then measure the gap between the

washer and circlip (see **FIG 6:40**). This should be from zero to .004 inch (0 to .05 mm) and a suitable washer should be selected to obtain this.

.119 to .121 inch (3.022 to 3.073 mm)
.122 to .124 inch (3.123 to 3.173 mm)
.125 to .127 inch (3.198 to 3.248 mm)
.128 to .130 inch (3.273 to 3.323 mm)

Refit the speedometer drive pinion and remove the special tool from the front of the gearbox.

Input shaft assembly:

Refit the selector forks and then install the input shaft assembly by reversing the order of removal as described earlier.

Lift the laygear cluster into alignment, making sure that the thrust washers are in position, and press out the dummy layshaft with the real layshaft, keeping the two shafts in constant contact throughout the operation. Secure with the roll-pin.

Rear extension:

This also is fitted in the reverse order of removal as described in the previous section. Make sure that the selector forks are correctly fitted to the outer sleeves of the synchro units and that the reverse operating lever engages correctly with the idler.

Do not forget the sealing washer on the bottom bolt securing the clutch housing.

Oil seals:

New oil seals should always be used when overhauling

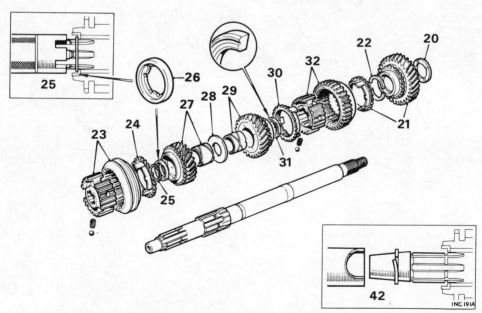

FIG 6:39 Showing the order of removal for the mainshaft assembly

Key to Fig 6:39 20 First-speed gear washer 21 First-speed gear and synchro cup 22 Split collars 23 Third-/fourth-speed synchro assembly 24 Third-gear synchro cup 25 Third-gear synchro assembly 26 Thrust washer 27 Third-gear and bush 28 Third-/second-gear selective washer 29 Second-gear and bush 30 Second-gear synchro cup 31 Second-gear washer 32 First-/second-speed synchro hub and reverse gear sleeve 42 Fitting the third-gear mainshaft circlip

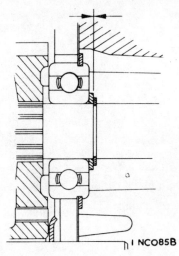

FIG 6:40 Measuring the gap between the selective washer and circlip

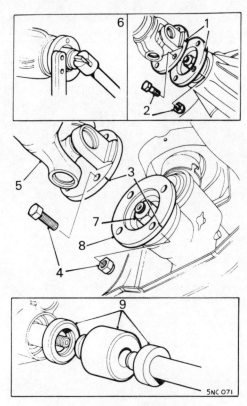

FIG 6:41 Renewing the rear oil seal

Key to Fig 6:41   1 Marking the rear flanges   2 Bolts and nuts   3 Marking the front flanges   4 Bolts and nuts   5 Propeller shaft   6 18G 1205   7 Flange nut   8 Mainshaft flange   9 Oil seal and 18G 134DR

the gearbox and normally no other replacements should be necessary. In the event of the rear oil seal developing a leak it can be removed without removing the gearbox as follows:

Refer to **FIG 6:41**. Jack-up the rear end of the car and place supports under the axle.

Mark the rear flange of the propeller shaft and the pinion flange 1 to ensure correct refitting and remove the four securing bolts 2.

Mark the front flange of the propeller shaft and the gearbox flange as shown at 3 and remove the four securing bolts 4. Remove the propeller shaft 5.

Use a tool as shown at 6, to hold the gearbox flange and remove the flange nut and washer 7. Withdraw the flange 8 from the gearbox mainshaft.

Extract the oil seal from the rear extension, using suitable tools.

Before fitting the new seal, make sure that the face on which it operates is not damaged or scored, then dip the seal in oil and press it as shown at 9 using the special or similar tool.

Complete the operation by reversing the removal procedure, tightening the flange nut to a torque of 90 to 100 lb ft (12.4 to 13.8 kgm). Finally check the gearbox oil level.

6:9 Fault diagnosis

(a) Jumping out of gear

1 Broken spring behind locating plunger
2 Excessively worn detent in selector shaft

3 Worn coupling dogs
4 Fork to selector shaft screw loose

(b) Noisy gearbox

1 Insufficient oil
2 Excessive end float in countershaft gear
3 Worn or damaged bearings
4 Worn or damaged gear teeth

(c) Difficulty in engaging gear

1 Worn clutch
2 Worn synchromesh cones

(d) Oil leaks

1 Damaged gaskets or oil seals
2 Faces damaged on castings

NOTES

CHAPTER 7

PROPELLER SHAFT, REAR HUBS, DIFFERENTIAL AND SUSPENSION

7:1 Description

Transmission from the gearbox to the rear axle is through a two-piece propeller shaft. It is supported at the centre by an encased roller bearing. The encasement is bolted to the underside of the body. Three universal joints are incorporated to couple the shafts together and connect them at each end to the differential and gearbox. The universal joints compensate for any propeller shaft misalignment that is induced by the rear axle when travelling on rough roads. A splined yoke allows for any longitudinal movement to counteract the same conditions. The sliding joint must not be dismantled and any excessive wear in the splines will mean renewing the propeller shaft-half completely.

The drive to the rear wheels is through a differential consisting of hypoid bevel gears which are housed in a malleable iron casting. Splined halfshafts transmit the drive to the rear wheels. The rear axle tube casing assembly is insulated from the rear suspension by rubber mountings.

The rear suspension shown in **FIG 7:22** has a four link system. The lower suspension members carry the combined coil springs and telescopic dampers. The upper radius rods are linked to the axle casing and body; the linkages having inner sleeve type rubber bushes. The radius rods combine the functions of torque reaction links and stiffening members.

7:2 Maintenance

Every 6000 miles (10,000 kilometres), check the level of oil in the differential. Refer to **FIG 7:1** to locate the combined filler and level plug. Clean the plug and surrounding area before removing it. The oil content is correct if the level of oil is in line with the lower edge of the filler hole. If necessary, top up to the correct level with SAE.90.EP oil or its equivalent. Use an oil can with a flexible nozzle. Allow any surplus oil to drain away before replacing the plug. In very cold climates where the temperature is 0°C or under, use SAE.80.EP or its equivalent.

Refer to **FIG 7:2** and recharge the sliding spline joint with grease.

Check the tightness of all the flange coupling bolts and the centre bearing attachment bolts.

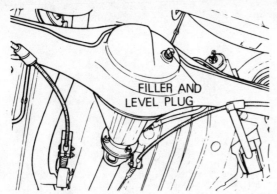

FIG 7:1   Location of rear axle filler and level plug

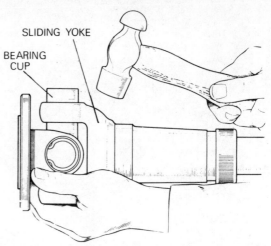

SLIDING YOKE

BEARING
CUP

FIG 7:4   Tapping the yoke to remove the bearing cup

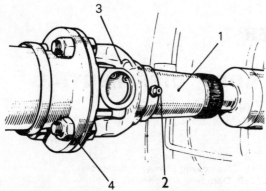

FIG 7:2   Lubricating point for sliding spline

Key to Fig 7:2   1 Sliding spline   2 Grease nipple
3 Yoke   4 Flange mating marks

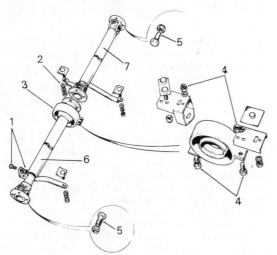

FIG 7:3   Propeller shaft components

Key to Fig 7:3   1 Front strap righthand connection
2 Rear strap righthand connection   3 Centre bearing
4 Centre bearing mounting brackets   5 Drive flange bolts
6 Front half   7 Rear half

7:3 The propeller shaft

Removing complete assembly:

1 Jack up the rear end of the car, secure with chocks under the front wheels and support the car on stands. Release the handbrake.

2 Refer to **FIG 7:3** and disconnect the righthand side of the front strap 1 from the floor panel (early models only).

3 Disconnect the righthand side of the rear strap 2 from the floor panel (early models only).

4 Remove the nuts, bolts and washers which secure the centre bearing 3 to the support brackets.

5 Support the propeller shaft and uncouple it from the gearbox and rear axle flanges. Before severing the connections, mark the adjoining flanges to ensure they are refitted in the same position.

Refitting:

6 Refit the shafts in the reverse order of removal but do not tighten the centre bearing housing bolts fully until the flanges are reconnected and tightened. Tighten the $\frac{5}{16}$ inch UNF flange bolts to a torque of 16 to 20 lb ft (2 to 3 kg m) and the $\frac{3}{8}$ inch UNF to a torque of 26 to 32 lb ft ($3\frac{1}{2}$ to $4\frac{1}{2}$ kg m).

7 Align the propeller shaft and tighten the centre bearing housing bolts to the same torque as the $\frac{5}{16}$ inch flange bolts.

Removing separate units:

The propeller shaft halves can be removed separately, if necessary, by disconnecting them at the centre flange. Mark the flanges before parting the joint to ensure they are refitted in the same position.

If only the front half is removed, remember to tighten the centre bearing bolts last, after aligning the two shafts.

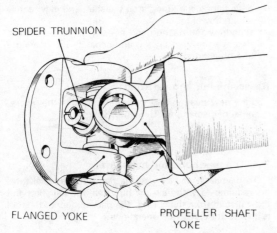

SPIDER TRUNNION

FLANGED YOKE

PROPELLER SHAFT YOKE

FIG 7:5 Fit the bearing cups and carefully press them into position

7:4 The universal joints

Removing and dismantling:

1 Take off the propeller shaft assembly or the half applicable for the removal of the universal joint (see **Section 7:3**).

2 Scrape off any paint, rust or dirt from around the vicinity of the bearing cups and circlips on the universal joints.

3 Remove the circlips and by referring to **FIG 7:4**, tap the yoke as shown. The shock from the hammer will cause the bearing cup to emerge from its recess. Remove the rest of the bearing cups in a similar fashion.

Reassembling and refitting:

4 If new spiders are being fitted, remove the bearing cups from the new spider and check that they are one third full of the approved lubricant and that the needle bearings are in position.

5 Locate the spider in the propeller shaft yoke, fit the bearing cups and carefully press them into position (see **FIG 7:5**). Repeat this operation to reconnect the second yoke.

6 Using two flat adaptors of slightly smaller diameter than the bearing cups, press or tap the cups into position until they reach the lower land of the circlip grooves. Do not press them below this point or damage may be caused to the cups and seals. Refit the circlips.

7 Refit the propeller shaft(s) as described in **Section 7:3**.

7:5 The centre bearing

Removing and dismantling:

1 Remove the front propeller shaft and refer to **FIG 7:6**.

2 Extract the splitpin 1 and unscrew the nut 2. Withdraw the drive flange 3 and remove the key 4. The

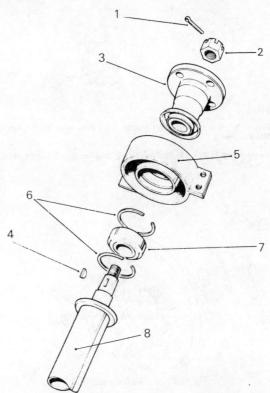

FIG 7:6 Components of centre bearing

Key to Fig 7:6 1 Splitpin 2 Nut 3 Drive flange 4 Key 5 Bearing housing 6 Wire clips 7 Bearing 8 Propeller shaft

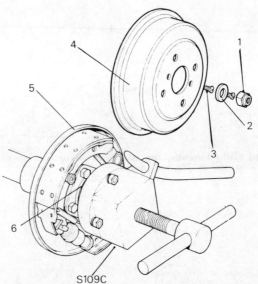

S109C

FIG 7:7 Withdrawing the rear hub with tool S109C

Key to Fig 7:7 1 Axle shaft nut 2 Washer 3 Drum retaining screws 4 Brake drum 5 Backplate 6 Oil catcher

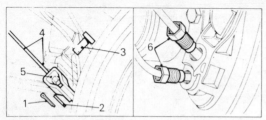

FIG 7:8 Disconnecting handbrake cable and hydraulic fluid pipes

Key to Fig 7:8   1 Splitpin   2 Washer   3 Clevis pin
4 Cable   5 Fork   6 Pipe unions

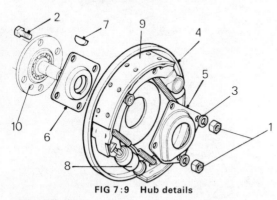

FIG 7:9   Hub details

Key to Fig 7:9   1 Nuts   2 Bolts   3 Spring washers
4 Backplate   5 Oil catcher   6 Oil seal housing   7 Key
8 Wheel cylinder   9 Brake shoe liner   10 Axle flange

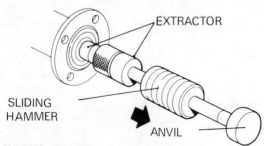

EXTRACTOR

SLIDING
HAMMER

ANVIL

FIG 7:10   Removing the axle shaft bearing with extractor tool S4235A and adaptor

AXLE CASING
OIL SEAL

HUB SEAL

FIG 7:11   Fit the axle casing oil seal with the lip facing inwards and position the hub seal in its housing as shown

---

drive flange is a taper fit on the shaft and may require a withdrawal tool.

3 Withdraw the bearing and housing 5 from the shaft.

4 Remove the wire clips 6 and separate the bearing 7 and housing.

Reassembling and refitting:

5 Fit a new bearing and replace the parts in the reverse order of dismantling. Use a new splitpin 1.

7:6 The rear hubs and halfshafts

To dismantle and service the rear hubs, special tools are required to withdraw the hub from the halfshaft and the halfshaft from the casing. The part number of the tool is quoted at the relevant operations.

Removing and dismantling:

1 Block the front wheels, jack up the rear of the car and support it on safety stands. Remove the wheels and release the handbrake.

2 Refer to **FIG 7:7,** unscrew the axle shaft nut 1 and plain washer 2. Remove the two screws 3 retaining the brake drum 4. If it is necessary to slacken off the brake adjustment to release the drum, refer to **Chapter 10.**

3 Fit the hub withdrawal tool S109C as shown in the illustration and separate the hub from the axle shaft.

4 Refer to **FIG 7:8,** extract the splitpin, collect the washer and remove the clevis pin from the handbrake cable fork and wheel cylinder operating lever. Disconnect the hydraulic fluid pipes from the wheel cylinder.

5 Refer to **FIG 7:9** and remove the four nuts 1, bolts 2 and spring washers 3 which secure the backplate 4 to the axle casing. Remove the oil catcher 5 and lift off the backplate and brake assembly. If any work is to be done in the brakes, refer to **Chapter 10.** During the process of dismantling the hub or the brakes, avoid contaminating the brake linings with grease or oil. If they are so contaminated, wash them immediately in petrol or trichlorethylene but make sure that these solvents do not come into contact with the rubber parts of the wheel cylinder.

6 Take off the rear hub oil seal and housing assembly 6. Extract the key 7 from the axle shaft.

7 Place a container under the end of the axle casing. The purpose of this is to catch the oil, which will spill out when the halfshaft and oil seal are removed.

8 Refer to **FIG 7:10,** fit the extractor tool S4235A and the adaptor S4235A-1 and withdraw the halfshaft. Remove the inner oil seal.

9 Press the bearing off the axle shaft.

10 Never refit old oil seals, always renew them whatever their condition. Check the bearing for wear and renew it if it is at all suspect.

Reassembling:

11 Pack the bearing with lithium-based grease. Press the bearing onto the shaft until it is positioned 2.84 inch (69.94 mm) from the end.

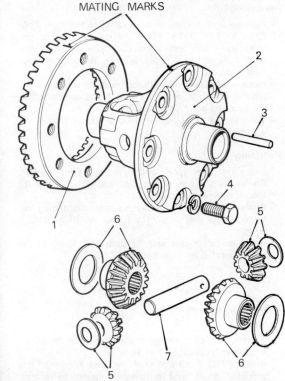

MATING MARKS

FIG 7:12 Components of differential

Key to Fig 7:12 1 Crownwheel 2 Differential cage
3 Pinion pin locking peg 4 Retaining bolts 5 Planet gears
and thrust washers 6 Sun gears and thrust washers
7 Pinion pin

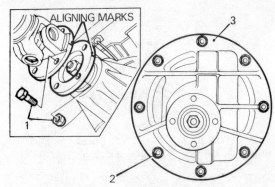

FIG 7:13 Removing differential

Key to Fig 7:13 1 Drive flange securing bolts
2 Differential housing securing nuts 3 Differential housing

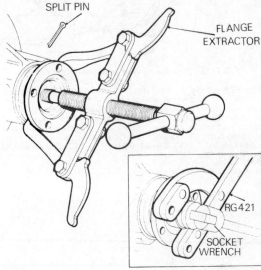

FIG 7:14 Extracting differential pinion drive flange

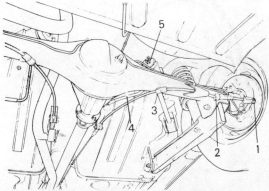

FIG 7:15 Removing rear axle assembly (part)

Key to Fig 7:15 1 Handbrake lever connection
2 Handbrake cable connection to suspension bracket 3 Cable
connection to rear axle tube 4 Flexible hose connection
5 Torque rod connection

12 Refer to **FIG 7:11**, dip the axle casing oil seal in light
oil and position it in the casing with the lip of the seal
facing inwards.

13 Refit the parts in the reverse order of dismantling.
Do not forget to fit the new hub seal into its housing
and fit a new hub joint washer. Tighten the backplate
securing nuts to a torque of 18 lb ft ($2\frac{1}{2}$ kg m) and
the axle shaft nut to 90 to 120 lb ft (12.4 to 16.6
kg m).

14 Readjust and bleed the brakes to the instructions given
in **Chapter 10**.

7:7 The differential assembly

The details of the differential are shown in **FIG 7:12**.
However, it is extremely unwise for the average owner
to attempt to fully dismantle or service the unit. The
meshing of the pinion and crownwheel is set by the
accurate measurement and shimming of the parts, for
which specialized equipment is essential. On many rear
axles the differential gears may be removed from the
casing but on the Triumph range a special tool is required to spread the casing by exactly the right amount
to allow the parts to be removed.

If the unit causes any trouble, other than oil leaks, the
unit (or car) should be taken to a suitable equipped
garage. The fitting of an exchange unit should also be
considered.

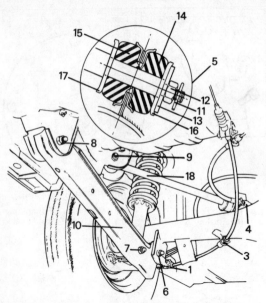

FIG 7:16   Removing rear axle assembly (part)

Key to Fig 7:16   Items 1, 3, 4 and 5 (see Key to **FIG 7:15**)   6 Suspension arm connection to axle   7 Damper lower mounting anchorage   8 Suspension arm connection to body   9 Radius rod connection to body   10 Suspension arm.   11 Radius rod spring pin   12 Radius rod to axle securing nut   13 Washer   14 Outer rubber bush   15 Inner rubber bush   16 Dished washer   17 Dished washer   18 Radius rod

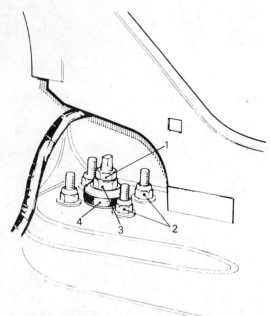

FIG 7:17   Disconnecting the spring and damper mounting flange. Do not unscrew the nuts 1 and 3

Key to Fig 7:17   1 Locknut (damper)   2 Mounting plate nuts   3 Nut (damper)   4 Upper rubber bush

Removing:

1 Remove both halfshafts as detailed in **Section 7:6**.
2 Refer to **FIG 7:13**. Mark the drive flange of the propeller shaft and differential pinion to ensure correct alignment when recoupling. Remove the four nuts and bolts.
3 Place a container of sufficient size to catch the $1\frac{1}{4}$ pints of oil which will drain from the differential when the nuts and bolts are removed.
4 Remove the eight nuts and bolts and withdraw the assembly.

Refitting:

5 Clean the joint faces and fit a new joint washer. Smear the surfaces of the joint washer with a slight film of sealing compound.
6 Replace the parts in the reverse order; tightening the casing bolts and nuts to a torque of 20 lb ft (2.7 kg m).
7 Refill the differential with $1\frac{1}{4}$ pints (.71 litres) of the recommended oil (see **Section 7:2**).

7:8 The pinion oil seal
Removing:

1 If there is no pit or ramps available, jack up the car as described in operation 1 of **Section 7:3**.
2 Refer to **FIG 7:13** and mark the drive flanges of the propeller shaft and differential pinion to ensure correct alignment when recoupling.
3 Refer to **FIG 7:14**. Extract the drive flange nut splitpin. Secure the flange, either by using the special tool RG421 as shown in the inset, or by inserting two long bolts into the flange and positioning a lever between them whilst the flange nut is loosened and removed.
4 Place a container under the flange to catch the escaping oil when the drive flange is withdrawn with an extractor.
5 Take out the oil seal from the drive flange housing.

Refitting:

6 The new seal should be immersed in light oil for one hour before fitting. Fit the seal with the lip facing inwards.
7 Fit the remaining parts in the reverse order of dismantling. Tighten the drive flange nut to a torque of 90 lb ft ($12\frac{1}{2}$ kg m) and the four $\frac{3}{8}$ inch UNF flange nuts to a torque of 26 to 32 lb ft ($3\frac{1}{2}$ to $4\frac{1}{2}$ kg m).
8 Top up the differential with oil (see **Section 7:2**).

7:9 Removing rear axle assembly

1 Chock the front wheels. Jack up the rear of the car and support it firmly on safety stands. Remove the road wheels and release the handbrake.
2 Disconnect the propeller shaft from the drive pinion flange. Place a mobile jack under the differential.
3 Refer to **FIGS 7:15** and **7:16**. Disconnect the handbrake cables at the brake backplate lever 1, rear

suspension bracket 2 and the rear axle tube clip 3. Disconnect the hydraulic brake pipe union at the flexible hose 4 and detach the flexible hose from the support bracket. Seal the ends of the pipes to prevent any dirt from entering. Remove the spring pin, nut, washers and bushes 5 (inset) securing the radius rods to the axle casing. Remove the bolts and nuts 6 securing the suspension arms to the axle.

4 Raise the axle assembly on the jack and move it carefully rearwards to clear the suspension arms.

Dismantling:

5 If the rear axle is to be dismantled, remove the half-shafts as described in **Section 7:6** and the differential as described in **Section 7:7**. Take off the hydraulic brake pipe, pull off the breather cap and unscrew the breather stem. Remove the filler/level plug.

Refitting:

6 If necessary, refit the parts to the axle casing. Position the assembly under the car and support it on a jack.

7 Raise the jack and engage the radius rods through the retaining brackets, fit the bushes, washers, nuts and pins.

8 Reconnect the lower suspension arms 6.

9 Reassemble in the reverse order of dismantling.

10 Bleed the brakes as described in **Chapter 10.**

11 With the car standing on its wheels, tighten the suspension arm bolts, 6 and 8, to the correct torque (see **Technical Data**).

7:10 Rear dampers and springs

Removing:

The damper and spring are removed from the car as an assembly and it would not be advisable to try and separate them in an attempt to save effort and time during removal operations. A special spring compressor is used to contract the spring when the parts are being separated, but the tool can be used only when the assembly is removed from the vehicle.

1 Support the body and rear axle with stands and jacks. Refer to **FIG 7:17** and working inside the boot, unscrew the four nuts 2 which secure the mounting flange to the body, collect the four flat washers.

2 Refer to **FIG 7:16,** unscrew the nut 7 and take out the bolt which anchors the lower damper mounting to the suspension arm. Remove the nut and bolt 8, lower the suspension arm and lift out the damper and spring assembly.

3 If necessary, the whole assembly can be taken to a service garage which will have the necessary equipment to separate the spring and damper and, if requested, give an opinion as to the serviceability of the damper and spring. If either is condemned by the garage then the opposite side must be renewed also. If it is possible to obtain the spring compressor tool S4221A and adaptors 5 and 18 continue as follows:

4 Refer to **FIG 7:18**, fit the tool, mount the assembly in a strong vice and compress the spring.

5 Refer to **FIG 7:19**, take off the locknut and nut 3 that secure the damper rod to the mounting flange.

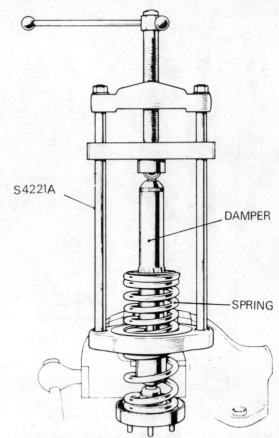

S4221A

DAMPER

SPRING

FIG 7:18   Compressing the spring prior to removal

Lift off the mounting flange, complete with the upper rubber bush 2, washers and the insulating ring 4. Withdraw the lower rubber bush and washer 5. Release the tension off the spring and separate the components.

6 Examine the rubber bushes and insulating rings for wear and signs of deterioration. Check the rubber bearing bush in the damper lower mounting and, if necessary, use a hand press to extract the bush and fit a new one. If the damper or spring are suspect, get them checked at a service garage. Refer to **Chapter 8** to carry out any preliminary checks on the damper.

Refitting:

Reassemble the parts in the reverse order of dismantling and note the following points:

Make sure the damper upper mounting washers are fitted so that the collars engage the mounting flange.

Tighten the $\frac{7}{16}$ inch UNF mounting bolts to a torque of 30 to 37 lb ft (4 to 5 kg m), the $\frac{5}{16}$ inch UNF mounting bolts to a torque of 16 to 20 lb ft (2 to 3 kg m) and the $\frac{1}{4}$ inch UNF mounting bolts to a torque of 7 to 9 lb ft (1 to $1\frac{1}{4}$ kg m).

Do not fully tighten the anchorage bolts 7 and 8 in **FIG 7:16** until the weight of the car is supported on the road wheels.

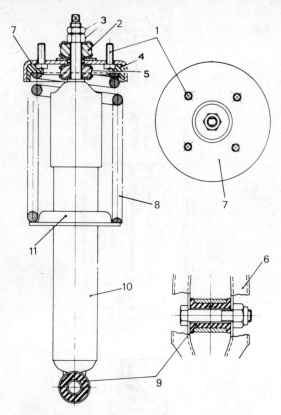

FIG 7:19   Spring and damper mountings

Key to Fig 7:19   1 Mounting studs   2 Upper rubber bush
3 Damper securing nuts   4 Insulating ring   5 Lower rubber
bush   6 Suspension arm   7 Mounting flange   8 Spring
9 Lower mounting bush   10 Damper   11 Lower retaining
flange

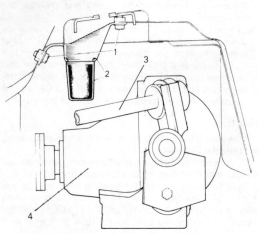

FIG 7:20   The bump stop

Key to Fig 7:20   1 Bracket support nuts   2 Rubber stop
and bracket   3 Torque rod   4 Differential casing

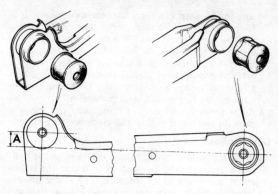

FIG 7:21   Suspension arm mounting bushes

Key to Fig 7:21   A = 1 inch (25.4 mm)

7:11 The bump stop
Removing:

1 Refer to **FIG 7:20** and remove the two nuts and
bolts 1, collect the spring washers. Take off the bump
stop complete with bracket 2.
2 Separate the bump stop and bracket by removing the
nut and spring washer.

Refitting:

3 Reverse the instructions 1 and 2.

7:12 The suspension arm
Removing:

1 Jack up the rear of the car, chock the front wheels,
support the car on stands and place a jack under the
rear axle.
2 Remove the nuts and bolts, 6, 7 and 8 in **FIG 7:16**.
3 Withdraw the suspension arm.
4 Refer to **FIG 7:21** to renew the rubber bushes and
note the different types. Use a hand press to extract the
old bushes and fit the new ones.
5 Reassemble in the reverse order, tightening the bolts
to the correct torques but do not fully tighten until
the weight of the car is supported on the road wheels.

7:13 The radius rod
Removing:

1 Chock the front wheels, jack up the rear of the car
and support the body on stands.
2 Refer to **FIG 7:16** and remove the spring pin, nut,
plain washer and outer rubber bush on early models,
later models are as shown in the diagram. Disconnect
the anchorage to the body by removing the nut and
bolt 9.
3 Withdraw the radius rod and remove the inner rubber
bush and two dished washers, one on later models,
from the screwed end.
4 If necessary, renew the body mounting rubber bush.
Use a hand press to extract the old one and also to
fit a new one.

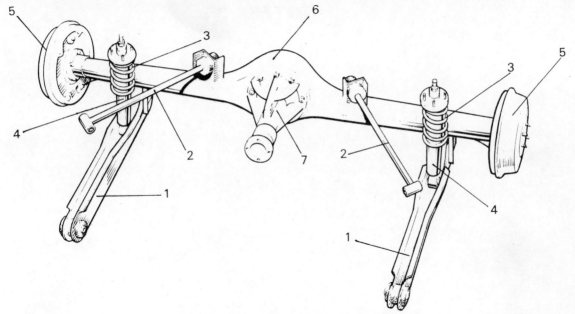

FIG 7 : 22   Rear suspension and axle assembly

Key to Fig 7 : 22   1 Suspension arms   2 Torque rods   3 Springs   4 Dampers   5 Drums and hubs   6 Rear axle casing
7 Differential casing

Refitting:

5 Fit the two dished washers, one on later models, to the
screwed end noting their position from the illustration.
Fit the inner rubber bush with its plain face to the
dished washers.

6 Locate the radius rod in position in the car, fit the
bolt and nut 9 to the body mounting. Fit the outer
rubber bush with the stepped face to the axle bracket.

7 Fit the dished washer on later models, and tighten the
washer and nut, secure with the spring pin and tighten
the body bracket anchorage.

7 : 14 Fault diagnosis

(a) Noisy axle

1 Insufficient or incorrect lubricant
2 Worn bearings
3 Worn gears

(b) Excessive backlash

1 Worn gears or bearings
2 Worn axle shaft or side gear splines
3 Worn universal joints
4 Loose or broken rear wheel studs

(c) Oil leakage

1 Defective seal in axle tube
2 Defective drive pinion oil seal
3 Defective differential cover gasket
4 Distorted differential cover

(d) Vibration

1 Propeller shaft out of balance
2 Worn universal joint bearings

(e) Rattles

1 Intermediate bearing mountings worn
2 Dampers loose
3 Defective coil spring damper rings

NOTES

CHAPTER 8

THE FRONT SUSPENSION AND HUBS

8:1 Description

The front suspension assembly complete with sub-frame is shown in **FIG 8:1**. The suspension is fully independent with coil springs controlled by hydraulic telescopic dampers, operating on the upper wishbone suspension member. The hubs are linked to the subframe by the upper suspension member and a lower suspension arm. A radius rod connected to the lower arm and the front of the subframe gives additional support, and checks any fore and aft movement of the hubs. Hinge deflection in the suspension members is cushioned by rubber mounting bushes.

The hubs are connected to the suspension members by a vertical link and ballpins, on which the hubs swivel in response to steering direction. A stub-axle bolted to the vertical link supports the taper roller bearings and the hubs.

8:2 Maintenance

Very little maintenance in the way of lubrication is required, as the swivel ballpins are packed with grease and sealed during production. The ballpins swivel in nylon cups which are renewable. Grease can be injected into the upper ball joint if necessary, by removing the plug and washer (see **FIG 8:5**) and fitting a grease nipple. The plug and washer must be refitted afterwards. No such facility exists on the lower ball joint.

The hubs and vertical link swivels should all be tested for wear with the road wheel fitted. Check that the wheel nuts are tight and then jack up the front of the car. Grasp the tyre at the six and twelve o'clock positions and try to rock the top of the tyre in and out. There should be very little play, and if it is excessive it is caused by either worn, maladjusted bearings or wear in the vertical link swivels. Repeat the test, this time grasping the wheel at the nine and three o'clock positions. Play, not to be confused with movement of the steering, indicates that the hub bearings are the source. If the play has gone then the most likely cause is wear in the vertical link swivels. Spin the wheel and check that the bearings rotate smoothly and freely. Noises from the brake should not be confused with the noise from a defective bearing. If the bearings are suspect then the hub should be removed and the bearings checked visually.

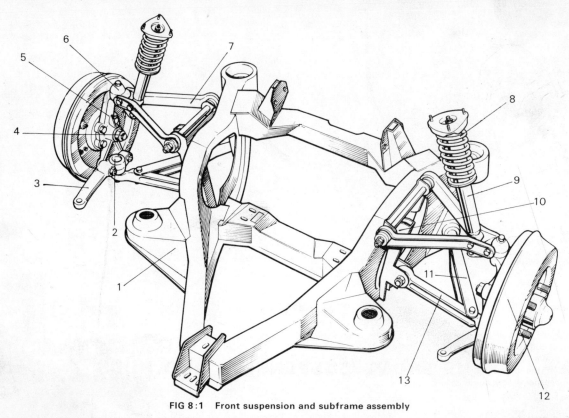

FIG 8:1   Front suspension and subframe assembly

Key to Fig 8:1   1 Subframe   2 Lower ball joint   3 Steering arm   4 Stub axle   5 Vertical link   6 Upper ball joint
7 Suspension upper wishbone   8 Spring   9 Damper   10 Support bracket   11 Radius rod   12 Brake drum   13 Suspension
lower arm

8:3 Front hubs

Removing:

1 Apply the handbrake, jack up the front of the car and
remove the road wheel.

2 Refer to **Chapter 10** to remove the brake caliper unit
(disc brakes), or remove the two screws securing the
brake drum and pull off the drum.

3 **FIGS 8:2** and **8:3** illustrate the hub details in
component form (disc) and in sectional detail (drum).
Prise off the hub cap 1 and wipe the grease away
from the end of the stub axle. Extract the splitpin 2,
loosen and unscrew the stub axle nut 3 and take off
the washer 4.

4 Withdraw the hub complete with bearings and oil seal.
Take care that the inner race 9 does not drop out of the
hub as it is freed from the stub axle.

Inspecting:

5 If necessary the bearing tracks 6 and 8 can be forced
out of the hub with a soft metal drift. The servicing of
the brakes can also be carried out at this stage, in
which case refer to **Chapter 10**. It is very important
that the linings and the rubbing surfaces of the disc
or drum should not become contaminated with
grease. If grease does come in contact with the

linings or pads, it should be washed off immediately
with petrol or other solvent. Do not allow these
solvents to come in contact with the rubber parts of
the wheel cylinders.

6 Before reassembling the parts, thoroughly clean them
in fuel or solvent. Wash the bearings separately so
that no dirt from the hub is washed into them.
Examine the surfaces of the tracks and rollers and
reject the complete bearing if either show signs of
pitting, fretting or wear. Rotate the inner race in the
track while pressing them firmly together and any
roughness in running will be more easily detectable.
Ideally both bearings should be renewed if either one
shows a fault.

Reassembling:

7 Drive the tracks 6 and 8 back into position in the hub,
so that they seat fully against the internal flange and
the largest diameter of the taper faces outwards.
If it has been removed then refit the brake disc, making
sure that the mating surfaces between the disc and
hub are scrupulously clean and free from particles.

8 Cover the inner bearing 9 with BP Energrease L2, or
any other brand equivalent, and fit the bearing in the
track 8. Fit the inner bearing shield 12, oil the new
felt seal 11, squeeze out any surplus and fit the seal
into the hub.

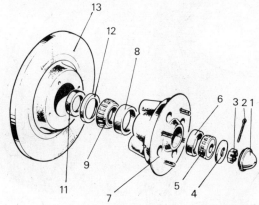

FIG 8:2 Hub components (disc brakes)

Key to Fig 8:2 1 Hub cap 2 Splitpin 3 Nut
4 Washer 5 Outer bearing 6 Track 7 Hub 8 Track
9 Inner bearing 11 Oil seal 12 Bearing shield 13 Disc

9 Pack the inside of the hub with new grease and then
slide the assembly into position on the stub axle. This
must be done very carefully, otherwise the oil seal may
become dislodged or damaged as it is seated over the
collar 10 of the vertical link 15.

10 Fit the outer bearing 5, covered in grease, fit the
washer 4 and tighten the nut 3 to a torque of 5 lb ft
(.70 kg m).

Hub bearing end float:

11 After tightening the nut to the correct torque, this is
only a little over fingertight, mount a dial gauge so
that the stylus touches the washer. Zero the gauge
and adjust the nut to give an end float of between .002
and .005 inch (.05 and .130 mm). If the nut has been
tightened to the correct torque, this will mean
slackening the nut one flat only.

12 Fit a new splitpin, fill the hub cap with new grease
and press it into position.

13 Refer to **Chapter 10** to replace the caliper unit
(discs). Fit the brake drum and complete the operation by fitting the road wheel.

8:4 The steering ball joints

Upper, removing:

1 Apply the handbrake, jack up the front of the car and
support it securely with stands. Remove the road
wheel.

2 Refer to **FIG 8:4**, remove the nut 2, washer and brake
hose bracket 3 from the upper wishbone ball joint
shank 4. Separate the ball joint shank from the
vertical link 5 (see instruction 6).

3 Support the hub assembly with a cord or wire to
avoid stressing the flexible brake hose.

4 Slacken the bolt and nut 6 which secures the damper
lower mounting to the wishbone.

5 Remove the two bolts and nuts 7 which anchor the
ball joint to the wishbone arms. Withdraw the ball
joint.

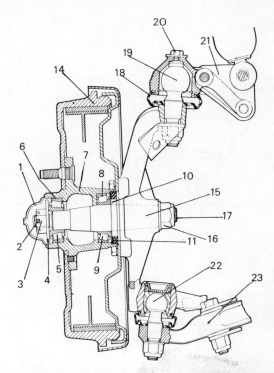

FIG 8:3 Cutaway section of hub (drum brakes)

Key to Fig 8:3 1 Hub cap 2 Splitpin 3 Nut 4 Washer
5 Outer bearing 6 Track 7 Hub 8 Track 9 Inner
bearing 10 Vertical link collar 11 Oil seal 14 Brake drum
15 Vertical link 16 Retaining nut 17 Stub axle 18 Rubber
boot 19 Upper ballpin 20 Plug 21 Triangular plates
22 Lower ballpin 23 Lower suspension arm

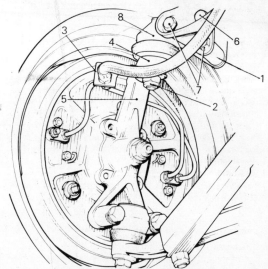

FIG 8:4 Removing upper ball joint

Key to Fig 8:4 1 Distance piece 2 Ballpin nut 3 Bracket
4 Ball joint shank 5 Vertical link 6 Damper lower mounting
bolt 7 Ball joint and upper wishbone securing bolts
8 Ball joint

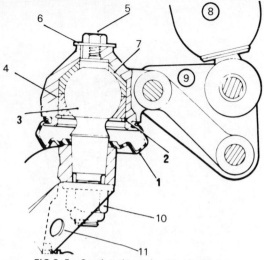

FIG 8:5   Section through upper ball joint

Key to Fig 8:5   1 Rubber boot   2 Circlip   3 Ballpin
4 Nylon lower seat   5 Plug   6 Washer   7 Nylon upper seat
8 Damper   9 Triangular plates   10 Nut   11 Support
bracket for flexible hose

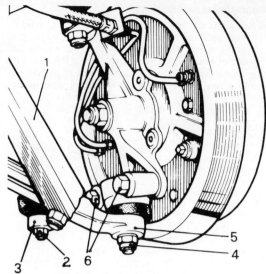

FIG 8:6   Removing lower ball joint

Key to Fig 8:6   1 Radius rod   2 Nyloc nut   3 Ball joint
shank   4 Nyloc nut   5 Lower suspension arm
6 Securing bolts

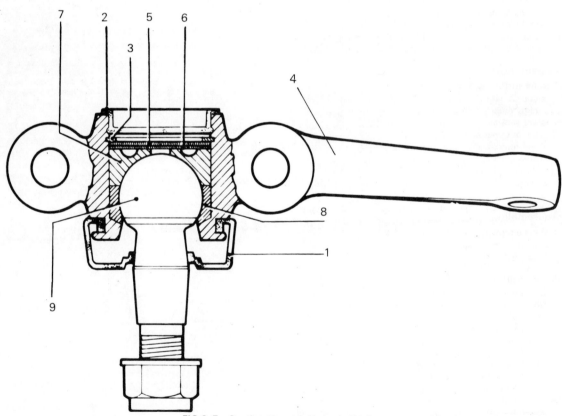

FIG 8:7   Section through lower ball joint

Key to Fig 8:7   1 Rubber boot   2 Sealing cap   3 Circlip   4 Steering arm   5 Top cover   6 Spring disc   7 Upper nylon seat
8 Lower nylon seat   9 Ballpin

Separating tapers on ball joints:

6 Ball joints are fitted where two parts are required to swivel about each other while motion or pressure is also being transmitted from one to the other. On one member a socket can rotate freely about the ball head end of a tapered pin. The tapered end of the pin fits into a very accurately machined mating taper on the other member and the two tapers are pulled into tight contact by the action of a nut. The nut has a locking system to ensure that it does not come free and allow the parts to separate.

With use the two tapers bed together and can be extremely difficult to separate after the nut and washer have been removed. Extractors are obtainable but they may not be readily available. Do not fall into the trap of hammering on the end of the tapered pin, as even with a slave nut fitted there is danger of damaging the threads or even the ball and socket. Instead use a wedge, such as a screwdriver, or some other method to pull the two members firmly apart. To prevent distortion, lay a block of metal against one side of the tapered eye (so that it is parallel to the tapered pin) and give the opposite side of the tapered eye a few smart blows with a copper-faced hammer. By this action the tapers will be quickly and safely freed. If hand pressure is used to pull the parts apart it is a wise precaution to leave the securing nut on the last few threads of the pin. This is to prevent the parts from flying apart suddenly and the hands hitting sharp projections.

Dismantling:

7 Refer to **FIG 8:5**, remove the rubber boot 1 and the circlip 2. Note the position of the open end of the circlip. Withdraw the ballpin 3, shims and the plastic lower seat 4.

8 Take out the plug 5 and washer. Using a suitable chisel, remove the plastic upper seat 7. This operation is necessary only if excessive wear exists between the ball and the plastic seat. If it is necessary, avoid damaging the housing with the chisel.

Reassembling:

9 Press a new upper plastic seat 7 in position, using the ballpin as a plunger and squeezing the ballpin and housing between the jaws of a vice. Fit the plastic lower seat 4 and circlip 2.

10 The ballpin should articulate freely and have a maximum end float of .004 inch (.102 mm). Three alternative lower ball seat sizes are available, also shims of .005 inch (.127 mm) and .010 inch (.254 mm). Select a lower ball seat and shim of the correct size to obtain the end float dimension.

11 Remove the circlip, shims and lower seat. Lubricate the ball with a smear of clean grease and reassemble. The circlip must be fitted with its open end at right angles to the ballhousing shank.

12 Partially pack a new rubber boot 1 with clean grease and fit it to the ball housing. Screw a grease nipple in the plug hole 5 and recharge the assembly with grease. Remove the nipple and fit the washer and plug.

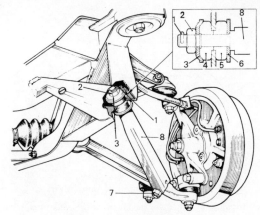

FIG 8:8   Removing radius rod

Key to Fig 8:8   1 Hairpin cotter   2 Securing nut
3 Dished washer   4 Outer rubber bush   5 Inner rubber bush
6 Washer   7 Nyloc nut   8 Radius rod

Refitting:

13 Refit the ball joint by reversing the instructions 1 to 5. Tighten the ballpin $\frac{1}{2}$ inch UNF nut to a torque of 50 to 65 lb ft (7 to 9 kg m) and the $\frac{3}{8}$ inch UNF nuts of the upper ball housing and the lower damper mounting to a torque of 20 to 24 lb ft (2.8 to 3.3 kg m).

Lower, removing:

1 Apply the handbrake, jack up the front of the car and support it securely on stands. Remove the road wheel.

2 Refer to **FIG 8:6** and unscrew the Nyloc nuts 2 and 4, collect the washers. Refer to instruction 6, 'Separating tapers on ball joints', at the beginning of the section.

3 Unscrew the two bolts 6 which secure the lower ball joint and steering arm to the vertical link. Remove the assembly from the vehicle.

Dismantling:

4 Refer to **FIG 8:7** and take off the rubber boot 1. Prise off the top sealing cap 2 and extract the circlip 3.

5 Push the ballpin upwards and force out the top cover 5, the spring disc 6 and the upper nylon seat 7.

6 Remove the lower nylon seat 8. Wash all the parts in paraffin. Refer to **Chapter 9, Sections 9:5** and **9:6** before servicing the tie rod ball joint.

Inspection:

7 Examine the ball and socket for any trace of roughness, renew any suspect and unserviceable items. Renew the rubber boot 1 and the Nyloc nuts if they turn easily on the ballpin threads.

Reassembling:

8 Fit the lower nylon seat 8, lubricate the ball with clean grease and insert it into the housing. Fit the upper ball seat 7, then the spring disc 6 with its concave side to the ball seat. Assemble the top cover, circlip and sealing cap.

9 Partially fill the rubber boot with clean grease and fit it to the housing.

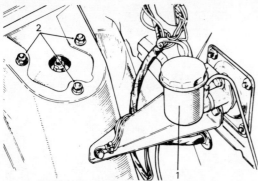

FIG 8:9   Removing upper mounting

Key to Fig 8:9   1 Brake fluid reservoir   2 Securing nuts

Refitting:

10 Reverse the instructions 1 to 3 and tighten the Nyloc ballpin nuts to a torque of 38 to 45 lb ft (5 to 8 kg m) and the bolts to a torque of 50 to 65 lb ft (7 to 9 kg m).

8:5 The radius rod

Removing:

1 Raise the front of the car on a jack and support it with either stands or blocks under the front wheel.
2 Refer to FIG 8:8 and remove the hairpin type cotter 1, nut 2, dished washer 3 and the outer rubber bush 4.
3 Unscrew the Nyloc nut 7, remove the bolt and detach the radius rod from the lower suspension arm. Pull the screwed end out of the subframe.

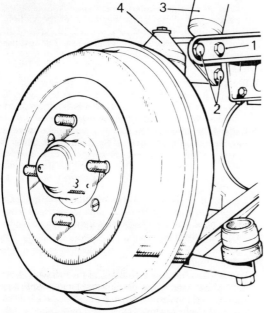

FIG 8:10   Removing lower mounting

Key to Fig 8:10   1 Damper lower mounting bolt   2 Upper wishbone to ball joint bolts   3 Damper   4 Ball joint

Inspecting:

4 Examine the rod for fractures and worn securing holes, check the rubber bushes for deterioration.

Refitting:

5 Fit the flat washer 6 with its radiused inner diameter away from the threaded end. Fit the rubber bush 5 with its plain face to the flat washer.
6 Insert the threaded end into the subframe and locate the other end with the bolt to the lower suspension arm. Fit the rubber bush 4 making sure the raised collar fits into the subframe orifice, check that the same condition applies to the other rubber bush.
7 Fit the dished washer 3 with its concave face to the rubber bush. Tighten the Nyloc nut 7 to a torque of 50 to 65 lb ft (7 to 9 kg m) and then tighten the nut 2 to a torque of 30 to 38 lb ft (4 to 5 kg m).

8:6 Road spring and damper

The damper and spring are removed from the car as an assembly and it is not advisable to try and separate them in an attempt to save time and effort during the removal operations. A special spring compressor is used to contact the spring when the parts are being separated, but the tool can be used only when the assembly is removed from the vehicle.

Removing:

1 Apply the handbrake, jack up the front of the car, support with safety stands and remove the road wheel.
2 Raise the engine bonnet, refer to FIG 8:9 and remove the three Nyloc nuts 2, collect the plain washers.
3 Refer to FIG 8:10 and remove the damper lower anchor bolt 1. Slacken only, the two nuts and bolts 2 which secure the upper wishbone to the ball joint.
4 Release the lower end of the damper and withdraw the damper and spring assembly downwards.
5 Refer to FIG 7:18 to fit the spring compressor tool S4221A.
6 Compress the spring until the upper mounting is free to revolve. Refer to FIG 8:11 and take off the locknut 1, nut 2, upper dished washer 3, rubber bush 4 and washer 5.
7 Withdraw the mounting flange 6 complete with spring insulating ring 7.
8 Release the spring tension, remove the tool and separate the spring and damper.

Inspection:

9 If a spring renewal is intended it is essential to check with the stores department of the service garage as to the type of spring employed. On some models the front springs do differ and an up to date parts list must be consulted to ascertain the part number and colour code. Check all rubber bushes for deterioration, renew them even if they are only slightly suspect. Renew the spring insulating ring.

The servicing of a spring damper is not generally practicable. The damper should be renewed if any of the following defects are apparent:

Damaged or dented body.
Bent piston rod.
Loosened mounting.
Fluid leakage.

If none of these defects is apparent, hold the unit vertically and carry out the following manual operations:

Slowly extend and compress the damper approximately 10 times, moving it to the limit of its stroke in both directions. There should be appreciable and constant resistance in both directions.

Renew damper units having the following defects: None or only slight resistance in one or both directions.

Excessive resistance; cannot be operated manually.

Pocket of no resistance when reversing direction.

Comparative performance can be assessed against the action of a new damper after taking care to expel air, but allowance must be made for greater resistance in the new unit due to the slightly increased friction between the piston rod and its oil seal.

Refitting:

10 Refer to the respective illustrations and reverse the operations 1 to 8. Tighten the nut and bolt on the damper lower mounting and the upper ball housing nuts to a torque of 20 to 24 lb ft (2.8 to 3.3 kg m).

8:7 Suspension wishbone

Removing:

1 Apply the handbrake, jack up the front of the car, support with stands and remove the front wheel.
2 Refer to **FIG 8:12,** remove the bolt and nut 1 which secures the end of the lower suspension arm 2 to the bracket 3.
3 Remove the three bolts and nuts 4 which secure the upper wishbone to the ball joint 5 and damper 6. Collect the triangular plates and distance piece.
4 Use rope or wire to support the hub assembly to the road spring to prevent undue strain on the flexible brake hose.
5 Remove the four bolts and nuts, three upper 7 and one lower, and take off the wishbone 8 complete with bracket assembly.

Dismantling:

6 Unscrew the Nyloc nut 9 and washer at the front end of the fulcrum shaft 10, take off the wishbone front half and washer 11. Unscrew the locknut 12 and nut 13. Take off the washer 14 and separate the wishbone rear half from the fulcrum shaft.

Servicing:

7 Renew the bushes by forcing out the old bush with either a hand press or large vice and suitable distance tubes. Use rubber grease or brake fluid when pressing in the new bush. Protect the bush by inserting a bolt through the centre and use a tube as a backing support, with sufficient internal diameter to clear the outside diameter of the bush. Check the support bracket 3 for fractures and the fulcrum shaft 10 and bracket 3 for fractures in the welded joints.

Refitting:

8 Pick up the fulcrum shaft 10 and fit the nut 13 and locknut 12, tighten and lock the nuts together so that

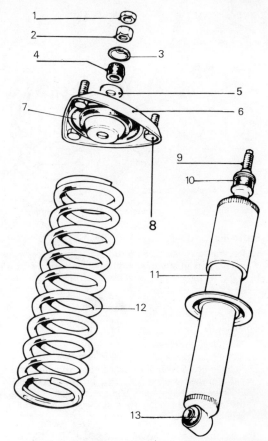

FIG 8:11   Components of damper and spring assembly

Key to Fig 8:11 1 Locknut 2 Nut 3 Upper dished washer 4 Rubber bush 5 Washer 6 Mounting plate 7 Insulating ring 8 Mounting bolts 9 Damper rod 10 Rubber bush 11 Damper 12 Spring 13 Damper lower mounting bush

there is one full thread (15) of the shaft projecting beyond the locknut. The tightening torque should be 30 to 38 lb ft (4.1 to 5.2 kg m) for the inner nut and 26 to 34 lb ft (3.6 to 4.7 kg m) for the locknut. Slide the plain washer 14 over the shaft, then, thread the shaft through the wishbone rear half, slide the plain washer 16 over the shaft and insert the shaft through the bracket holes.
9 Fit the plain washer 11 over the shaft then the wish-wishbone front half, fit the plain washer and Nyloc nut 9, but do not tighten the nut at this stage.
10 Fit the bracket assembly and shim(s) to the sub-frame and secure with the four bolts and nuts, three upper 7 and a lower one.
11 Fit the lower suspension arm 2 to the bracket 3, insert the bolt 1, fit the nut but do not tighten at this stage.
12 Locate the wishbone arms to the ball joint 5, insert the triangular plates, fit the three bolts 4 and nuts, not forgetting the distance piece in the lower one, and reconnect the lower damper mounting. Tighten the nuts to the torque given in **Technical Data.**

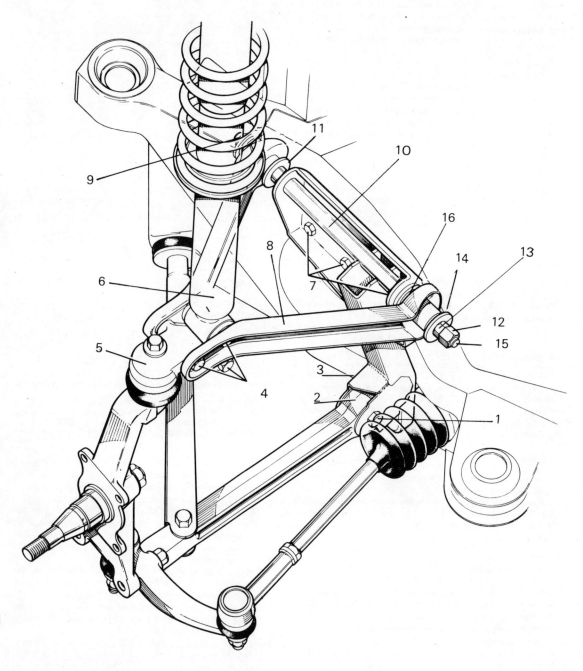

FIG 8:12   Removing upper wishbone

Key to Fig 8:12   1 Suspension arm to bracket bolt   2 Suspension arm   3 Bracket   4 Wishbone to ball joint bolts   5 Ball joint   6 Damper   7 Bracket securing bolts   8 Wishbone rear arm   9 Nyloc nut   10 Fulcrum shaft   11 Washer   12 Locknut   13 Nut   14 Washer   15 Fulcrum shaft   16 Washer

13 Take off the rope or wire that was used to support the hub, fit the road wheel, remove the stands and jack. Tighten the bolt 1 to a torque of 30 to 38 lb ft (4.1 to 5.2 kg m) and the Nyloc nut 9 to the same torque.

8:8 Lower suspension arm

Removing:

1 Apply the handbrake, jack up the front of the car and support the body on stands.
2 Refer to **FIG 8:13,** remove the Nyloc nut 1 and washer and detach the arm from the ball joint.
3 Refer to **FIG 8:8,** remove the hairpin type cotter 1 and slacken the nut 2.
4 Remove the nut and bolt 2 and the nut and bolt 3 in **FIG 8:13.**
5 Withdraw the lower suspension arm.

Servicing:

6 Press out the old bush and press in a new one using rubber grease or brake fluid to assist the entry. Ensure that the bush is centred correctly.

Refitting:

7 Refit the suspension arm in the reverse order, operations 1 to 5. Do not tighten the nut and bolt 2 until the jack has been removed and the weight of the car is on the wheels.

8:9 Suspension geometry

The term 'steering geometry' refers to the layout of the steering mechanism and any of its dimensions, linear or angular, which contribute to the required behaviour of the steering system. The steering system is always designed to comply with the specification of the front suspension, in order that the best possible steering behaviour is obtained under all conditions.

Departure from any steering/suspension dimensions may result in unsatisfactory steering and/or abnormal wear of tyres, steering and suspension components.

Poor steering and tyre wear are often caused by unbalance of the tyres themselves.

Camber:

This is the amount in degrees by which the wheels are inclined from the vertical, when viewed from the front of the car. Camber angle is defined as positive when the tops of the wheels lean outwards. The positive camber angle is increased by adding equal amounts of shims under the fulcrum brackets and decreased by the equal removal of shims.

Castor:

This is the angle in side elevation between the vertical and a line drawn through the two steering swivel points. Positive castor is when the steering axis is inclined backwards.

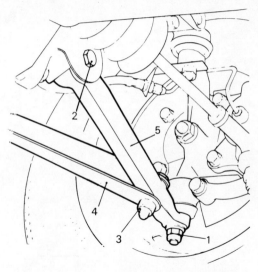

FIG 8:13   Removing lower suspension arm

Key to Fig 8:13   1 Nyloc nut   2 Arm to bracket bolt   3 Radius rod to suspension arm bolt   4 Radius rod   5 Lower suspension arm

Steering axis inclination (KPI):

This is the angle between the vertical and a line drawn through the steering swivel points, when viewed from in front of the car.

8:10 Fault diagnosis

(a) Wheel wobble

1 Worn hub bearings
2 Broken or weak front coil springs
3 Uneven tyre wear
4 Worn suspension linkage
5 Loose wheel fixings

(b) Bottoming of suspension

1 Check 2 in (a)
2 Dampers not working

(c) Heavy steering

1 Corroded or seized upper or lower swivels
2 Wrong suspension geometry

(d) Excessive tyre wear

1 Check 4 in (a), 2 in (b) and 2 in (c)

(e) Rattles

1 Check 2 in (a)
2 Rubber suspension bushes worn
3 Damper connections loose
4 Radius arm mountings loose or worn
5 Coil spring rubber insulators worn or compressed
6 Damper rubber bushes worn through

(f) Excessive rolling

1 Check 2 in (a) and 2 in (b)

NOTES

CHAPTER 9

THE STEERING GEAR

9:1 Description

A rack and pinion steering unit is fitted to all models of the Toledo. This type of unit, as opposed to the more common spiral cam and follower type, provides greater sensitivity on the steering as well as more accurate control. The pinion is turned directly by the steering column and as it turns it drives a rack from side to side of the car. The rack is in its turn directly connected to the tie rods, which act on the steering arms attached to the vertical links. As a result the system does not require drag links or steering idlers, and the motion is much more positive and direct. The maximum lock of the front wheels is controlled by the rack unit and there are no stops on the suspension.

The steering column is fitted with universal joints and is so designed, with an impact clamp, that the column collapses together in a serious accident instead of impaling the driver. The horn push and direction indicator switch are mounted on the head of the steering column. As the switches are mounted in the upper outer column they do not revolve with the steering wheel and the cables are led out of the column through a hole so that no stator tube is required in the column assembly.

9:2 Routine maintenance

1 At 12,000 mile intervals, clean the grease nipple in the steering rack unit (see **FIG 9:6**) and inject a maximum of five strokes of grease into the rack unit. Do not overgrease.

2 At regular intervals, inspect the rubber bellows on the steering rack and those on the tie rod ends. If they are split or damaged they should be renewed as soon as possible to prevent dirt from entering the assemblies. The tie rod ends are lubricated by packing their bellows with grease but this need only be done when the parts are dismantled for servicing or replacement.

9:3 Rack and pinion

Removing:

1 Apply the handbrake, jack up the front of the car and support with a safety stand on the steering wheel side of the car. Remove the righthand side road wheel if the car has righthand steering and the lefthand side road wheel if the car has lefthand steering.

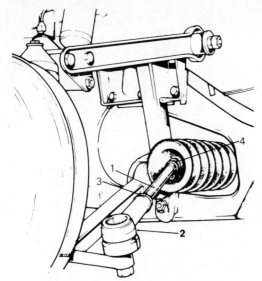

FIG 9:1 Tie-rod and tie-rod ball joint

Key to Fig 9:1   1 Tie-rod   2 Tie-rod ball joint   3 Locknut
4 Clip

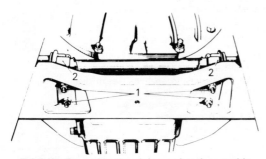

FIG 9:2 Removing the pinion and rack assembly

Key to Fig 9:2   1 Securing nuts   2 U-bolts

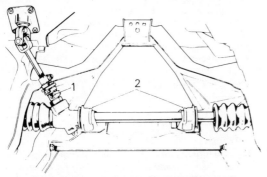

FIG 9:3 Uncoupling the intermediate shaft

Key to Fig 9:3   1 Clamp bolt   2 Rubber mountings

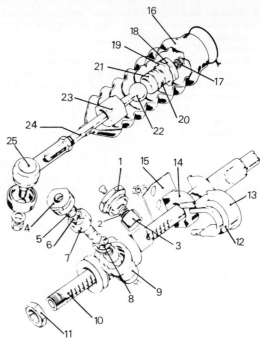

FIG 9:4 Component parts of rack and pinion assembly

Key to Fig 9:4   1 Plug   2 Spring   3 Plunger
4 Pinion end plug   5 O-ring   6 Circlip   7 Ballbearing
8 Pinion   9 Housing   10 Rack   11 Locknut   12 U-bolt
13 Retainer   14 Rubber mounting   15 Bearer plate   16 Gaiter
17 Spring   18 Locknut   19 Tabwasher   20 Shims   21 Cup
22 Ball-end   23 Cup nut   24 Tie-rod   25 Tie-rod ball
joint

2 Refer to **FIG 9:1** and disconnect the tie rod ball joints
from the steering arms (see operation 6, 'Separating
tapers on ball joints' in **Chapter 8, Section 8:4**).

3 Refer to **FIG 9:2** and unscrew the four nuts 1 which
secure the U-bolts and rack to the subframe, collect
the washers. Lift off the U-bolts 2 and the rack clamp
brackets.

4 Refer to **FIG 9:3** and scribe a line over the steering
column components, so that when the pinch bolt 1 is
removed and the column is separated from the
splines of the rack pinion shaft, it can be reassembled
to its original position.

5 Remove the pinch bolt, ease the rack forward to
disengage the splines and manoeuvre the rack
assembly from underneath the car.

9:4 Dismantling

1 Refer to **FIG 9:4** and unscrew the plug 1, withdraw
the spring 2, shims and plunger 3.

2 Unscrew the plug 4 and ease out the O-ring from
inside the plug. Screw two short bolts into the tapped
holes at the side, invert the plug and screw it back
into the pinion shaft. The idea of this, is to prise out the
shaft using the bolts as a fulcrum point as shown in
FIG 9:5.

3 When the shaft has been extracted, unscrew the plug and remove the two bolts. Take off the circlip and withdraw the ballrace.

4 Slacken off the gaiter clips and slide the rubber gaiters outwards. Slide the pinion housing clear and hold the rack shaft in a vice using soft jaw adaptors. Refer to **FIG 9:4,** slacken the locknuts 11 and release the tie rod inner ball joints by unscrewing the nut 23. Collect the ball cup 21, shims 20, tabwasher 19 and the spring 17. Remove the other tie rod and slide the pinion housing 9 off the rack.

5 Unscrew the grease nipple from the pinion housing.

9:5 Inspecting and servicing

1 Thoroughly clean and examine all components for wear or distortion, particularly the gear teeth of the rack and pinion. Renew any defective parts and if necessary the rack bearing bush in the end of the housing. This may prove to be a little difficult as the only method is to drift it out and press in a new one.

2 Similarly the lower bush in the pinion-housing may be renewed by the same method (see **FIG 9:6**) except that the end cover will have to be renewed also. The recessed end of the bush, when fitted into the housing, is adjacent to the end cover.

3 Check the pinion bearing for wear and renew it if its condition is doubtful. Renew the O-ring whatever the condition. Examine the rubber gaiters for signs of cracking or swelling, do not take chances regarding their serviceability, if there is the slightest doubt renew them, as they are largely responsible for keeping out abrasive properties such as road dirt, sand and mud.

4 The tie rod ball joints are renewable as a service item, they are unscrewed from the track rods after slackening the locknut. If they are faulty, make enquiries at the service stores regarding the availability of new component parts; it might be quicker in this instance to renew the ball joint complete. When refitting them to the track rod, position them so that the distance between the centres of the inner tie rod ball, and the ball joint, is $9\frac{3}{16}$ inch (233.4 mm) (see **FIG 9:7**).

9:6 Reassembly of the steering rack unit

1 Refer to **FIG 9:6,** insert the rack into the tube and refit the pinion. Make sure the pinion meshes correctly, adjust the position of the rack if necessary.

2 Adjust the pinion pressure pad by first fitting the pad 3, spring 2 and the cap nut 1 to the rack tube, then by tightening the plug fingertight to just eliminate any side movement in the rack.

3 Use feeler gauges to measure the clearance between the cap nut and housing face. Rack side movement should be .004 to .008 inch (.102 to .203 mm).

4 Remove the cap nut and pad.

5 Fit the shims equal to the established clearance **plus** .006 inch (.15 mm) to obtain the correct rack side movement.

6 Pack the unit with a recommended type grease, assemble the cap nut 1, shims, spring 2 and pad 3 to the housing 9 and then tighten the cap nut.

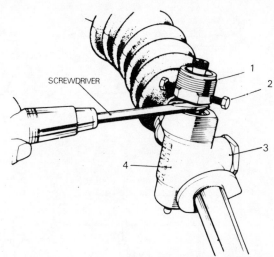

FIG 9:5 Extracting the pinion from the housing

Key to Fig 9:5   1 Inverted plug   2 Bolts   3 Plug
4 Housing

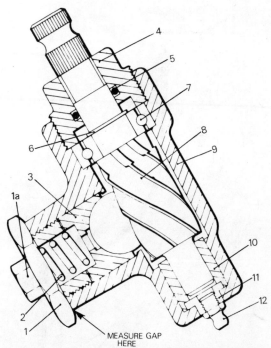

FIG 9:6 Sectional drawing of housing assembly

Key to Fig 9:6   1 Cap nut   1a Plug   2 Spring
3 Pad   4 Pinion end plug   5 O-ring   6 Circlip
7 Ballbearing   8 Pinion   9 Housing   10 Bush   11 End cover   12 Grease nipple

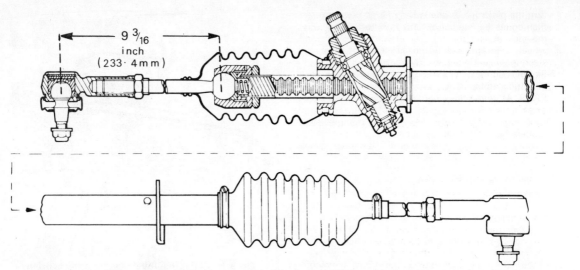

FIG 9:7 The distance between the centres of the inner tie-rod ball and the ball joint is $9\frac{3}{16}$ inch (233 mm)

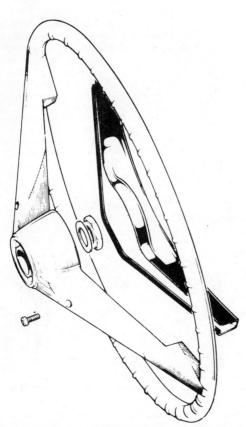

FIG 9:8 Steering wheel assembly

7 Lubricate the inside of the ball housing and insert the ballrod. Refer to **FIG 9:4** and fit the ball seat 21, shim(s) 20, a new tabwasher 19 and the adaptor 18. Tighten the adaptor to a torque of 80 lb ft (11 kg m).

8 Check the ball end for end float and articulation. Hold the nuts in a soft jawed vice and push and pull the tie rod to estimate the approximate amount of ball lift, which should be between .0005 inch (.0127 mm) and .003 inch (.0762 mm). There should be no tight spots in articulation. Add or remove shims to obtain these conditions. Shims are available in sizes of .002 inch (.05 mm), .004 inch (.102 mm) and .010 inch (.254 mm).

9 If the end float and articulation are satisfactory lock the adaptor and cup nut with the tabwasher.

10 Slide the spring 17 into the adaptor, fit the locknut 11 to the rack, then screw on the ball housing as far as it will go. When tightening the locknut it is essential that the rack shaft is held with a spanner at the other end to prevent its rotation, otherwise undue stress will be applied to the rack pinion. Tighten the locknut to 80 lb ft (11 kg m).

11 Pack grease around the ball joint, fit both gaiters, making sure they are the correct way round, and fit the gaiter and clips over the completed inner tie rod assembly. Fit the track rod ball joint.

12 Complete the assembly and checks on the other tie rod assembly.

13 Inject grease into the rack and pinion housing.

9:7 Refitting to the car

1 Carefully locate the rack assembly into position and guide the pinion shaft splines into the intermediate shaft coupling, to the previously made location marks. If the marks are obliterated and lost it will be necessary to centralize the rack and ensure that the steering wheel is in the straight-ahead position. To do this,

turn the pinion shaft one way as far as it will go and then count the number of turns from lock to lock. Set the rack at half the number of turns. The steering wheel is in the straight-ahead position when the steering wheel bar is perfectly horizontal.

2 Fit and tighten the pinch bolt. Position the rack mounting rubbers and fit the bearer plate (see 15 in **FIG 9:4**), under the mounting rubber that is furthest away from the pinion. This applies to both lefthand and righthand steering. Check that the mounting rubbers are correctly positioned and tighten the U-bolts. Reconnect the tie rod ball ends to the steering arms. Check for full and free movement from lock to lock.

3 Fit the road wheel and refer to **Section 9:12** to reset the front wheel track.

9:8 The steering wheel

Removing:

1 Refer to **FIG 9:8** and remove the two screws from the underside of the wheel spokes. Lift off the steering wheel pad.

2 If the steering is in the locked position, turn the ignition key to unlock it and then unscrew the retaining nut at the top of the column. Collect the washer.

3 Scribe a locating mark across the column and steering wheel to ensure the wheel is replaced in the correct position. Take out the ignition key.

4 Refer to **FIG 9:9** and remove the three screws which secure the nacelle halves together.

5 Use a suitable extractor and withdraw the wheel from the column splines.

Refitting:

6 Reverse the instructions 1 to 5 and make sure the scribe marks are aligned when the wheel is relocated on the column. If the marks were omitted, set the road wheels in the straight-ahead position and fit the wheel with the spokes positioned perfectly horizontal.

9:9 The steering column

A modification to the steering column has made the removal operations slightly different between the earlier and later models. From Commission No. T244 DG lefthand steer and T1754 DG righthand steer shearhead bolts are fitted to the steering column clamp bracket. The bolt heads twist off when they are fitted and tightened. To remove them the shanks must be drilled and the bolts removed with an extractor. Operations relating to this type of column, where they are extra to the removal of the earlier type, are noted in the instructions.

Removing:

1 Disconnect the battery.

2 Refer to **FIG 9:10** and **9:11,** which illustrate the earlier and later type respectively, and disconnect the plug-in connectors 2 for the ignition, starter, horn and direction indicator lights. Take out the ignition key.

3 Take out the three screws which clamp the nacelle halves 4 together, separate and remove the two halves.

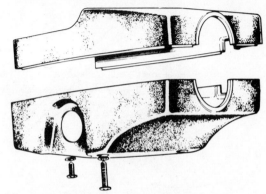

FIG 9:9   The nacelle covers

Late type:

4 Remove the direction indicator and horn stalk complete with brackets.
Refer to **Chapter 12** and remove the parcel shelf.

5 Refer to **FIG 9:12** and remove the pinch bolt and nut 1 which clamp the lower end of the column to the universal joint.

6 Refer to **FIG 9:13** and **9:14** and note the difference between the clamping arrangement of the two types.

7 Dealing first with the earlier type, unscrew the two nuts 1 which secure the clamp bracket 2 to the support bracket 3. Detach the clamp bracket and spring clip 4. Lift out the steering column complete. Refer to **FIG 9:14** and drill down the centre of the shanks of the two bolts 1. Drill far enough for an Easiout type extractor to obtain a good grip. Withdraw the bolts. Detach the clamp brackets 2 and 3 and the spring clip 4. Lift out the steering column complete.

8 To dismantle the steering column refer to the next section.

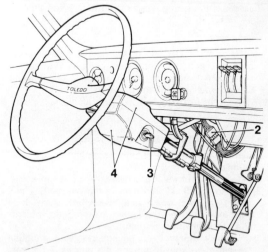

FIG 9:10   Early type steering column assembly in position

Key to Fig 9:10   2 Plug-in connectors   3 Ignition key
4 Nacelle covers

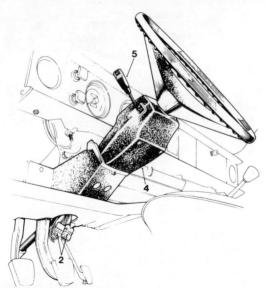

FIG 9:11 Later type steering column assembly in position

Key to Fig 9:11   2 Plug-in connectors   4 Nacelle covers
5 Direction and horn switch

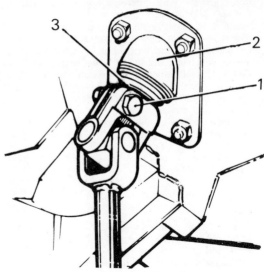

FIG 9:12   Upper universal joint

Key to Fig 9:12   1 Clamp bolt   2 Bushed plate
3 Nylon thrust washer

Refitting:

9 Refer to **FIG 9:12** and locate the steering column in the bushed plate 2 fitted to the scuttle. Fit the nylon washer to the lower end of the column. With the wheels in the straight-ahead position and the steering wheel spokes perfectly horizontal, insert the column splines into the mating splines of the universal joint. Fit and tighten the pinch bolt and nut.

10 On the earlier type, referring to **FIG 9:13,** fit the spring clip 4 and clamp bracket 2 to the column, assemble the spring washers and nuts 1 and tighten.

Late type:

Refer to **FIG 9:14,** fit the spring clip 4, clamp bracket 2 and two new shear bolts 1. Tighten the shear bolts evenly until the heads snap off. Refer to **Chapter 12** and refix the parcel shelf.

11 Reverse the instructions 1 to 4 for both types.

9:10 Dismantling the steering column

1 Remove the steering column assembly as described in the previous section.

2 Refer to **Section 9:8** and take off the steering wheel.

3 Refer to **FIG 9:15** and remove the two bolts 1 and spring washers which hold the safety clamp 2 in position. Withdraw the lower column 3 downwards and out of the upper column 5.

4 Carefully withdraw the upper column from the tubular housing 6 without disturbing the bushes. To extract the bush 7 from the tubular housing, depress the rubber dowel out of its location. To remove the lower bush 8, push out the end cap 9 and remove the bush by the same method.

Refitting:

5 If necessary fit new bushes to the tubular housing and replace the end cap.

6 Insert the upper column very carefully into the tubular housing, then insert the lower column very carefully into the upper column. Fit the nylon thrust washer 10 above the slot.

7 Align the milled flat of the lower column with the slot in the upper column, fit the safety clamp 2, but do not fully tighten the clamping bolts at this stage (see **FIG 9:16**).

8 Telescope the upper and lower columns to reduce the overall length as far as they will go, but do not use force otherwise the collapsible tube will be damaged. Slide the tubular housing downwards so that it butts the safety clamp against the edge of the slot and push the lower column upwards to prohibit any axial float in the collapsible tube. Make sure a turning clearance exists between the safety clamp and the tubular housing interspaced by the nylon washer 10. Tighten the clamp bolts in the safety clamp.

9 Refit the steering column into the car (see previous section) and refit the steering wheel as described in **Section 9:8.**

9:11 The intermediate shaft

Removing:

1 Refer to **FIG 9:17,** remove the upper pinchbolt 1 and the lower pinch bolt 2.

2 Take off the U-clamps which secure the rack housing to the subframe.

3 Ease the rack forward to disengage the splines at the flexible coupling and detach the intermediate shaft from the steering column.

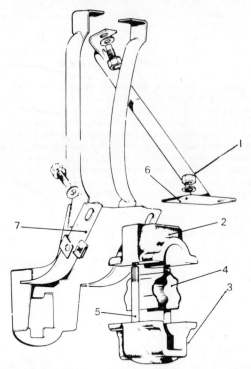

FIG 9:13 Steering column clamping arrangement, early type

Key to Fig 9:13 1 Clamp nuts 2 Upper clamp 3 Lower clamp 4 Spring clip 5 Clamp stud 6 Clamp plate and support 7 Support bracket

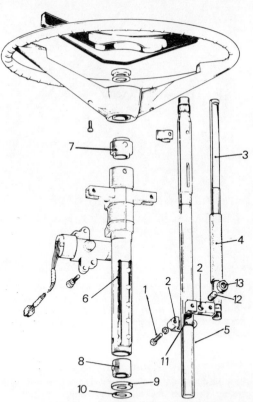

FIG 9:15 Steering column assembly

Key to Fig 9:15 1 Clamp bolt 2 Clamp bracket 3 Milled flat of lower column 4 Collapsible spacer 5 Upper column 6 Tubular housing 7 Upper bush 8 Lower bush 9 End cap 10 Nylon thrust washer 11 Slot 12 Plug 13 Locknut

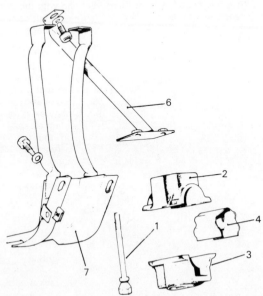

FIG 9:14 Steering column clamping arrangement, late type

Key to Fig 9:14 1 Shear bolt (see Key to **FIG 9:13**)

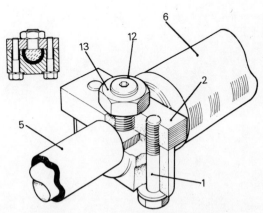

FIG 9:16 Details of clamping arrangement

Key to Fig 9:16 1 Clamp bolt 2 Clamp bracket 5 Upper column 6 Tubular housing 12 Plug 13 Locknut

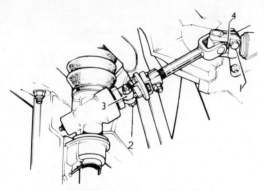

FIG 9:17   The intermediate shaft

Key to Fig 9:17   1 Upper clamp bolt   2 Lower clamp bolt
3 Clamp   4 Column splines

Refitting:

4 Refit the shaft in the reverse order of removing. Ensure that the front wheels are in the straight-ahead position and the steering wheel spokes are perfectly horizontal before engaging the flexible coupling splines.

9:12   Front wheel alignment (track)

An indication that the front wheels are not in correct alignment is when the tyres wear unevenly and the treads have a feathered appearance on the edges of one side.

On all the models covered by this manual the correct wheel alignment is 0 to $\frac{1}{16}$ inch (0 to 1.59 mm) toe-in in either an unladen or laden condition. Adjustment is by slackening the locknuts 3 and clips 4 on the tie rods (see **FIG 9:1**) and rotating the tie rods so that they screw either in or out of the tie rod ends thus effectively altering the length of the assemblies. Unless the adjustment required is very small, both tie rods should be adjusted by equal amounts to ensure that the steering wheel will still be in the straight-ahead position when the front wheels are so.

The wheel alignment is best checked using a proper gauge but if care is taken then the measurements can be taken without special equipment. With the car on level ground and the wheels in the straight-ahead position, roll it forwards for a few yards to settle the suspension and bearings.

Measure, as accurately as possible, the distance between the inside wheel rims on the front of the front wheels and at wheel centre height. Mark the point of contact of the tyre with the ground with a piece of chalk and roll the car forwards so that the wheels turn exactly half a revolution. **Never push the car backwards or the measurements will be inaccurate.** Again measure the distance between the rims at wheel centre height but at the rear of the front wheels. The difference between the two dimensions gives the wheel alignment.

9:13   Fault diagnosis

(a)   Wheel wobble

1 Unbalanced wheels and tyres
2 Slack steering connections
3 Incorrect steering geometry

(b)   Wander

1 Check 2 and 3 in (a)
2 Damaged suspension or chassis
3 Uneven tyre pressures
4 Weak dampers or springs

(c)   Heavy steering

1 Check 3 in (a)
2 Very low tyre pressures
3 Neglected lubrication
4 Wheels out of track
5 Steering rack unit incorrectly adjusted
6 Steering column bushes tight
7 Seized tie rod ends

(d)   Lost motion

1 Loose steering wheel
2 Worn splines
3 Worn steering coupling
4 Worn ball joints
5 Worn vertical link swivels

CHAPTER 10

THE BRAKING SYSTEM

10:1 Description

The braking system on all Toledo models is the Girling hydraulic type. Power assistance, through the medium of a vacuum servo, is provided on all 1500 export four door models, but on the British market and 1500 two door models it has been a standard fitment only since October 1972. When the footbrake pedal is depressed, pressure is applied, either manually or power assisted, to a master cylinder; from which fluid is transmitted through rigid and flexible pipes to the four wheel cylinders. Flexible hoses are fitted to allow for suspension movement.

The vacuum servo and master cylinder assembly is mounted on the engine bulkhead in line with the footbrake pedal arm. The purpose of the servo is to assist the manual pressure applied to the brake fluid, to retard the speed or stop the car. Braking action is still effective even if there is a breakdown in the servo unit, as the brake pedal can operate directly upon the master cylinder. The increased manual pressure required to operate the brake under these circumstances is physically obvious, but not alarmingly so and the car can be driven safely providing the driver is fully aware that the braking action is fractionally slower.

The handbrake is centrally mounted between the front seat and operates in the rear wheels only by a mechanical linkage. Adjustment on the home market models, is automatically taken up when the rear shoes are adjusted. The 1500 export models have a self-adjusting device, operated by the handbrake, to take up excess clearance between the shoes and the drum.

The pre-October 1972 British market models have expanding brake shoes and friction drums fitted on all four wheels. The later models are now equipped with self-adjusting fixed caliper disc brakes on the front wheels. The front brake on the early models incorporates the 'two leading shoe' system with individual single piston wheel cylinders to operate each shoe. The rear brakes on early and late models are the leading and trailing type, both operated by a single floating piston.

The 1500 export four door models and the later two door models have self-adjusting disc brakes on the front. Self-adjusting rear drum brakes have been a standard fitment on both four and two door models throughout.

A ratchet wheel attached to the closed end of the wheel cylinder is stroked by a lever connected to the handbrake linkage. As increasing wear in the liners and drum begins to exceed the normal free running requirement, the lever causes the ratchet to rotate one tooth and extend the overall length of the cylinder. The self-adjusting mechanism is so designed that a limit of adjustment is imposed to prevent the liners wearing beyond the point of renewal. An indication of this, is

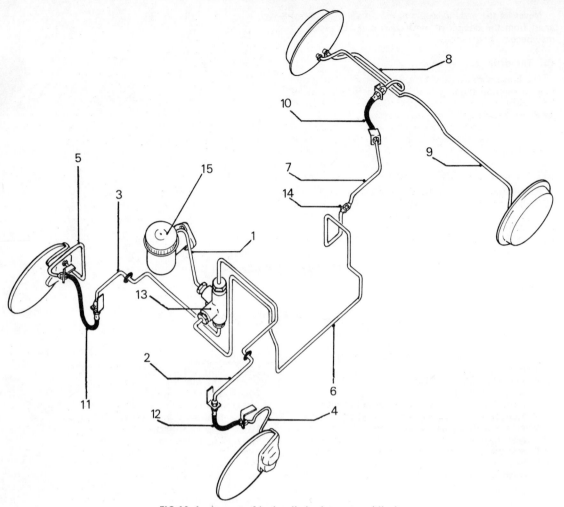

FIG 10:1   Layout of hydraulic brake system (disc)

Key to Fig 10:1   1 Master cylinder to four-way connector   2 Four-way connector to lefthand front hose   3 Four-way connector to righthand front hose   4 Lefthand front hose to caliper (or wheel cylinder)   5 Righthand front hose to caliper (or wheel cylinder)   6 Four-way connector to union adaptor   7 Union adaptor to rear hose   8 Rear hose to righthand wheel cylinder   9 Transger pipe righthand to lefthand wheel cylinder   10 Rear flexible hose   11 Righthand front flexible hose   12 Lefthand front flexible hose   13 Four-way connector   14 Union adaptor   15 Master cylinder

when the handbrake travel becomes excessive and when this stage is reached liner renewal is imminent. **Do not attempt to adjust the handbrake linkage to compensate.**

The layout of the hydraulic pipes and hoses is shown in **FIG 10:1,** it is similar for both systems although the illustration shows the disc brake type. The recommended fluid is Castrol Girling Green.

10:2 Routine maintenance and adjustment

(a) The hydraulic system

1 Periodically check the level of the fluid in the master cylinder reservoir and maintain this at the correct level. **Use only the recommended fluid for this operation.**

2 Check the tightness of all pipe unions but use only spanners of short length to prevent overtightening.
3 Check for leakage of fluid at wheel and master cylinders and if apparent, rectify by dismantling and fitting new seals as described in this Chapter.
4 Every 10,000 miles, check the flexible fluid pipes for chafing or deterioration and renew if necessary.
5 Every 40,000 miles (or three years) completely drain and refill the system with new fluid as described under 'bleeding the system'.

(b) The front disc brakes:

These are self-adjusting but every 10,000 miles the pads should be inspected for wear. When the friction pads have worn to between $\frac{1}{8}$ and $\frac{1}{16}$ inch in thickness they should be replaced as described later in this chapter.

Never let the pads wear down more than $\frac{1}{16}$ inch as, apart from the danger of ineffective braking, the discs may become badly scored.

(c) The drum brakes (1300):

The brake shoes on the 1300 may be adjusted at any time to keep optimum braking efficiency which is partly dependant upon a minimal clearance being maintained between the lining and the brake drum.

Each brake backplate has an adjuster which protrudes from it. These are shown, for the front and rear brakes respectively, in **FIGS 10:2** and **10:3**.

(d) The rear drum brakes (1500):

As mentioned previously, the rear drum brakes are self-adjusting, the only indication of excessive wear in the brake shoe liners is when the self-adjusting mechanism has reached its limit and results in an ever increasing travel in the handbrake lever. Renew the liners or brake shoes as soon as practicable and reset the self-adjusting mechanism.

10:3 Adjusting the 1300 drum brakes

Front:

1 With the handbrake released, apply the footbrake several times to centralize the shoes. Jack up the front of the car, making sure beforehand that the handbrake is applied and the jack is not likely to collapse.
2 Refer to **FIG 10:2** and working on the front adjuster 1, rotate it in a clockwise direction and spin the wheel at the same time. When the wheel becomes locked, slacken back (anticlockwise) the adjuster until the wheel becomes free.
3 Repeat this operation on the second shoe adjuster 2.
4 Repeat the whole operation on the other front wheel.
5 If the rotation of the adjuster, clockwise, fails to lock the road wheel it would indicate that the linings on the brake shoes are critically worn.

Rear:

1 Apply the handbrake several times to centralize the shoes. Release the handbrake and chock the front wheels. Jack up the rear end of the car, making sure it is stable and support the rear axle with blocks.
2 Refer to **FIG 10:3** and turn the single adjuster in a clockwise direction, spin the wheel at the same time. When the wheel becomes locked, slacken off (anticlockwise) the adjuster until the wheel spins freely.
3 Repeat the operation on the other rear wheel.
4 Check the handbrake application.
5 Read item 5 in the front brake adjustment.

10:4 Removing, refitting brake shoes (1300)

Front:

1 Apply the handbrake. Jack up the front wheel of the car until it is almost clear of the ground, slacken the wheel nuts. Raise the car until the wheel is clear and support the vehicle further by positioning firm blocks or stands under the subframe. Unscrew the wheel nuts and remove the road wheel.

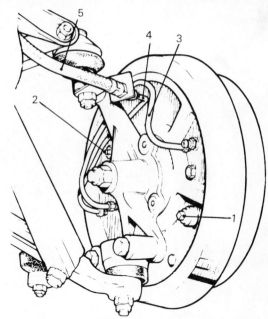

FIG 10:2 Front brake adjusters (early 1300)

Key to Fig 10:2 1 Front shoe adjuster 2 Rear shoe adjuster 3 Transfer pipe, rear to front cylinder 4 Supply pipe 5 Flexible hose

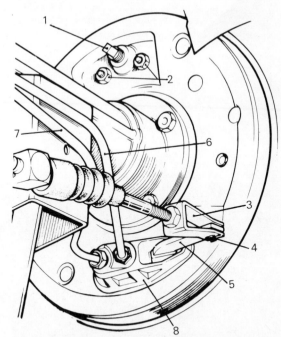

FIG 10:3 Rear brake adjuster, view from inboard of righthand rear wheel (1300)

Key to Fig 10:3 1 Adjuster 2 Adjuster unit retaining nuts 3 Handbrake cable fork end 4 Clevis pin 5 Handbrake lever 6 Rear hose to righthand wheel cylinder pipe 7 Transfer pipe, righthand to lefthand wheel cylinder 8 Rubber boot

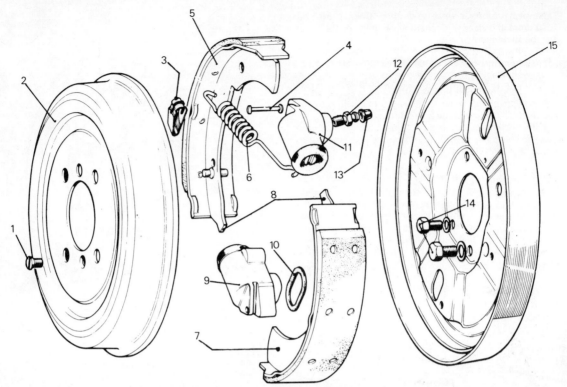

FIG 10:4   Components of front brake (early 1300)

Key to Fig 10:4   1 Drum retaining screw   2 Drum   3 Spring clips   4 Steady pin   5 Shoe   6 Return spring (upper)   7 Shoe
8 Leading points   9 Lower wheel cylinder   10 Gasket   11 Upper wheel cylinder   12 Bleed screw   13 Dust cap   14 Backplate
retaining screws   15 Backplate

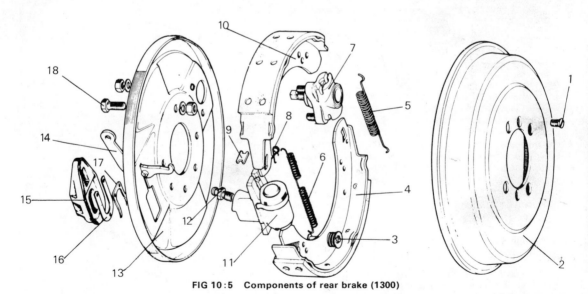

FIG 10:5   Components of rear brake (1300)

Key to Fig 10:5   1 Drum retaining screw   2 Drum   3 Steady pin and spring   4 Trailing shoe (positioned at front)   5 Upper
return spring   6 Lower return spring   7 Adjuster unit   8 Retaining spring   9 Lever plate   10 Leading shoe (positioned at rear)
11 Wheel cylinder   12 Bleed screw   13 Backplate   14 Handbrake lever   15 Rubber boot   16 U-clip   17 Spring plate
18 Backplate retaining bolts

2 Remove the two countersunk screws which secure the drum to the hub. Withdraw the friction drum.

3 If the friction area inside the drum is ridged or worn, difficulty may be experienced in pulling the drum away from the shoes. In this instance slacken off the brake shoe adjusters.

4 Refer to **FIG 10:4** and prise the spring plate retainers 3 off the shoe steady pins 4. Take out the steady pins.

5 Pull the leading edge of the lower shoe 7 away from its location in the piston and, against the pressure of the upper spring 6 lift it clear of the cylinder. Pull the trailing edge of the shoe away from its slotted location at the back of the other cylinder. Release the tension on the spring and unhook it from the shoe and backplate. If the shoe is to be refitted, mark it for correct location.

6 Repeat operation 5 in the other shoe.

7 It is advisable, if the shoes are to be left off for some time, to secure the pistons in the wheel cylinder by binding string or wire around the cylinder; strong elastic bands may also suffice. Do not press the foot-brake pedal whilst the shoes and drums are removed.

Avoid contaminating the liners with grease or oil as it will seriously effect the braking efficiency. Wash off any such contamination immediately with petrol, or if it is obtainable, trichlorethylene. If the liners are already contaminated and have apparently been so for some time, renew them and also the other side irrespective of their condition, to maintain breaking stability. Always when renewing the brake shoes or drums on a particular wheel, renew the corresponding parts on the opposite wheel also.

8 Use a high pressure air-line or foot pump to blow away all loose dust from the mechanism, use a dry clean cloth to wipe dust from the inside of the drums. Hard stubborn mud or dirt can be removed with a stiff brush.

9 If the liners are worn down to the rivet heads, renew them. Don't attempt to reline the shoes, obtain a complete set on an exchange basis. Heavily scored or worn friction drums should be renewed on an exchange basis and in this instance it is advisable to renew the shoes and liners also. Renew weak or distorted springs.

Refitting:

10 Slacken off the snail cam adjusters and position the bottom shoe so that the narrow end of the shoe web will enter the piston slot. Connect the return spring to the shoe web and backplate. Engage the broad end of the shoe web into its locating slot at the back of the wheel cylinder and pull on the spring to engage the narrow end of the web into the piston slot. Repeat this operation in the other shoe, bearing in mind that the narrow edge of the shoe web locates in the piston slot.

11 Reassemble the remaining parts and adjust the brakes to the instructions given in **Section 10:3**.

Rear:

1 Chock the front wheels, release the handbrake and jack up the rear wheels. Support the vehicle with a safety stand or firm blocks.

2 Refer to **FIG 10:3** and slacken off the brake adjuster.

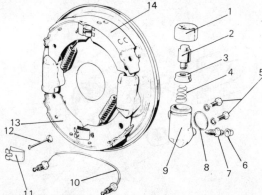

FIG 10:6 Wheel cylinder components, front (early 1300)

Key to Fig 10:6   1 Protective cover   2 Piston   3 Seal   4 Spring   5 Retaining bolts   6 Dust cap   7 Bleed screw   8 Gasket   9 Cylinder housing   10 Transfer pipe   11 Spring clip   12 Shoe steady pin   13 and 14 Brake shoes

3 Unscrew the two countersunk screws which secure the brake drum to the hub and withdraw the drum.

4 Refer to **FIG 10:5** and push the retainer plate of the steady pins against the pressure of the spring, turn it and release it from the steady pin. Remove the spring and steady pin.

5 Release the small spring 8 which secures the handbrake lever plate 9 to the rear brake shoe web.

6 Pull one shoe against the tension of the springs and release it from its location in the adjuster slot. Release the other end from its location in the wheel cylinders. Release the tension and unhook the springs from the shoes. Mark the shoes so that they will be replaced in the correct position; unless they are being renewed.

7 Refer to operations 7, 8 and 9 under the removal of the front brake shoes. Check that the wheel cylinder slides

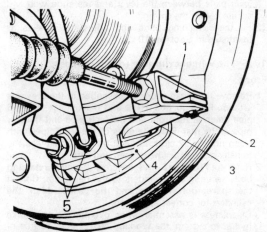

FIG 10:7 Handbrake cable connection to righthand rear wheel

Key to Fig 10:7   1 Handbrake cable fork end   2 Clevis pin   3 Handbrake operating lever   4 Rubber boot   5 Hydraulic pipe connections

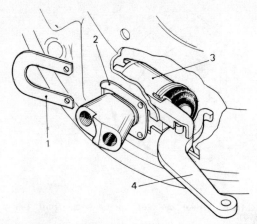

FIG 10:8 Removing wheel cylinder from backplate

Key to Fig 10:8 1 U-clip 2 Spring plate 3 Cylinder
4 Handbrake operating lever

freely in the backplate. If the adjuster mechanism is
to be overhauled refer to **Section 10:6**. Check the
free movement of the handbrake lever.

Refitting:

8 Arrange the shoes so that the blanked out slot at the
end of the rear shoe web will be positioned to the rear
of the wheel cylinder and the blanked out slot at the
end of the front shoe web will be positioned to the
front of the adjuster.

9 Fit the upper spring to the shoe webs, on the inboard
side of the shoes, and fit the assembly to the backplate. Engage the ends of both shoes in the adjuster.

10 Engage the handbrake lever in the bottom end of the
rear shoe, fit the lower spring inboard of the shoes
with its smallest length of the coil to the rear. Engage
the lower ends of both shoes in the wheel cylinder.

11 Fit the steady pins and the springs. Fit the handbrake
lever plate between the lever and the shoe web and
secure it with the spring.

12 Fit the remaining parts and adjust the brakes as
instructed in **Section 10:3**.

10:5 The wheel cylinders (drum brakes):

Front:

1 Remove the brake shoes as described in the previous
section. Refer to **FIG 10:2** and disconnect the feed
pipe union at the front and the feed pipe and transfer
pipe at the rear. Plug the ends of the feed pipes with
clean non-fluffy cloth to keep out dirt and place the
transfer pipe somewhere clean and safe.

2 Refer to **FIG 10:6** and unscrew the two retaining
bolts securing the cylinders to the backplate. Collect
the shakeproof washers and the gasket. Mark the
cylinders for correct relocation.

3 Cleanliness is essential when overhauling the brake
hydraulic system, the working area should be free of
dirt and the hands must be kept perfectly clean. If
particles of dirt enter the cylinders they will scratch
the highly polished bores and piston sides, which will
provide an escape route for the fluid when it is under
pressure. The components should be washed only

in methylated spirits or clean brake fluid, petrol or
other solvents will have a detrimental effect on the
seals, and dust covers, although it is advisable to
renew the seals, whatever the condition, once the
cylinders have been dismantled.

4 Take off the rubber dust cover and withdraw the
piston, seal and spring.

5 Clean and examine the cylinder bores and the pistons
for score marks and wear. Use a magnifying glass
if there is one available. Renew the cylinder assembly
if there is the slightest doubt in its serviceability.

6 Lubricate the cylinder bore, new seal and piston with
clean brake fluid; not the fluid they have been washed
in. Fit the spring, the seal and piston with the lip of the
seal inwards and make sure it does not curl back, fix
the new rubber dust cover and check that the piston
and seal move freely in the bore.

7 Refit the parts in the reverse order of dismantling.
Before refitting the transfer pipe, blow compressed air
through it. Adjust the brakes as described in **Section
10:3** and bleed the hydraulic system as described in
Section 10:12. After bleeding the system, get a
second operator to press the foot brake pedal, whilst
a check is made for leaks around the reassembled
parts.

Rear (1300):

1 Remove the brake shoes as described in the previous
section. Refer to **FIG 10:7** and disconnect the handbrake by removing the clevis pin from the fork end
and lever attachment.

2 Disconnect the fluid feed pipe at the wheel cylinder.
If the work is on the righthand side, disconnect the
transfer pipe union also. Take off the wheel cylinder
rubber boot from the inboard side of the backplate.
Refer to **FIG 10:8** and extract the horseshoe clip 1
which secures the wheel cylinder to the backplate.
  Remove the spring plate 2 and withdraw the
cylinder assembly complete with handbrake lever.

3 Refer to **FIG 10:9** and take off the spring clip around
the rubber dust cover, remove the cover and extract
the piston and seal.

4 Complete operations 3, 5 and 6 under overhauling the
front wheel cylinders. Refit the parts in the reverse
order of dismantling and note the following points.

5 Ensure that the mounting faces of the wheel cylinder
and backplate are clean and smear them with a light
coating of zinc-based grease. When fitting the spring
plate (see **FIG 10:8**), position it with the open end
to the front of the car and the dimple projections
facing inboard. Fit the horseshoe clip with the opend
end to the rear of the car and make sure the dimples
locate with the dimples in the spring plate, locking
them together. Check that the cylinder moves freely
in the backplate.

6 Read and complete operation 7 under overhauling
the front wheel cylinder, but before blowing compressed air through the transfer pipe, make sure both
ends are disconnected.

10:6 The rear brake adjuster (1300):

Whilst the brakes are dismantled it is advisable to
remove the adjuster mechanism and check the cams and
adjuster screw for wear. Unscrew the two nuts which

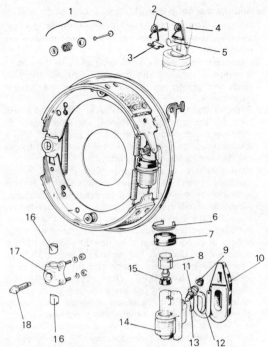

FIG 10:9   Wheel cylinder components, rear (1300)

Key to Fig 10:9   1 Steady pin assembly   2 Retaining spring
3 Lever plate   4 Brake shoe   5 Operating lever   6 Clip
7 Protective cover   8 Piston   9 Dust cap   10 Rubber boot
11 Bleed screw   12 U-clip   13 Spring plate   14 Cylinder
housing   15 Seal   16 Tappet   17 Adjuster housing
18 Adjuster screw

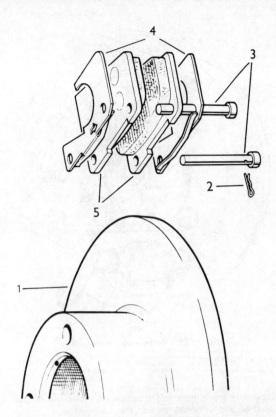

FIG 10:11   Brake pads and disc

Key to Fig 10:11   1 Disc   2 Retainer clips   3 Pad
retainers   4 Damping shims   5 Pads

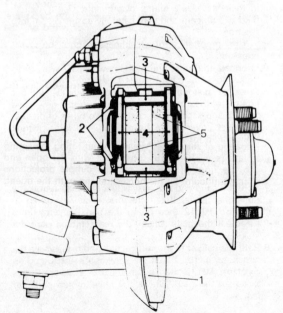

FIG 10:10   The caliper unit

Key to Fig 10:10   1 Disc   2 Retainer clips   3 Pad
retainers   4 Damping shims   5 Pads

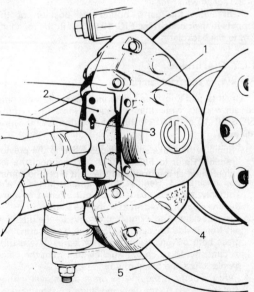

FIG 10:12   Fitting the brake pads

Key to Fig 10:12   1 Caliper unit   2 Pad retainer
3 Arrow pointing in direction of wheel rotation   4 Pad
5 Disc

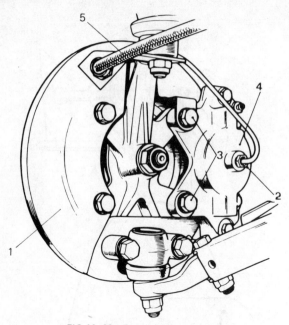

FIG 10:13 Removing caliper unit

Key to Fig 10:13　　1 Disc shield　　2 Pipe union
3 Securing bolts　　4 Caliper　　5 Flexible hose

secure the mechanism to the backplate, collect the spring washers and withdraw the adjuster.

Extract the tappets and take the screw out of the body, clean the parts thoroughly and renew worn ones. Smear, very lightly, the faces of the tappets and the tapered face of the screw with grease.

Reassemble the parts, noting the position of the tappets in their bores (see **FIG 10:9**). Refit the mechanism to the backplate.

10:7 Disc brakes:

Renewing the friction pads:

The total pad thickness (including backplate) must not be allowed to wear thinner than $\frac{3}{8}$ inch (3.17 mm). **FIGS 10:10** and **10:11** show the method of renewing the pads.

1 Securely jack up the front of the car and remove the road wheels.
2 Take out the spring clip retainers 2 and withdraw the pad retainers 3. Remove the damping shims 4 and withdraw the brake pads 5. Do not attempt to reline the brake pads. Avoid intermixing the shims.
3 Use an air-line and a brush to remove all the dust and dirt from inside the caliper. Open the bleed screw and press both pistons back into their bores. Use a tube or container to catch the fluid ejected from the bleed nipple. Close the bleed nipple.
4 Refit the parts in the reverse order of removal, noting that the arrows on the damping shims must point in the direction of forward rotation. Make sure the angled edge of the shim rests on the brake pad (see **FIG 10:12**).
5 If necessary, bleed the brakes (see **Section 10:12**).

Servicing the caliper unit:

1 Refer to **FIG 10:13.** Jack up the front of the car, secure it with a stand or firm blocks and remove the road wheel.
2 Disconnect the brake pipe union 2 and seal the end of the pipe to prevent dirt entering. Remove the two bolts and spring washers 3 and lift off the caliper assembly 4.
3 Remove the friction pads. Refer to **FIG 10:14** and take off the circlips 4 securing the dust cover 5. Remove the covers and extract the pistons 6. Use a low pressure air-line if the pistons are difficult to get out. Do not intermix the pistons.
4 Very carefully, prise out the cylinder seals 7; the operator must be extremely cautious with this operation to prevent scoring or damaging the bores.
5 Absolute cleanliness is essential in all operations involving the hydraulic system. Use only the recommended cleaning fluids and lay the parts on clean sheets of paper so that they cannot pick up dirt or contaminant. Use only the recommended brake fluid, Castrol Girling (Green) Clutch and Brake Fluid or to specification SAE.70.R3. Other brake fluids will attack the material of the seals causing them to fail. Bores of cylinders must be smooth and highly polished. If the bore shows pitting, scoring or wear the whole assembly must be renewed. The only fluids that should be used for cleaning the parts are methylated spirits (denatured alcohol), brake fluid or Girling hydraulic cleaning fluid. When internal parts are refitted they should all be dipped into clean hydraulic fluid and refitted wet. Seals must be replaced using only the fingers and worked around so that they are fully and squarely onto their recesses. It is advisable to discard all old seals and fit new ones in their place as a matter of principle. Use hydraulic fluid as lubricant and very carefully ease the seal into the bore.

The importance of cleanliness cannot be overstressed.

6 Lubricate the bores and fit the new seals 7 with clean brake fluid, install the seals using the fingers only. Press the pistons into the cylinders, evenly, without tilting, to their original locations. Fit the new dust cover 5 and secure with circlips. Two types of pistons and dust covers have been fitted, the later pistons having a lip for securing the dust cover in position.

The later type dust cover can be used on early pistons, but the early type dust cover must not be fitted to the later type pistons.

7 Refit the caliper to the vertical link and reassemble the remaining parts. Bleed the brakes as instructed in **Section 10:12** then pump the pedal several times to adjust the pads. Check the reassembled parts for leaks.
8 Refit the caliper to the vertical link and reassemble the remaining parts. Bleed the brakes as instructed in **Section 10:12** then pump the pedal several times to adjust the pads. Check the reassembled parts for leaks.

The brake disc:

Before this can be removed from the wheel hub, the

hub must be removed from the suspension as instructed in **Chapter 8, Section 8 : 3.**

A scored brake disc will cause poor braking and excessive pad wear. If the damage is only shallow, it can be machined off provided that no more than .020 inch (.0508 mm) is removed from each face. A very high standard of finish is required, so the machining must be left to firms specializing in this sort of work.

If the scoring is too deep to be machined off then the disc must be renewed. When the disc and hub have been refitted to the car, with the correct end float, mount a DTI (Dial Test Indicator) on the caliper. Set the DTI so that the stylus rests vertically on the outer face of the brake disc at a distance of .5 inch (12.7 mm) from the outer edge of the disc. Press the hub assembly inwards to take up the end float and rotate it so that the runout on the brake disc is measured. The runout must not exceed .004 inch (.10 mm) and if this figure is exceeded check the mating surfaces of the disc and hub for dirt. Re-assemble the disc to the hub, aligning different securing holes. If the runout is still excessive the disc will either have to be machined or scrapped.

10 : 8 The self-adjusting rear brake (1500)

Removing brake shoes:

1 Refer to **Section 10 : 4,** complete operations 1 and 3 for the 1300 rear brakes.

2 Refer to **FIG 10 : 15** and spring the ratchet operating lever 2 away from the ratchet wheel, rotate the wheel to release the brake adjustment.

3 To release the brake shoes from the anchor pins and wheel cylinder locations, use the method described in **Section 10 : 4** for the 1300 rear brakes, operation 4 and 6. Complete also operations 7, 8 and 9 as described for the front brakes.

Refitting:

4 Place the shoes in the position they will occupy on the backplate, fit the upper spring inboard of the shoe webs with the long hook to the front shoe. Lift the shoes and spring together and engage the upper ends in the anchor plate.

5 Fit the lower duplicated coil spring inboard of the shoe webs, engage the handbrake operating lever in the rear shoe web ensuring that the lever pad is properly located. Engage the front shoe on the ratchet spindle and the rear shoe on the cylinder piston.

6 Reassemble the remaining parts and after completing the other side, operate the handbrake lever several times to adjust the brake.

Wheel cylinders:

Remove the brake shoes and carry out the instructions given for the removal of the rear wheel cylinders on the 1300 models (see **Section 10 : 5**). The extra operation will be to ensure that the ratchet wheel spins freely on the screwed rod. Make sure it is slackened off completely when refitting.

10 : 9 The master cylinder

Reference should be made to **FIG 10 : 16** to observe the sequence of component parts but it will be helpful if the principle of operation of the master cylinder is first understood by reference to **FIG 10 : 17** which shows:

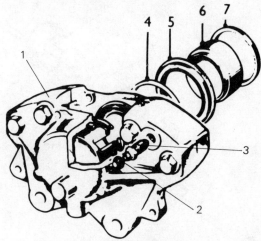

FIG 10 : 14   Caliper unit components

Key to Fig 10 : 14   1 Caliper housing   2 Dust cap
3 Bleed screw   4 Circlip   5 Dust cover   6 Piston   7 Seal

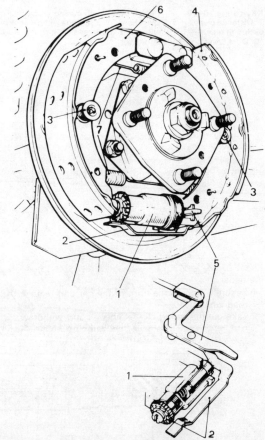

FIG 10 : 15   Rear brake self-adjusting mechanism (1500)

Key to Fig 10 : 15   1 Wheel cylinder   2 Ratchet operating lever   3 Steady pin and spring   4 Leading shoe
5 Handbrake operating lever   6 Trailing shoe   7 Shoe return springs

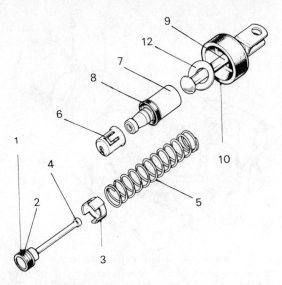

FIG 10:16   Master cylinder, components

Key to Fig 10:16   1 Valve seal   2 Spring (valve seal)
3 Distance piece   4 Valve shank   5 Plunger return spring
6 Spring retainer   7 Plunger   8 Plunger seal   9 Pushrod
10 Dust cover   12 Pushrod stop

(A) Brakes released condition:

When the brake pedal is released, hydraulic pressure created by the brake shoe pull-off spring, plus the plunger return spring 5, causes the plunger 7 to return to its rear stop 12. The last $\frac{1}{32}$ inch of movement withdraws the valve shank 4 rearwards, lifting the seal 1 from its seat on the end face of the cylinder, thus permitting recuperation of the hydraulic fluid to the reservoir via the drilled passage.

(B) Brakes applied condition:

Pressure applied to the pushrod 9 by operation of the pedal, forces the plunger 7 forward. This in turn allows the valve shank 4 to move forward under the influence of the spring 5 until the valve spacer contacts the end face of the cylinder. The spring washer 2 then forces the valve shank and seal 1 forward until the seal contacts the end face and closes the passage to the reservoir.

Continued movement of the piston displaces fluid through the hydraulic pipe lines and applies the brakes, the valve shank 4 passing further into the hollow centre of the piston as the latter moves down the cylinder bore. **During dismantling, make a note or sketch of the method of fitting seals, etc. with particular reference to contours, lips, etc.**

Removing:

The master cylinder removal operations vary slightly when a vacuum servo unit is installed. The different installations are shown in **FIGS 10:18** and **10:19**.

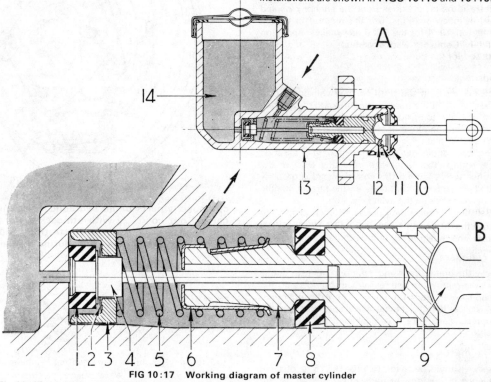

FIG 10:17   Working diagram of master cylinder

Key to Fig 10:17   1 Valve seal   2 Spring (valve seal)   3 Distance piece   4 Valve shank   5 Plunger return spring   6 Spring retainer   7 Plunger   8 Plunger seal   9 Pushrod   10 Dust cover   11 Circlip   12 Pushrod stop   13 Identification rings   14 Fluid reservoir

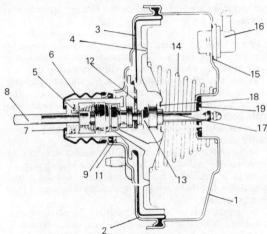

FIG 10:18   Vacuum servo unit

Key to Fig 10:18   1 Front shell   2 Rear shell
3 Diaphragm   4 Diaphragm plate   5 Filter   6 Dust cover
7 End cap   8 Valve operating rod assembly   9 Seal
10 Bearing between seal and retainer (not shown) 11 Retainer
12 Valve retaining plate   13 Reaction disc   14 Diaphragm
return spring 15 O-spring 16 Non-return valve 17 Pushrod
18 Retainer sprag washer   19 Seal and plate assembly

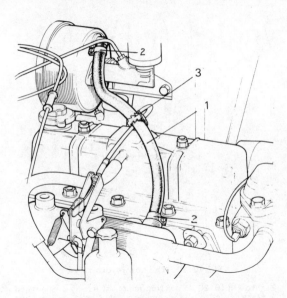

FIG 10:19   The vacuum hose

Key to Fig 10:19   1 Vacuum hose   2 Retaining clips
3 Retaining strap

1 (Non-servo). Remove the splitpin and the clevis pin
which secures the master cylinder pushrod to the
brake pedal.

2 (Both). Disconnect the brake fluid pipe at the master
cylinder. Plug the orifice to prevent fluid from
escaping and cover the pipe union to prevent dirt
entering.

3 (Non-servo). Slacken the bolt securing the master
cylinder bracket to the front spring turret and remove
the two bolts which secure the bracket and master
cylinder to the scuttle.

4 (Servo). Take out the bolt securing the earth wires
and the front end of the master cylinder bracket to the
valance. Unscrew the two mounting nuts securing the
master cylinder to the servo. Collect the shakeproof
washers.

5 (Both). Withdraw the master cylinder and drain the
reservoir.

Dismantling:

1 Remove the dust cover 10 shown in **FIG 10:16**.

2 Depress the pushrod 9 and withdraw the circlip.

3 Withdraw the pushrod together with the circlip and
the pushrod stop.

4 On a piece of wood, gently tap out the plunger and
valve assembly. Alternatively apply a tyre pump to the
fluid outlet port.

5 Lift the locating clip on the spring retainer 6 to release
the retainer, spring and valve assembly from the
plunger.

6 Detach the valve shank 4 by passing it through the
offset hole in the spring retainer 6.

7 Remove the spring 5, distance piece 3 and spring
washer 2 from the valve shank.

8 Take off the seal 1 from the valve shank 4 and then
remove the seal 8 from the plunger 7.

9 Inspect all component parts for scoring or wear and
if apparent, renew the complete unit on an exchange
basis.

10 Clean all components if unworn in clean brake fluid
and observe strict cleanliness.

11 Renew all seals and refit seals 1 and 8 to the valve
shank 4 and the plunger 7 respectively using only the
fingers for manipulation.

12 Fit the spring washer 2 exactly as shown in **FIG
10:17** together with the distance piece 3 and the
spring 5 to the valve shank 4.

13 Attach the spring retainer 6 and fit the assembly to
the plunger 7.

14 Liberally apply clean hydraulic fluid and fit this
component assembly to the master cylinder body
bore. Fit the pushrod 9 with stop plate 12 circlip 11
and the dust cover 10.

**It cannot be too strongly emphasised that the
fitting of valve seals, plunger seals and the other
component parts of all hydraulic units must be
carried out correctly with utmost regard to lips
and contours as shown in illustrations and from
observations and notes made, during dismantling.**

Refitting:

Reverse the instructions for removal, fill the master
cylinder reservoir with clean fluid and bleed the brakes
as described in **Section 10:12**.

10:10 The vacuum servo unit

A mechanically operated vacuum servo unit is fitted
between the master cylinder and the brake pedal to assist
the driver in applying increased force to the brake master
cylinder.

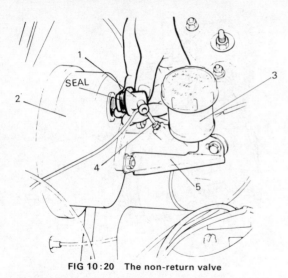

FIG 10:20   The non-return valve

Key to Fig 10:20   1 Non-return valve   2 Servo unit
3 Master cylinder   4 Hydraulic supply pipe   5 Mounting
bracket

Referring to **FIG 10:18** and when the footbrake is in
the 'off' position, the diaphragm 3 is suspended in a
partial vacuum; created by the inlet manifold evacuating
air from the chamber via a non-return valve.

When the brakes are applied, the rod 8, which is connected to the pedal, is pushed forward to close the
the vacuum port at the rear of the diaphragm and
subsequently open another port to atmosphere. Contact
also takes place between the rod 8 and the hydraulic
pushrod 17. Assistance is given in pushing the rod 17
forward, by atmospheric pressure at the back of the
diaphragm, which pushes the diaphragm and plate

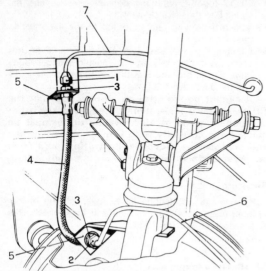

FIG 10:21   Front flexible hose

Key to Fig 10:21   1 and 2 Rigid pipe union
3 Locking nuts   4 Flexible hose   5 Support bracket
6 and 7 Caliper or wheel cylinder supply pipe

forward in an attempt to occupy the vacuum space in the
chamber.

The brakes are held on by the back pressure from the
pushrod 17 which reacts against the disc 13 causing it to
extrude at the centre. This extrusion pushes back the
valve operating rod 8 to close the port to atmosphere.

When the brake pedal is released, the atmospheric
port is closed and the vacuum port is opened. The
diaphragm return spring 14 pushes the diaphragm and
plate back to the 'off' position. Air is evacuated from the
chamber and the diaphragm is again suspended in a
partial vacuum.

In the event of a servo failure, the mechanical contact
between the rod 8, reaction disc 13 and pushrod 17
ensures a hydraulic braking operation without servo
assistance, but there will be a noticeable difference in the
effort required.

A service kit is available to maintain the servo in peak
condition. It consists of a new dust cover 6, end cap 7,
filter 5, O-ring 15 and a seal and plate assembly 19. A
tube of Rykan O-grease is also included in the kit.

Any other maintenance is not recommended, if the kit
fails to cure a suspect servo it should be replaced on an
exchange basis.

Removing, fitting vacuum hose:

1 Depress the footbrake pedal several times to destroy
  any vacuum in the system.
2 Refer to **FIG 10:19** and slacken the hose clips at the
  induction manifold and the servo non-return valve.
  Release the hose from its retaining strap.
3 Refit the hose, making sure the clips are secure and
  that there are no leaks.

Removing, fitting non-return valve:

4 Take off the vacuum hose (see operations 1 to 3).
5 Refer to **FIG 10:20** and twist the non-return valve
  from the servo body. The valve is held by a rubber
  sealing and fixing lug, it may be necessary to 'work'
  the valve inside the body to break the seal. Turn it one
  third of a turn to release the fixing lug.
6 Renew the rubber sealing and press the valve into the
  servo body, turn it clockwise one third of a turn to
  secure the lugs. Reconnect the hose.

Removing servo:

7 Disconnect the hose at the servo non-return valve.
8 Remove the master cylinder as described in **Section
  10:9** and disconnect the pushrod from the footbrake
  pedal.
9 Remove the four mounting nuts and spring washers
  securing the servo to the scuttle. Lift the servo away.

Removing filter:

10 Refer to **FIG 10:18** slide the rubber boot and end cap
   along the pushrod, away from the housing. Extract
   the old filter from the neck of the housing and scrap it.
   Make no attempt to clean it.
11 Cut the new filter obliquely from the periphery to the
   centre hole. This is to enable the filter to be pushed
   over the rod and fitted into the neck of the diaphragm
   housing.
12 Slide the end cap and rubber boot back into position.

Renewing seal and plate assembly:

13 To remove the seal and plate assembly from the front shell, grip the centre rib with a pair of pointed nose pliers.

14 Lubricate the new seal with the grease supplied in the kit and press it into the recess.

10:11 The flexible hoses

Special care should be exercised when either removing or fitting flexible brake hoses, otherwise kinking and twisting will occur and quickly spoil their reliability. In the case of the front hoses refer to **FIG 10:21** and unscrew the rigid pipe unions 1 and 2 whilst keeping the flexible hoses quite still with another spanner on their hexagon ends. Now remove the locking nuts and lockwashers 3 from the support brackets in a similar fashion and withdraw the hoses.

With the rear hoses refer to **FIG 10:22** and unscrew the rigid pipe unions 1 and then withdraw the locknuts and washers 2 using two spanners. Do not twist the hose.

10:12 Bleeding the brakes

Before bleeding the system on the 1300 model equipped with drum brakes, release the handbrake, fully slacken off the adjustment on the front wheels and fully expand the shoes, with the adjusters, to lock the rear wheels.

On the 1300 and 1500 models equipped with disc brakes and a vacuum servo, do not bleed the system with the servo in operation, that is, with the engine running.

Obtain a clean transparent jar and a length of tubing, either rubber or plastic, with an inside diameter small enough to fit over the bleed screws. Fit the tube to the bleed screw as shown in **FIG 10:23,** and trail the other end in the glass jar, which has sufficient hydraulic fluid in it to cover the open end of the hose.

1 Fill up the master cylinder reservoir as full as possible with the correct grade of fresh clean hydraulic fluid. Throughout the operation fluid will be pumped out of the system and the reservoir level will fall, so after every few strokes top up the reservoir again to prevent the level from falling so low that air is again drawn into the system. **Do not use the fluid that has been bled from the system.**

2 On the drum brake models start on the lefthand rear wheel, then to the righthand rear wheel. Follow on with the lefthand front wheel and finish on the righthand front wheel. On the disc brake models start on the front wheel furthest away from the master cylinder and follow with the other front wheel. Then, if the car is a righthand steer, bleed the cylinder on the lefthand rear wheel, if it is a lefthand steer, bleed the cylinder on the righthand rear wheel. Bleed the cylinder on the remaining wheel. In each case, open the bleed screw 90 to 180 deg.

3 Have a second operator pump the brake pedal with full fast strokes, leaving a short pause between each stroke. At first a mixture of fluid and air will be ejected from the bleed tube, but carry on pumping until the fluid comes out air free. Tighten the bleed nipple on a down stroke. Repeat the bleeding operation on the remaining nipples.

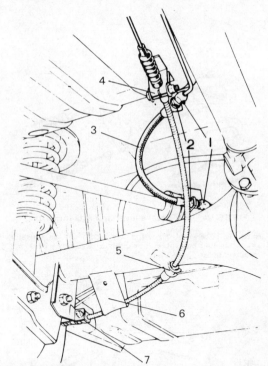

FIG 10:22 Rear flexible hose and handbrake cable attachments

Key to Fig 10:22   1 Rigid pipe unions   2 Locknuts   3 Flexible hose   4 Cable pinchbolt and bracket   5 Rubber bush and bracket retainer   6 Axle casing brackets   7 Cable supports

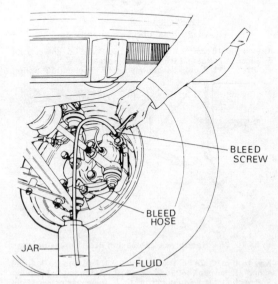

FIG 10:23   Bleeding the system

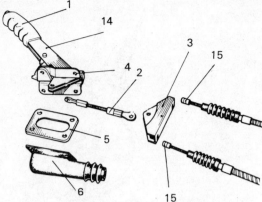

FIG 10:24 Handbrake lever and attachments

Key to Fig 10:24 1 Handgrip 2 Rod 3 Compensator 4 Lever retaining bracket 5 Lower plate 6 Gaiter 14 Lever 15 Cable nipples

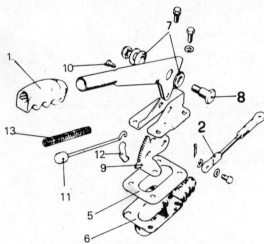

FIG 10:25 Handbrake components

Key to Fig 10:25 1 Handgrip 2 Rod 5 Lower plate 6 Gaiter 7 Nut and washers 8 Fulcrum pin 9 Ratchet 10 Pin 11 Button release rod 12 Pawl 13 Spring

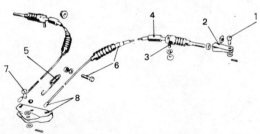

FIG 10:26 Handbrake cables and attachment points

Key to Fig 10:26 1 Clevis pin 2 Fork end 3 Cable support to suspension bracket 4 Rubber bush 5 Spring 6 Pinchbolt and fixing point 7 Compensator swivel pin 8 Cable nipple and attachment point

4 If after bleeding, the pedal still feels spongy or air is continuously ejected, then alter the technique slightly. Leave the nipple closed and have the second operator press down on the brake pedal. Open the nipple so that the fluid and air is forced out under higher pressure. When the pedal has reached the end of its stroke, close the bleed nipple and allow the pedal to return under its own action. Repeat this method until all the air has been expelled.

Keep the reservoir constantly topped up and do not return fluid that has been bled through the system directly to the reservoir.

10:13 The handbrake

Removing lever, pawl and ratchet

1 Refer to **Chapter 12** and take out both front seats and the seat runners. Roll back the carpet to clear the handbrake.
2 Refer to **FIG 10:24**, slide off the handgrip 1 and take off the gaiter. Release the handbrake.
3 Remove the splitpin and clevis pin securing the brake rod 2 to the compensator 3.
4 Unscrew and remove the four bolts and spring washers which secure the bracket 4 to the floor of the car. Lift out the handbrake lever and bracket assembly.
5 Take off the rod 2, the lower plate 5 and gaiter 6.
6 Refer to **FIG 10:25** and take off the nut and washers 7, extract the fulcrum pin 8 and withdraw the ratchet 9 and bushes from the lever.
7 Drill through or file off the riveted end of the pawl fulcrum pin 10, depress the button 11 and secure it with sticky tape, remove the pin 10 and the pawl 12.

Reassembling and refitting:

8 Assemble and fit in the reverse order of dismantling. Fit a new pawl fulcrum pin and rivet over. Make sure the pawl is in the right position and engages with the button release rod.

Adjusting the handbrake cables:

As previously mentioned, the handbrake is automatically adjusted during the process of rear brake shoe adjustment but after long service additional adjustment may become necessary due to cable stretch. The following operations should be carried out to effect the adjustment.

1 Chock the front wheels, jack up the rear of the car and support with stands. Release the handbrake.
2 Refer to **FIG 10:3** and remove the splitpin and clevis pin attaching the fork end to the handbrake lever.
3 (Manually adjusted brakes only). Operate the handbrake lever at the rear of the backplate to expand the shoes and obtain the minimum clearance between liners and drum.
4 Ensure that the compensator (see 3 in **FIG 10:24**) is centrally positioned and adjust each cable fork so that new clevis pins can be entered in the fork and lever without straining the cables.

5 (Self-adjusting brakes only). Check the free rotation of the rear wheels to ensure they are not binding or dragging.
6 Tighten the locknuts and fit new splitpins.

Removing the handbrake cables:

1 Chock the front wheels, jack up the rear of the car and support with stands.
2 Refer to **FIG 10:26,** remove the splitpins and clevis pins attaching the forks to the handbrake levers, detach the cable supports 3 from the suspension brackets and release the cable sheaths and rubber bushes 4 from the clips on the axle housing.
3 Pull the cable forks through the axle casing brackets.
4 Unscrew the pinch bolt nut at the cable sheath front brackets (see also **FIG 10:22**). Pull the cable sheath rearwards until they are clear of the front brackets and ease the cable wires downwards.
5 Release the cable nipples 8 from the compensator and withdraw the cables.

Refitting:

6 Refit the cables in the reverse order of dismantling. Do not tighten the pinch bolt 6 too tightly and before refitting the cable fork ends to the backplate levers, adjust the cables as described in the previous subsection.

10:14 Fault diagnosis

(a) Spongy pedal

1 Leak in the system
2 Worn master cylinder
3 Leaking wheel cylinder
4 Air in the system
5 Gaps between shoes and underside of linings

(b) Excessive pedal movement

1 Check 1 and 4 in (a)
2 Excessive lining wear
3 Very low fluid level in supply reservoir
4 Too much free movement of pedal

(c) Brakes grab or pull to one side

1 Brake backplate loose
2 Scored, cracked or distorted drum
3 High spots on drum
4 Unbalanced shoe adjustment
5 Wet or oily linings
6 Front suspension loose
7 Rear suspension loose
8 Worn steering connections
9 Mixed linings or pads of different grades
10 Uneven tyre pressures
11 Broken shoe return springs
12 Seized handbrake cable

NOTES

CHAPTER 11

THE ELECTRICAL EQUIPMENT

11 : 1 Description

A 12-volt negative earth system is incorporated in all Toledo models. The alternator and possibly some accessories contain polarity-sensitive components. These components may be irreparably damaged if they are subjected to the wrong polarity. Always make sure that the battery earth lead is connected to the battery negative terminal. To prevent any damage to components, do not make or break any connection in the charging circuit, this includes the battery leads, whilst the engine is running. If necessary, the engine can be run with either all the connections made or with the unit completely disconnected.

Details are given in this Section on how to dismantle and service some of the electrical components, such as, the alternator and the starter. It must be emphasized, however, that the necessary test equipment must be available to the operator. If not, the components should be taken to a service garage or a Lucas agency for testing. In any event the alternator should not be tampered with unless the operator has the knowledge and skill with which to effect his purpose.

Before stripping down a component to renew some known defect part, always consider and enquire into the possibility of obtaining a replacement unit on an exchange basis. Sometimes it is often quicker and consequently cheaper to do this than have to wait for what seems an intolerably long period for some supplementary detail.

11 : 2 The battery

This is a 12-volt, 9 plate type of 39 amp/hr rating (20 hr rate).

The original battery design incorporated the Aqualock device and a weekly check of the electrolyte level should be carried out.

The vent chamber cover should remain in position at all times, except when topping up and taking specific gravity readings (see **FIG 11 : 1**).

If the acid level in any of the cells is below the bottom of the filling tube, top up as follows:

Remove the vent chamber cover and pour distilled water into the trough until all the filling tubes are full. and the trough is just covered.

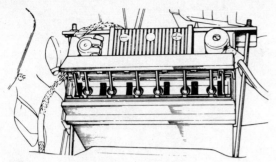

FIG 11 : 1   The Aqualock type battery with vent chamber cover raised

Immediately replace the cover to allow the water in the trough and tubes to flow into the cells. Each cell will automatically receive the right amount of water.

With a battery of conventional design, the electrolyte level should be maintained at just above the tops of the separators.

Never use a naked light to inspect the interior of a battery.

Keep the outside of the battery casing clean, the terminal connections tight and lightly covered with petroleum jelly.

If the battery is subjected to long periods of discharge without suitable opportunities for recharging, a low state of charge can be expected. A defect in the charging system can also result in a discharged battery.

Checking the specific gravity of the electrolyte is a simple method of assessing the state of charge of a battery.

Electrolyte:

Never add concentrated acid to the battery. Electrolyte of the correct specific gravity should only be added to the battery to replace any that has been lost by spillage or leakage, and distilled water only is required to replace evaporation losses. It is best to obtain ready mixed electrolyte, but if it is to be made up from concentrated sulphuric acid and distilled water take great care in handling the acid as it is extremely dangerous. Use a suitable container as a great deal of heat is given off in the mixing, and **add the acid to the water. Never add water to concentrated acid.**

The condition and specific gravity of the electrolyte will give a great deal of information on the battery. Use an hydrometer to measure the specific gravity, drawing up sufficient electrolyte to ensure that the float is suspended freely. The indications of the readings are as follows:

For climates below 32°C (90°F)	Specific gravity
Cell fully charged	1.270 to 1.290
Cell half-discharged	1.190 to 1.210
Cell discharged	1.110 to 1.130

Replace spillage with electrolyte of specific gravity 1.270.

For climates above 32°C (90°F)	Specific gravity
Cell fully charged	1.210 to 1.230
Cell half-discharged	1.130 to 1.150
Cell discharged	1.050 to 1.070

Replace spillage with electrolyte of specific gravity 1.210.

These figures are given for a standard electrolyte temperature of 16°C (60°F) and for accurate results the reading should be converted to standard by adding .002 for every 3°C (5°F) rise and subtracting for every increment fall in temperature.

All the cells should give approximately the same readings and if one is out then that cell is suspect. If the electrolyte appears dirty or full of small specks then this is another indication of a faulty cell.

11 : 3 The alternator

The alternator is a delicate piece of equipment and should not be tampered with in an attempt to rectify a suspect charging fault unless the operator concerned has sufficient knowledge and the correct test equipment to carry out the necessary checks.

Routine maintenance is confined to ensuring that the air cooling vents are clear and that the belt is maintained at the correct tension. No lubrication is required.

The alternator details are shown in **FIG 11 : 2**. Never disconnect or reconnect any part of the charging circuit when the engine is running otherwise the components may be damaged.

Before checking the alternator for defects check the following points:

1 The drive belt must be at the correct tension and not slipping on the pulleys.
2 Check the condition of the battery and the battery terminals.
3 Run the engine at 2480 rev/min (alternator running at 6000 rev/min), switch on the headlamps and check that the voltage drop between the alternator (+) blade and the battery positive terminal does not exceed .5 volt. Similarly check that the voltage drop between the alternator (—) blade and the battery negative terminal does not exceed .25 volt.

Alternator checks:

This method tests only the alternator, leaving the control unit inoperative. If the equipment is not available to carry out the check then a diode check should be carried out as described later. If the alternator is found to be defective on test this diode check should be carried out before any other checks.

1 Disconnect the multi-socket connectors and remove the moulded cover 1. Connect up a test circuit as shown in **FIG 11 : 3** taking great care to observe the correct polarity of the circuit. Leave the variable resistor 3 disconnected until just before starting the engine otherwise it will drain the battery.
2 Start the engine and gradually increase its speed. At 620 engine rev/min (1500 alternator rev/min) the light 4 should go out.
3 Hold the engine speed steady at 2480 rev/min (6000 alternator rev/min) and adjust the variable resistance 3 until the voltmeter reads 14 volts. Leave the alternator to attain its normal operating temperature and check that the voltmeter still reads 14 volts. The ammeter should then be reading 28 amps.
4 If the ammeter reading does not reach 28 amps then there is a fault in the alternator. Provided that the alternator is satisfactory, stop the engine, replace the cover 1 and carry out a control unit check.

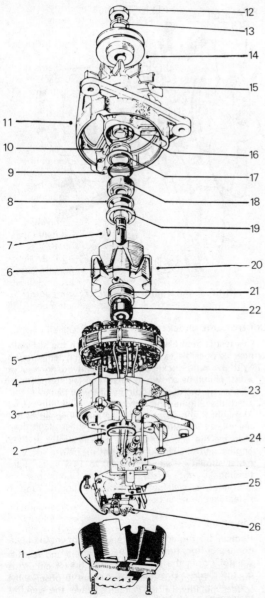

FIG 11:2   The 15ACR Lucas type alternator

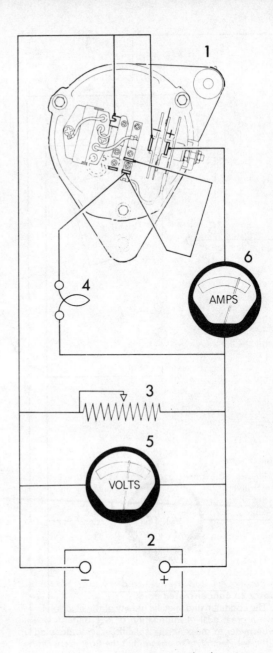

FIG 11:3   Alternator test circuit

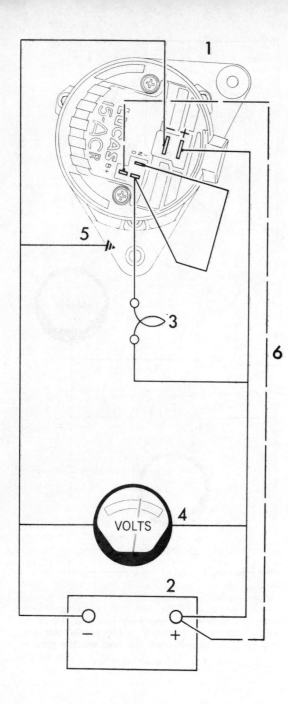

FIG 11:4 Control unit check

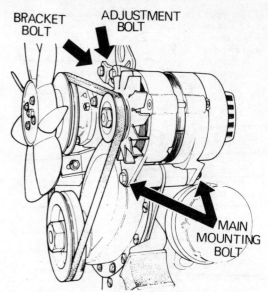

BRACKET BOLT

ADJUSTMENT BOLT

MAIN MOUNTING BOLT

FIG 11:5 Alternator removal, securing points

Control unit check:

This test should also be performed with the alternator as near as possible to its normal operating temperature.

1 With the multi-socket connector removed, connect up a test circuit as shown in **FIG 11:4** taking great care to observe the correct polarity of the circuit.

2 Start the engine and gradually increase the speed. The light 3 should go out at an engine speed of 620 rev/min (1500 alternator rev/min).

3 Increase the speed and then hold it steady at 2480 engine rev/min (6000 alternator rev/min). The voltmeter should be steady at 14.0 to 14.4 volts. If the reading is not steady within the limits but the alternator is satisfactory then the control unit is defective and must be renewed.

Diode check:

1 Remove the moulded cover and disconnect the Lucar connector from the rectifier pack 24.

2 Carefully note the position of the three stator wires on the diodes. Unsolder the wires from the diodes, carefully gripping the pin with a pair of pliers so that they act as a heat sink.

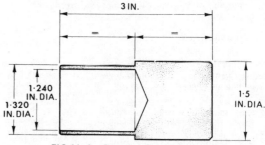

3 IN.

1·240 IN.DIA.

1·320 IN.DIA.

1·5 IN.DIA.

FIG 11:6 Details of extractor tool

Key to Fig 11:4   1 Alternator   2 Battery (12-volt)
3 Bulb (12-volt—2.2 watt)   4 Voltmeter (0-20 volt)
5 Earth connection to alternator body

3 Test each diode in turn by connecting a bulb and 12-volt battery. Test with the voltage in one direction and then reverse the polarity. The bulb should light in one direction only. If it does not light at all or lights in both directions, then the diode is faulty and the complete rectifier pack must be renewed.
4 Refit the rectifier pack and solder back the stator wires using a pair of pliers as a heat sink and carrying out the soldering as rapidly as possible.

11 : 4 Removing, dismantling alternator

Refer to **FIG 11 : 5** and disconnect the multi-socket connectors. Slacken the main mounting bolt assembly and the two adjustment bracket bolts.

Push the alternator towards the engine. If the alternator is tight on the slackened mountings, do not lever the body with a bar, use a piece of wood and use the drive end bracket as the pressure point. Take off the fan belt.

Take out the adjustment bolt nearest the alternator and also the main mounting bolt. Support the weight of the alternator to withdraw the latter.

Dismantling the alternator:

1 Remove the alternator from the car, take off the cover 1 and remove the rectifier pack as described in Diode Check. Remove the brush box and control unit assembly from the rectifier pack by unscrewing the three screws. The control unit may be removed, if required, after noting the position of the three wire eyelets, removing the three screws securing the eyelets and the screw securing the control unit.
2 Place an extractor tool, as shown in **FIG 11 : 6** so that it engages with the outer race of the bearing 21. Surplus solder may have to be filed away from the connections on the slip ring moulding 22 to allow the tool to pass over the moulding. Get an assistant to hold the slip ring end bracket 3 and carefully drive the bearing out of the bracket by tapping the end of the extractor tool. Leave the rubber O-ring 2 in place unless it is damaged. Remove the stator windings 5 from the drive end bracket 3.
3 Wrap the pulley 14 with a length of old fan belt and grip it carefully in a vice. Unscrew the nut 12, remove the washer 13 and pulley 14. Extract the key 7 from the shaft.
4 Use a press to remove the rotor 20 from the drive end bracket 11. Do not hammer on the end of the shaft otherwise the threads will become damaged. The renewal of the bearings will be dealt with separately. Reassemble the alternator in the reverse order of dismantling.

Brush gear:

Check that the brushes protrude at least .2 inch from the brush box when free. Use a modified spring balance to check that the spring pressure is 7 to 10 oz when the faces of the brushes are flush with the brush box. Renew the brush box assembly if either of these limits are not reached.

Clean the brushes with petrol-moistened cloth and check that they move freely in the brush box. If necessary polish the sides of the brush lightly, using a smooth file.

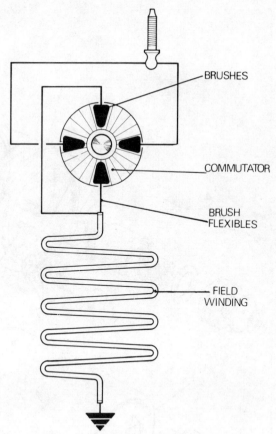

FIG 11 : 7   Starter motor field winding and brushes

Slip rings and rotor:

Check that the slip rings are smooth and clean, cleaning them with a petrol-moistened cloth. If the slip rings show any burn marks, polish these off using very fine glasspaper. Never use emerycloth, as this will leave particles imbedded in the slip ring, and do not machine the slip rings as this may affect the high speed performance of the alternator.

The resistance of the field coil winding can be measured between the slip rings and this should be 4.33+5 per cent ohm at 20°C. A 110-volt AC test lamp may be used, beteeen each slip ring and the rotor to ensure that the insulation has not broken down. Renew the rotor if it is defective.

The stator:

After removing the stator the windings may be checked. Connect a 12-volt battery and 36 watt test bulb in series with any pair of stator wires. The bulb should light. Repeat the test by disconnecting any one wire and replacing it with the third wire, and again the bulb should light. A 110-volt AC test bulb may be used to test the insulation between the wires and the stator core. Renew the stator if it is defective.

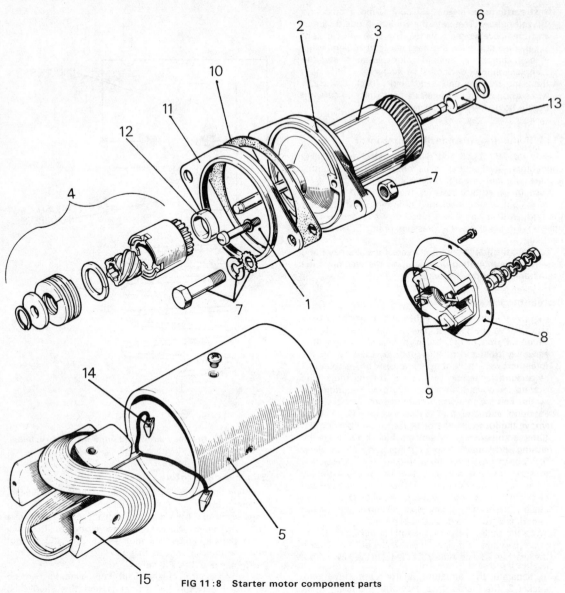

FIG 11 : 8 Starter motor component parts

Key to Fig 11 : 8 1 Slot-head bolts   2 Drive bracket   3 Armature   4 Inertia drive assembly   5 Yoke or body   6 Thrust washer
7 Supporting bolt, washers and nut   8 Commutator end bracket   9 Brushes   10 Shim   11 Packing   12 Bush   13 Bush
14 Bush   15 Field coil

The bearings:

Dismantle the alternator as far as is required.

Unsolder the two field winding connections to the slip
ring moulding 22 and remove the moulding from the
shaft. Use a suitable extractor to remove the bearing 21
from the slip ring end bracket 3. Pack the new bearing
with Shell Alvania RA grease or equivalent and use a
suitable tube to drive the inner race of the bearing into
position on the rotor shaft. Replace the slip ring moulding
22 on the shaft ensuring that the slot in the shaft engages
in the projection in the moulding. The moulding may be

fitted either way round. Resolder the connections using
Fry's HT 3 solder.

Use a large screwdriver to remove the circlip 19 and
take out the bearing retaining plate 8. Push out the
bearing 18 and its associated parts. Pack the new bearing
with Shell Alvania RA grease and reassemble it in the
reverse order of dismantling.

Refitting:

Replace the alternator in the car to the reverse order of
removal. Adjust the fan belt to the correct tension as
described in **Chapter 4, Section 4 : 2.**

11:5 The starter motor

A Lucas, series wound, four brush motor with an extended shaft carrying an inertia drive, or a type with pre-engage drive for cold climate markets, is fitted to the Toledo models. The armature shaft rotates in two porous bronze bushes, one end of the shaft is squared and protrudes from the commutator drive end to accept a spanner fitting so that it can be turned to clear any jamming. A face-type moulded commutator is a feature of this type, which means the four brushes bear on the end face of the commutator rather than the perimeter.

A plastic brushbox is riveted to the commutator end bracket which holds four wedge-shaped brushes and captive coil springs. The brushes are keyed to ensure a correct fitting.

Referring to FIG 11:7, the field winding is a continuously wound strip with no joints. One end is attached to two brush flexibles and the other end is earthed to the yoke or body.

The yoke has no inspection windows, which means the starter will have to be removed to check the brush gear. There are no through-bolts, instead, the commutator end bracket is held by four screws and the drive end bracket is attached by two slot-headed bolts. The tappings for the screws and bolts are in the yoke.

11:6 Removing the starter

1 Disconnect the battery and the single lead from the terminal post on the starter.
2 Note the position of the starter, shims if fitted and the packing in relation to the clutch housing.
3 Jack up the front of the car and support with safety stands. From above the engine remove the upper mounting bolt and nut. Working below the engine remove the lower mounting bolt and nut, support the starter and withdraw it downwards complete with packing and shims if fitted.

11:7 Dismantling, reassembling starter

1 Refer to FIG 11:8 and remove the two slot-headed bolts 1 and spring washers. Withdraw the drive end bracket 2, armature 3 and the inertia drive assembly 4 from the yoke 5. Take off the thrust washer 6.
2 Unscrew the four 4BA bolts and lift off the commutator end bracket 8, take the two field winding brushes 9 out of their holders.
3 To separate the armature 3 from the drive end bracket 2, the inertia drive assembly 4 must first be removed.

Removing inertia drive:

4 Refer to FIG 11:9 and using a suitable hand press, compress the spring 3 and ease the jump ring 1 off the shaft. For information, a special tool S4221A and adaptor S4221A-14 is used to compress the spring.
5 Withdraw the components from the shaft.

Inspecting:

The brushes:

6 Renew the brushes if they are near or less than .375 inch (9.53 mm) in length.
   Clean the brushes and the brush box with a petrol moistened cloth, check that the brushes move freely

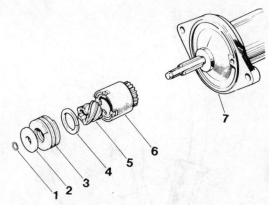

FIG 11:9   Inertia drive components

Key to Fig 11:9   1 Jump ring 2 Shaft collar 3 Main spring
4 Buffer washer   5 Screwed sleeve   6 Pinion and barrel
7 Drive end bracket

in the brush box by holding the flexibles and sliding the brushes backwards and forwards in their housings. If the brushes stick, polish their sides with a fine file. Examine the springs and test the spring pressure, this should be done with a new brush as shown in FIG 11:10. Position the brush so that the top protrudes .06 inch (1.5 mm) above the brush box, obtain a spring balance and push down on the brush and spring. The spring pressure should be 28 oz (800 grams). Repeat the test on the remaining three springs, if the pressure is low on any of the springs, renew the commutator end bracket. The springs are not supplied separately as a service item.

To change old brushes for new ones and dealing first with the two brushes attached to the terminal end post on the commutator bracket, brushes are supplied attached to a new terminal post. Remove the

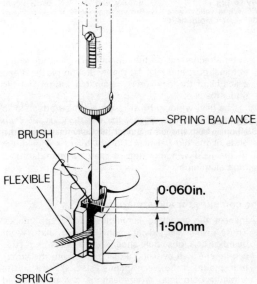

FIG 11:10   Testing the brush spring pressure

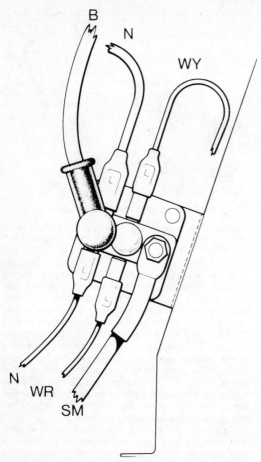

FIG 11 : 11   The solenoid switch connecting wires

Key to Fig 11 : 11   **B** Battery lead   **N** Brown wire
WY White/yellow wire   **N** Brown wire   **WR** White/red wire
SM Starter motor lead

outer attachments on the terminal post, withdraw the terminal post and take off the insulation piece. When assembling the new ones, retain the longer flexible under the clip.

The field winding brushes are supplied attached to a common flexible. Severe the old flexibles .25 inch (6 mm) from the joint. Solder the new flexibles to the ends of the old flexibles. Do not try to solder direct to the field winding strip, it may be manufactured from aluminium.

The commutator and armature:

7 Inspect the armature laminations for score marks. These marks will indicate either a bent shaft, worn bearings or a loose pole shoe. If the shaft is bent (this can be checked by using a dial gauge with the armature mounted between centre stocks) renew the armature complete. Worn bearings can be renewed by referring to operation 8. Loose pole shoe screws

must be tightened with a wheel type screwdriver, if this tool is unobtainable consult your service garage.

Clean the commutator with a petrol moistened cloth, its condition should be smooth and without pits or burnt spots. If not, skim the commutator by mounting it in a lathe, use a high speed and a sharp tool. Take only a light cut each time and do not exceed a minimum commutator thickness of .080 inch (2.03 mm). Polish the skimmed surface with fine glass-paper, not emerycloth, and do not undercut the insulators between the segments. Clean with a petrol moistened cloth.

The bronze bush bearings:

8 To renew the commutator end bracket bush, drill out the two rivets which retain a plate and felt seal around the bearing orifice. Scrap the plate and seal and obtain new ones complete with rivets. Screw a $\frac{1}{2}$ inch tap into the bush to withdraw it. A new bush should be immersed in thin oil for a period of 24 hours before it is fitted. Using a highly polished shouldered mandrel with the spigot end a clearance fit in the bush, press the new bush into the end bracket. Do not ream the bush after fitting otherwise the porosity may be impaired. Fit the new felt seal and plate and secure with the rivets.

Renew the drive end bracket bush using the same method. Instead of using a tap, the bush can be pressed out of the bracket.

Field windings:

9 Checking the field windings in the yoke requires a 110-volt AC test lamp circuit. This type of test should be a job for your service garage or a Lucas agency. If there is a fault, renewing the field windings requires a special wheel-type screwdriver to loosen and tighten the securing screws.

The inertia drive:

10 Refer to **FIG 11 : 9** and inspect the parts for wear. Renew the sleeve 5 and pinion 6 as a pair, not individually, if either one is suspect. Before assembling, lightly lubricate the bronze bush in the drive end bracket. Assemble the parts in the order shown in the illustration. Don't use oil or grease on the splines or the components, otherwise dirt and grit will stick to the rubbing surfaces and promote rapid wear.

Reassembling:

11 Reassemble the remaining components in the reverse order of dismantling, operations 1 and 2.

11 : 8   The starter solenoid

Removing and refitting:

1 Disconnect the battery connections. The heavy positive cable from the battery runs directly to the solenoid switch (see B in **FIG 11 : 11**). Note also the other wire positions on the solenoid and their colour codes. This is important to ensure the correct operation of the ballast resistor starter system, when the wires are replaced.

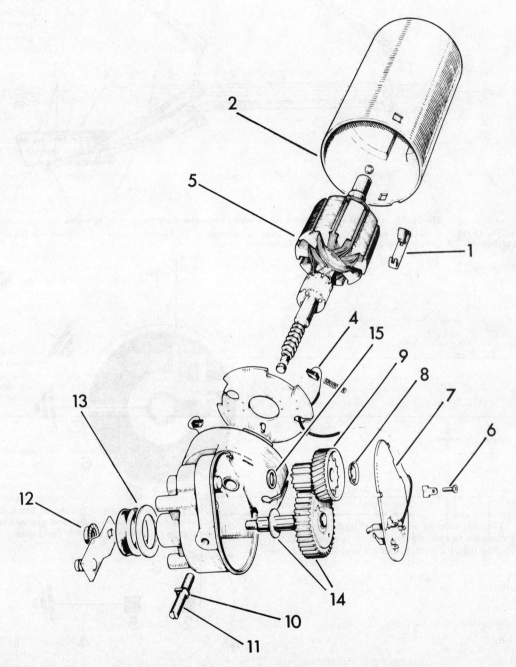

FIG 11 : 12   Windscreen wiper motor and gearbox components

Key to Fig 11 : 12   1 Clips   2 End frame   4 Brush   5 Armature   6 Screw   7 Gear cover   8 Retainer   9 Helical gear and pinion   10 Locknut   11 Thrust screw   12 Crank arm nut   13 Sealing ring and washer   14 Final gear and thrust washer 15 Thrust washer

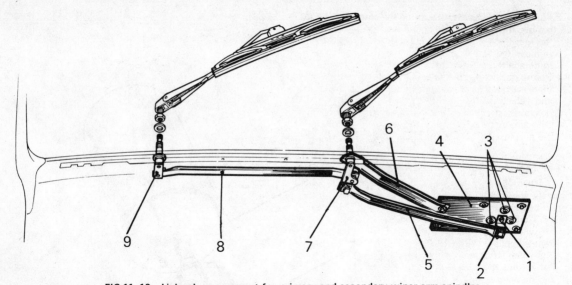

FIG 11 :13   Linkrod arrangement for primary and secondary wiper arm spindles

Key to Fig 11 :13   1 Crank arm nut   2 Crank arm   3 Motor securing nuts   4 Support bracket   5 Linkrod   6 Support rod   7 Pendulum arm   8 Linkrod to secondary wiper   9 Pendulum arm

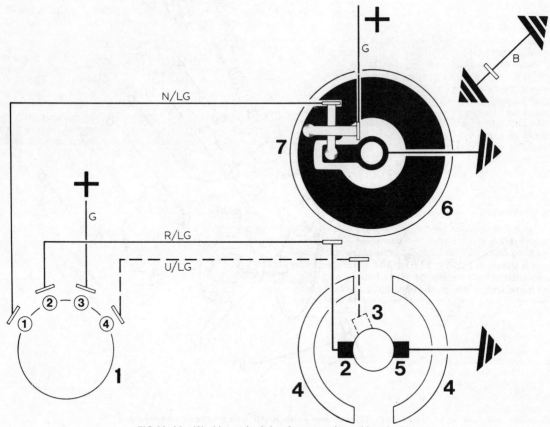

FIG 11 :14   Working principle of automatic parking device

Key to Fig 11 :14   1 Facia switch (terminal 4 not used with single-speed wiper)   2 Normal supply brush   3 High-speed brush (two-speed wiper only)   4 Permanent magnet   5 Earth brush   6 Final gear slip ring arrangement   7 Static contacts

2 Pull back the rubber protector on the battery lead and remove the two nuts and spring washers. Disconnect the four Lucas connectors and the starter motor lead.

3 Remove the two securing screws and spring washers to detach the solenoid from the vehicle.

4 Before positioning the solenoid in the car, make sure there is a good electrical contact between the solenoid and vehicle body. Replace the wires in their correct positions, check with the illustration and the wiring diagrams in the Appendix if the previously made notes are misplaced.

11:9 Starter motor—Lucas type M35J.PE

On this type of starter which is fitted to some Toledo models the motor section is similar to that already described in **Section 11:5** but the method of engagement is different in that the drive pinion is brought into mesh with the starter ring gear before the main starter current is applied.

The solenoid assembly is mounted on the top of the motor casing and operates a fork-shaped lever which slides the drive pinion forward to engage the ring gear on the flywheel. When this engagement is complete the main current is applied to the motor to turn the drive shaft and pinion.

The position of the drive engaging lever in the end bracket is preset and cannot be altered. This eliminates the necessity of setting the pinion position to obtain the correct operation of the solenoid. The lever swivels on a non-adjustable pivot pin retained in the drive end bracket by means of a special pin and retaining ring.

A roller clutch is included as a free wheel device to prevent the motor from being rotated at excessive speed after the engine has started and before the pinion has moved out of engagement.

As with other types of electric motors, the brushgear should be examined from time to time and replacement should be made when brushes are worn down to $\frac{3}{8}$ inch (9.5 mm). Brush spring tension should be 28 oz with a new brush protruding $\frac{1}{16}$ inch (1.5 mm) from the brush box.

11:10 The windscreen wiper motor

The AC Delco wiper motor consists of a permanent magnet motor and an integral gearbox unit which drives a rotating crank arm. An exploded view of the component parts is shown in **FIG 11:12**. The drive spindle assembly is mounted, at the armature end, in an internally magnetized end frame and, at the spindle end, into a gearbox casing. The worm gear on the spindle drives a helical gear, which is splined to the projecting hub of a small pinion. The pinion is in constant mesh with a final drive gear.

The geared down rotary motion is converted to reciprocating motion, by using a cranked lever affixed to the motors final drive shaft and a link rod between the cranked lever and a pendulum arm which is affixed to the primary wiper spindle. Reciprocating movement is transferred to the secondary wiper spindle by another linkrod connected between the primary and a secondary pendulum arm (see **FIG 11:13**).

On some lefthand steer models and later British market models a two-speed wiper motor is incorporated. The motor is provided with a third brush. When high

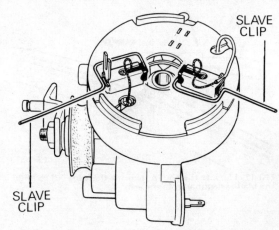

FIG 11:15 To hold the brushes in place during assembly retain them with wire or bent paper clips

speed is selected, the positive supply is transferred from the normal speed brush to the high speed brush.

A feature of the switchgear provides automatic parking of the wiper arms, irrespective of their position, when the switch is turned to the off position.

The working principle is shown in **FIG 11:14**. The facia switch 1 has four contacts but the fourth contact is used only when a two speed wiper and an electric washer pump are fitted.

The two static contacts 7 are swept by a slipring arrangement 6 on the final gear. When the switch is selected 'off' the motor will continue to run until the slipring break aligns with the inner static contacts. At this point no contact is made, but this lasts only momentarily as the inner static contact then aligns with the earthed projection; causing a regenerative braking of the armature which maintains a consistent parking of the blades.

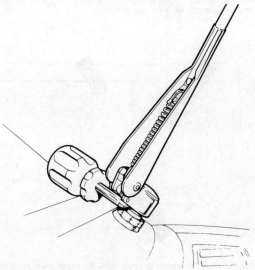

FIG 11:16 Removing wiper arm and blade

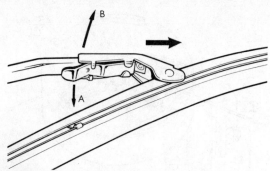

FIG 11 :17   Lift the clip 'A' and tilt the cage 'B' to slide the blade assembly from the arm

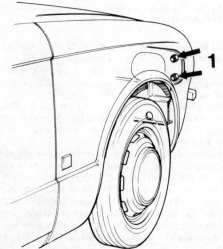

FIG 11 :18   Two of the retaining nuts and bolts which secure the headlamp assembly to the body. Four other screws which secure the grille end headlamp rim moulding must also be removed

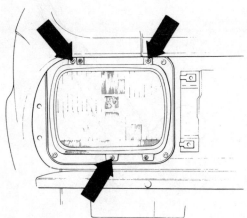

FIG 11 :19   The three screws which retain the rim and light unit

Removing the windscreen wiper motor:

1 Refer to **FIG 11 :13**. Disconnect the battery terminal.
2 Remove the motor shaft nut 1 and take off the cranked arm. Unscrew the three retaining screws to detach the motor.
3 Disconnect the four Lucar connectors and collect the six washers and three spacers.

Dismantling the motor:

4 Refer to **FIG 11 :12** and release the three clips 1 from the end frame 2. Withdraw the end frame approximately a $\frac{1}{4}$ inch (6 mm) and using two screwdrivers hold back the two brushes 4 so that they do not contact the armature drive spindle and become contaminated with grease. Withdraw the frame and armature.
5 Remove the two brushes and springs and pull the armature from the end frame, take care not to lose the thrust ball.
6 Remove the single screw 6 and the Lucar blade, take off the gear cover 7 and the brush plate which are joined together by a single wire.
7 Carefully lever the retainer 8 off the shaft and withdraw the helical gear and pinion assembly.
8 Using a pair of pliers unscrew the locknut 10 and unscrew the thrust screw 11 from the gearbox. Take off the rubber sealing ring and washer 13.
9 Withdraw the final gear and thrust washers 14 and 15.

Inspecting:

10 If the components are badly worn or the field coil requires renewal, serious consideration should be given to renewing the whole unit on an exchange basis. In most cases the unit is more readily obtained from suppliers than the component parts. To renew the brushes, unsolder the connections and resolder the new brush connections. Examine the commutator surface and clean with a petrol moistened cloth. Clean off any burning or pitting with very fine glass-paper and remove the dust with a cloth soaked in petrol.

Reassembling:

11 Lubricate the gear generously with a high temperature water resistant grease.
12 Reassemble in the reverse order of dismantling and note the following points.
13 Make sure the earth brush is not accidentally trapped under the brush plate and avoid contaminating the brushes or the commutator with grease. To hold the brushes in place whilst the armature is being assembled, refer to **FIG 11 :15** set them deep in their boxes, retaining them with wire or bent paper clips as shown. Don't forget to fit the thrust ball at the end of the armature shaft.
14 Insert the armature and end frame until it is approximately a $\frac{1}{4}$ inch (6 mm) from its seating then take off the retaining wires around the brushes. Push the assembly fully home and fit the retaining clips.
15 After replacing the gears and the gear cover, adjust the armature end float. Screw the thrust screw into the casing without loading it. Connect the motor in series

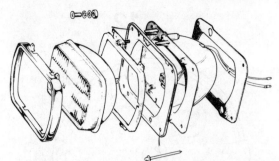

FIG 11:20 Component parts of the sealed beam unit

with a 12-volt battery and an ammeter. Run the motor and note the ammeter reading. Tighten the thrust screw slowly until the ammeter reading increases by .10 amp, hold this position and tighten the locknut.

Windscreen wiper arms and blades:

To remove the windscreen wiper arm and blade, hinge the assembly forwards and off the screen. Refer to **FIG 11:16** and with a small screwdriver lift the retaining clip from the spindle groove. Pull the arm and blade off the spindle.

To remove the blade from the arm, lift the arm and blade from the screen, refer to **FIG 11:17** and lift the clip 'A', tilt the cage 'B' and slide the blade off the arm.

11:11 The fuses

The fuses are situated in the engine compartment and and held in a junction box affixed to the bulkhead. Two 35 amp fuses control the multi-circuits as follows:

Battery control:

Horn; Headlamp flash; Luggage boot lamp; Roof lamp.

Ignition control:

Temperature control; Fuel indicator; Heater fan; Reverse lamp (if fitted); Windscreen wiper; Stop lights; Direction indicator lights.

To gain access to the fuses, pull off the plastic cover. To remove a defective fuse, lever it away from its spring contacts.

11:12 The lamps
Headlamps:

Two rectangular pre-focus type headlamps or two sealed beam headlamp units are fitted, which have a 75:60 watt rating. With sealed beam units, bulb failures are very rare but when they do fail the whole sealed beam unit must be renewed. To remove the headlamps, refer to **FIG 11:18** and remove the two nuts and washers 1 and the four screws and washers which secure the grille and headlamp rim moulding to the body. Refer to **FIG 11:19** and take out the three screws to release the retaining rim and light unit.

To detach the wires on the pre-focus type, pull the connector block from the bulb. Withdraw the bulb by disengaging the clip.

On the sealed beam unit type, pull the connector block from the light unit. The components of the sealed beam unit are shown in **FIG 11:20**.

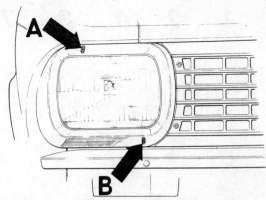

FIG 11:21 Headlight beam alignment screws

Key to Fig 11:21   A=Horizontal plane   B=Beam height

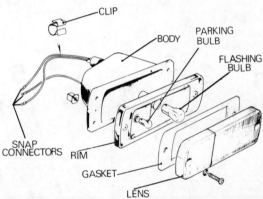

FIG 11:22 Components of front parking and flasher unit

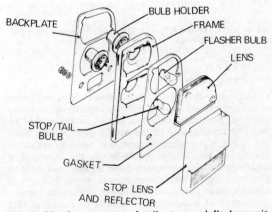

FIG 11:23 Components of tail, stop and flasher unit

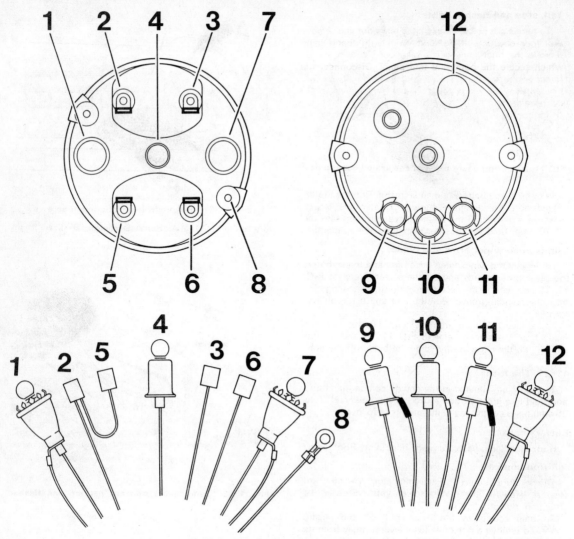

FIG 11 : 24   Gauges and warning light connections and bulb holders

Key to Fig 11 : 24 (Refer to the wiring diagrams in the Appendix for wiring colour codes in brackets)   **1** Righthand turn signal warning light (GW and B)   **2** Temperature indicator (LG)   **3** Temperature indicator (GU)   **4** Instrument illumination (R)   **5** Fuel indicator (LG)   **6** Fuel indicator (GB)   **7** Lefthand turn signal warning light (GR and B)   **8** Earth (B)   **9** Ignition warning light (W and NY)   **10** Oil pressure warning light (W and WN)   **11** Main beam warning light (UW and B)   **12** Instrument illumination (R and B)

Headlamp beam setting:

The owner-operator is not advised to reset the beam alignment himself, as the lighting regulations in many countries are strictly enforced, The alignment should be checked and adjusted by the service garages who have the necessary equipment and are familiar with the appropriate regulations. However, in the event of a headlamp misalignment presenting a hazardous light to oncoming traffic and, circumstances are such that the beams cannot immediately be reset by the service garage, an adjustment is provided on the rims as shown in **FIG 11 : 21**.

Two holes in the rim allow access to the alignment screws A and B. Screw A controls the horizontal plane and screw B controls the beam height.

Front parking and flasher lights:

To renew the bulbs refer to **FIG 11 : 22** and remove the two securing screws in the lenses. To take out the unit completely, lift the bonnet and from inside the engine compartment disconnect the snap connectors at the wiring harness break-out. Withdraw the lamp assembly from the panel.

Tail, stop and flasher lights:

To renew the bulbs, open up the rear boot and remove the floor covering. If working on the righthand lamp remove the floor panel also. Take out the two screws which secure the boot side trim panel. Disconnect the Lucar connector to the defective bulb and pull the bulb holder from the lamp base. Extract the bulb from the bayonet fitting.

To continue, and remove the lamp unit completely, refer to **FIG 11:23** and remove the four nuts, spring washers and washers. Withdraw the lamp assembly from the car.

Rear number plate lights:

To renew the bulbs, open up the boot lid and remove the cowled rim securing screws. Turn back the rubber lip and remove the lens. Extract the bulb. To remove the lamp, disconnect the wires from the snap connectors and manoeuvre the rubber body outwards from the panel.

When replacing, ensure that the cowled rim is fitted so that the light will be directed towards the number plate.

Interior roof light:

To renew the bulb on early vehicles rotate the lens until the two securing screws are visible. Take out the screws and lower the lamp. On later vehicles, squeeze the lens at the clip projections and remove. Remove the festoon bulb.

To remove the lamp, first disconnect the battery, note the wire colour codes and their positions, then on early vehicles disconnect the three Lucar connections. On later vehicles, disconnect the two terminal ends, remove the two screws to release the base.

When refitting the later type, position the earth tag under the appropriate screw head.

Instrument panel lights:

The bulbs illuminating the two informative gauges and warning lights are shown in **FIG 11:24** with corresponding numbers to their respective positions in the back of the instruments. The illustrations also shows the Lucar connections. The wiring colour codes are shown in the key and these can be deciphered from the wiring diagrams in the Appendix.

The bulb holders are pressed into position and held either by spring tags on the instruments (see 9, 10 and 11) or by spring serrated collars (see 1, 7 and 12) in the bulb holders. Probing behind the instruments to release a bulb holder may prove to be somewhat restricting due to the limited space and wiring. Refitting it in position can be even more difficult particularly if the sprung tags or serrations become distorted. If any difficulty is experienced, refer to **Section 11:13** to remove the instruments from the facia panel.

11:13 Removing temperature fuel gauge:

1 Disconnect the battery. Remove the trim board from under the facia panel, held by four spring clips.
2 The instrument is held to the facia panel by two circular knurled nuts. The inboard nut must be unscrewed and taken off the mounting screw with a

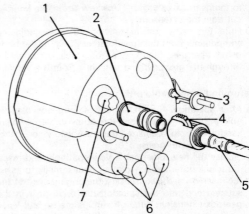

FIG 11:25   Rear view of speedometer

Key to Fig 11:25   1 Speedometer gauge   2 Boss
3 Knurled nut   4 Locking lever   5 Cable   6 Bulb holders (warning lights)   7 Trip reset nut

spring washer and a short clamp bracket. The outboard nut need only be slackened. Withdraw the instrument.
3 To remove the temperature and fuel gauges take out the two supporting screws.
4 When replacing the instrument, don't forget to replace the earth wire on the inboard screw. Check that all lights perform satisfactorily.

11:14 Removing speedometer and cable

1 Disconnect the battery.
2 Refer to **FIG 11:25** and unscrew the two circular knurled nuts, collect the spring washers and release the clamp brackets. Pull the instruments forward until it is possible to obtain access at the rear.
3 Pull out the panel light bulb holders (see **FIG 11:24**) and unscrew the trip reset knurled nut at the attachment to the facia support rail.
4 Depress the lever to release the catch from the annular groove in the boss. Pull the cable away from the instrument.
5 To remove the cable completely, jack up the car sufficiently high enough to allow a working access

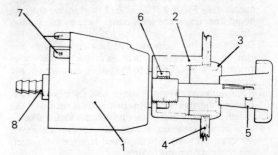

FIG 11:26   Windscreen wiper switch

Key to Fig 11:26   1 Switch   2 Spacer   3 Bezel
4 Facia panel   5 Knob lock plunger   6 Slotted ring
7 Lucas connections   8 Water pipe

to the gearbox extension. Unscrew the cable knurled nut from the extension.

6 Note the cable run in relation to other adjacent components from the speedometer down to the body panel aperture. Manoeuvre the cable downwards through the grommet and detach it from the vehicle.

Removing inner cable only:

5a After operation 4, with the aid of long-nosed pliers pull the inner cable from the outer cable. Be very careful not to damage the upholstery or other furnishings with grease.

6a Grease the new inner cable very sparingly and insert it into the outer cable. Rotate it occasionally to assist the insertion and also to assist the engagement of the squared end into the speedometer drive gear in the gearbox extension. Wipe off surplus grease and leave approximately one inch of the inner cable protruding so that the squared end can be engaged in the speedometer gauge.

Refitting speedometer:

7 Engage the inner cable to the speedometer and push the outer cable over the boss, ensure that the catch engages in the annular groove.

8 Refer to **FIG 11 : 24** to position the bulb holders. Reconnect the trip indicator and reverse operations 1 and 2.

11 : 15 The flasher unit

The flasher unit is mounted in a clip on the forward face of the facia panel, next to the washer-wiper switch. To remove it is to merely pull it from the clip and disconnect the Lucar connectors.

When refitting ensure that the green wire is connected to terminal 'B' and the light green and brown wire is connected to terminal 'L'.

11 : 16 Switches

Removing ignition:

Starter switch:

1 Disconnect the battery. Take out the two screws which secure the upper nacelle around the steering column and the single screw securing the lower nacelle (see **FIGS 9 : 10** and **9 : 11**). Remove the trim board from under the facia panel, held by four spring clips.

2 Disconnect the harness plug associated with the ignition-starter switch, check with the colour codes if necessary, by referring to the wiring diagrams in the Appendix.

3 Remove the parcel tray finisher, held by three screws. Unwind the two small Posidriv screws securing the switch assembly to the steering column lock.

4 Unwind any tape securing the harness to the column, withdraw the switch harness and remove the switch and harness from the column.

5 When refitting the switch to the steering column lock, take note of the position of the keyway and ensure the lock shaft and switch are aligned for correct engagement.

Removing head sidelamp switch:

1 Disconnect the battery.

2 In the underside of the knob there is a small hole in which is housed a spring clip. Insert a probe into the hole, depress the clip and pull off the knob.

3 Unscrew the bezel with a suitably sized tool.

4 Remove the switch from the facia and manoeuvre it into an accessible position. Note the colour codes of the wiring and their positions. Disconnect the Lucar connectors.

Removing windscreen wiper and washer switch:

1 Refer to **FIG 11 : 26** and follow the instructions given for the removal of the head and sidelamp switch. Note the water pipe positions by marking one of them with tape. There will be a slight drainage of water when the pipes are removed.

2 When replacing make sure the switch is fitted tightly to the spacer. If not tighten the slotted ring.

Removing stop lamp switch:

1 Disconnect the battery. The switch is adjacent to the brake pedal arm, above the steering column. Disconnect the two Lucar connectors and slacken the large hexagon nut.

2 Unscrew the switch from the nut. The nuts and washer can remain in position; retained by the spring-loaded pedal arm.

3 When replacing, do not overtighten the nut on the plastic threads.

4 With the brake pedal released adjust the clearance between the brake pedal and the face of the switch bracket to .060 inch (15.24 mm).

5 After completing, check the stop lamp lighting.

11 : 17 Fault diagnosis

(a) Battery discharged

1 Terminal connections loose or dirty
2 Shorts in lighting circuits
3 Generator or alternator not charging
4 Control box faulty
5 Battery internally defective

(b) Insufficient charging rate

1 Check 1 and 4 in (a)
2 Drive belt slipping

(c) Battery will not hold charge

1 Low electrolyte level
2 Battery plates sulphated
3 Electrolyte leakage from cracked case
4 Battery plate separators defective

(d) Battery overcharged

1 Control box needs adjusting

(e) Generator or alternator output low or nil

1 Belt broken or slipping
2 Control box out of adjustment
3 Worn bearings, loose polepieces

4 Commutator worn, burned or shorted
5 Armature shaft bent or worn
6 Insulation proud between commutator segments
7 Brushes sticking, springs weak or broken
8 Field coil windings broken, shorted or burned
9 Alternator diode(s) defective

(f) Starter motor lacks power or will not turn

1 Battery discharged, loose cable connections
2 Starter pinion jammed in flywheel ring gear
3 Starter switch or solenoid faulty
4 Brushes worn or sticking, leads detached or shorting
5 Commutator dirty or worn
6 Starter shaft bent
7 Engine abnormally stiff, perhaps due to rebore

(g) Starter runs but does not turn engine

1 Pinion engagement mechanism faulty
2 Broken teeth on pinion or flywheel gears

(h) Noisy starter pinion when engine is running

1 Pinion return mechanism faulty

(j) Starter motor inoperative

1 Check 1 and 4 in (f)
2 Armature or field coils faulty

(k) Starter motor rough or noisy

1 Mounting bolts loose
2 Damaged pinion or flywheel teeth
3 Pinion engagement mechanism faulty

(l) Lamps inoperative or erratic

1 Battery low, bulbs burned out
2 Faulty earthing of lamps or battery
3 Lighting switch faulty, loose or broken connections

(m) Wiper motor sluggish, taking high current

1 Faulty armature
2 Commutator dirty or shorting
3 Brushes worn or sticking, springs weak or broken
4 Lack of lubrication
5 Linkage worn or binding
6 Wiper motor fixing bolts loose
7 Motor transmission binding, no armature shaft end float

(n) Wiper motor runs but does not drive arms

1 Wiper linkage faulty
2 Transmission components worn

(o) Fuel, temperature or pressure gauges do not work

1 Check wiring for continuity
2 Check instruments and transmitters for continuity

NOTES

CHAPTER 12

THE BODYWORK

12:1 Description

The Toledo body is designed as a two or four-door, four seater saloon. It has a rust proofed steel panelled body of unitary construction with a separate front sub-frame. All the doors are forward hinged and they are fitted with high anti-burst load door locks. The handles are the push-button type and the winding side windows are of toughened safety glass. The front doors have pivoting anti-draught side vents. The curved windscreen is also of toughened glass with a zebra zone in front of the driver, which, if shattering does occur whilst driving, it does not immediately restrict the drivers vision.

The upholstery is made from expanded PVC leather cloth which can be cleaned with luke warm, non-caustic soapy water; do not use detergents or household cleaners. The separate front seats are adjustable fore and aft, on the two-door models the front seats are prevented from pitching forward by self-locking catches, which are released by a lever in the side of the seat squab. The rear seat is the divan type and the seat cushion is removable. There are seat anchor points for both front and rear seat passengers. To comply with the law the front seat harnesses should already be fitted, but if it is

desired to fit rear harnesses, the anchorage points are accessible when the rear seat cushion and squab are removed (see **Section 12:10**).

A heater and demister unit provides fresh air of a selected temperature to the interior of the car. Air flow can be increased by the use of a two-speed booster fan. Through-flow ventilation is provided by the use of interior ducts at the base of the back light. Two face-level air ducts are located each side of the facia panel and the ducts can be adjusted to suit the passengers requirements. Exterior non-return ducts at the top of the backlight assist rear window demisting.

One of the most infuriating things that can happen to any owner is the appearance of small dents and scratches which mysteriously occur on the bodywork of a well kept car. Although the damage is of a minor nature the apparently unrelating cost, when the bodywork is restored by experts, can be prohibiting. The following hints may be helpful to those people who would like to tackle the problem themselves.

Minor dents can still pose a problem. It is not advisable for the average owner to attempt to beat out the dents, as incautious or excessive hammering will stretch the metal

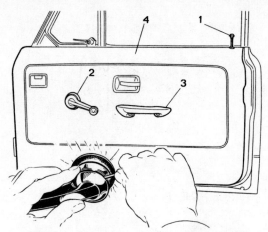

FIG 12:1   Removing window regulator handle

Key to Fig 12:1   1 Interior lock plunger   2 Regulator handle
3 Arm rest   4 Trim pad

and make things worse instead of better. Filling minor
dents and scratches is probably the best method of
restoring the surface. The touching-up of paintwork is
well within the powers of most owners, particularly as
self-spraying cans of paint are now readily available in the
correct matching colours for most models. Paint fades
and changes colour with age so although touching-up
paint is an exact match for brand new paint, it will not be
an exact match after the car has been in use for some time.
For this reason it may be better to spray a whole wing or
panel rather than to try to touch-up a small area.

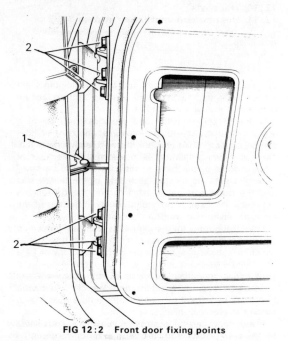

FIG 12:2   Front door fixing points

Key to Fig 12:2   1 Check strap rivet   2 Hinge support bolts

Before spraying it is essential to remove all traces of
wax polish with white spirits. Even more drastic treatment
will be required if silicone-based polishes have been used.
Mask off surrounding areas with newspaper and masking
tape to prevent spray dust from settling on them, and
spray in the cleanest and most dust free conditions
available. Lightly scuff the area to be sprayed. Use a primer
surfacer or paste stopper according to the amount of
filling required and, when it is dry, rub it down with 400
grade 'Wet or Dry' paper, using plenty of water as a
lubricant and cleaner. Spend plenty of time and patience
in obtaining the best surface possible, using more coats
of filler if required. Small blemishes which are hardly
noticeable on the matt surface will stand out glaringly
in the final polished surface.

Apply the final coat evenly to a complete panel, but
more lightly around the edges if only part of a panel is
being sprayed. Use two thin coats, rubbing down
between each coat, rather than apply one thick coat
which may run.

When the paint is hard and dry, use a cutting compound
to remove spray dust, and lightly polish the surface.
Leave the car for at least a week before applying wax
polish.

12:2 Working on the doors

Maintenance:

The only maintenance required is to periodically oil
the hinges, locks and door striker plates so that they all
work freely and prevent unnecessary wear. Make sure
that surplus oil is wiped away to avoid staining or
permanently damaging passengers' clothing.

Removing the door trim panel:

1 Refer to **FIG 12:1** and unscrew the interior lock
plunger knob 1.
2 Depress the bezel 2 on the window winding handle.
Press out the exposed pin and take off the handle and
bezel.
3 To remove the arm rest, unwind the two screws and
pick up the spring and plain washers.
4 Around the perimeter of the trim pad are sixteen
spring clips which locate in small holes in the door
panel. With a blunt screwdriver carefully placed under
the trim, prise loose each clip until the trim panel is
free.

Refitting:

5 To refit the panel reverse the instructions 1 to 4.

Removing a front door:

1 Disconnect the battery and remove the trim pad. Take
out the water curtain.
2 Refer to **FIG 12:2** and drill out the door check strap
rivet 1.
3 Support the door with blocks, mark the position of the
hinges, and unscrew the six hinge bolts 2. Take care
the door does not overbalance and fall as the last bolt
is removed.

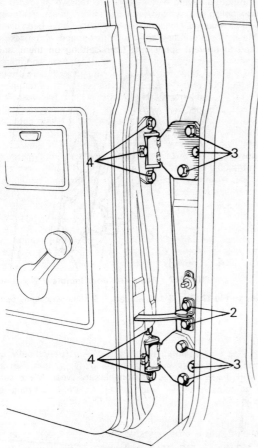

FIG 12 : 3   Rear door fixing points

Key to Fig 12 : 3   2 Check strap retaining bolts   **3** Pillar hinge bolts   **4** Door hinge bolts

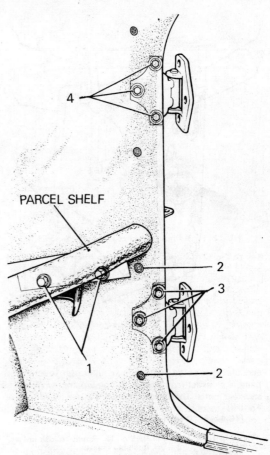

FIG 12 : 4   Front door hinge fixing points

Key to Fig 12 : 4   1 Parcel shelf retaining bolts   **2** Trim pad screws   **3** Lower hinge securing bolts   **4** Upper hinge securing bolts

Refitting :

4 Obtain a new rivet for the door check strap and reverse operations 1 to 3. Align the hinges to the previously made marks. Check the door closing action and adjust the striker plate if necessary.

Removing a rear door :

1 Disconnect the battery. Refer to **FIG 12 : 3** and remove the two bolts and spring washers retaining the check strap 2.
2 Support the door with blocks, mark the position of the hinges and unscrew the six hinge bolts 3 and spring washers. Take care the door does not overbalance and fall as the last bolt is being removed.

Refitting :

3 Reverse operations 1 to 3. Align the hinges to the previously made marks. Check the door closing action and adjust the striker plate if necessary.

Renewing hinges

Front door :

1 Remove the door as previously described.
2 Refer to **FIG 12 : 4** and unscrew the two bolts 1 and collect the spring and plain washers. Remove the two screws 2 and washers to allow the trim pad to be moved, so that access can be made to the lower fixings.
3 Ease the parcel shelf upwards slightly and unscrew the lower hinge bolts 3. Withdraw the hinge.
4 Unscrew the three bolts 4 to withdraw the upper hinge.

Refitting :

5 Reverse the operations 1 to 4 and check the closing action of the door. Adjust the striker plate if necessary.

Rear doors :

1 Remove the door as previously described and unscrew the six bolts 4. Mark the position of the hinges on the door before finally removing

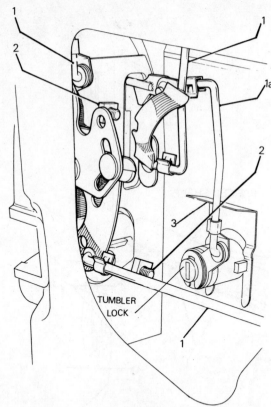

FIG 12:5   Door lock linkages and mechanism

Key to Fig 12:5   1 Linkages   1a Handle to lock linkage
2 Securing bolts   3 Lock retaining bracket

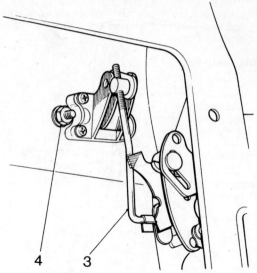

FIG 12:7   Removing door handle

Key to Fig 12:7   3 Linkage rod   4 Handle retaining bolt

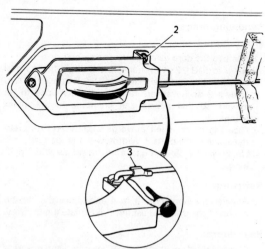

FIG 12:6   Front door lock remote control

Key to Fig 12:6   2 Retaining screws   3 Securing clip

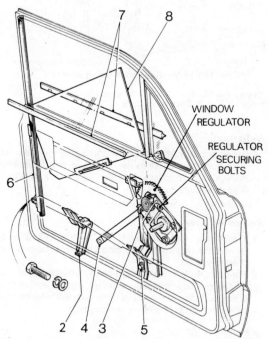

FIG 12:8   Removing front door glass and window
regulator mechanism

Key to Fig 12:8   2 Glass stop   3 Stiffener   4 Regulator arm
5 Bolt   6 Channel   7 Waist seals   8 Glass

Refitting:

2 Locate the new hinges to the previously made marks and secure them with the six bolts. Refit the door as described earlier.

The door locks:

Removing, front or rear:

1 Remove the trim pad as described earlier in the Section. Take out the water curtain.
2 Refer to **FIG 12:5** and release the linkages 1 and 1a.
3 Remove the four screws 2 and pull the lock clear.

Tumbler lock:

4 To remove the tumbler lock, complete operation 1 and release the linkage 1a. Withdraw the clip 3 and push the lock out of the door.

Refitting:

Reverse the operations 1 to 4. Check the door closing and locking action.

Remote control, front door lock:

1 Remove the trim pad as described earlier in the Section.
2 Refer to **FIG 12:6** and unwind the three screws 2. Collect the spring and flat washers and detach the handle.
3 Spring the clip 3 off the control rod.

Refitting:

4 Reverse the instructions 1 to 3. Check the closing and locking action of the door.

The door handles:

Removing, front or rear:

1 Remove the door trim pad as described earlier in the Section. Take out the water curtain.
2 Refer to **FIG 12:7** and release the linkage 3, unscrew the two nuts 4, collect the spring and plain washers and pull the handle out of the door.
3 To detach the push button, unscrew the two nuts.

Refitting:

4 Reverse the instructions 1 to 3. Check the closing and locking action of the door.

12:3 Door windows and regulators

Removing front door glass:

1 Remove the door trim pad as described in **Section 12:2**. Take out the water curtain.
2 Refer to **FIG 12:8** and unscrew the three screws which secure the glass stop 2. Unscrew the three screws which secure the stiffener 3 (early models only).
3 Wind the glass down fully and detach the regulator arm 4 from the channel.
4 Remove the bolt and plain washer 5.
5 To detach the channel 6 take out the single bolt and its spring and plain washer.
6 Take off the inner and outer door waist seals 7 by detaching them from their securing clips.

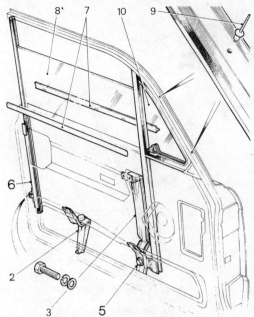

FIG 12:9   Removing front door quarter vent

Key to Fig 12:9   2 Glass stop   3 Stiffener   5 Bolt
6 Channel   7 Waist seals   8 Glass   9 Pop-rivet
10 Quarter vent

7 Turn the glass 8 sideways and lift it upwards and out of the window frame.
8 If the glass is being taken out for some other reasons apart from renewal, take care not to scratch it on the seal clips when it is withdrawn.

Refitting:

9 To fit a new glass follow the instructions 1 to 8 in the reverse order. Extra care should be taken when fitting the new glass to avoid scratching the surface or placing an undue strain on it which might cause it to shatter.
10 Lightly grease the moving parts of the regulator mechanism.

Removing front door quarter vent:

1 Complete operations 1 to 6 for removing the door glass, but it is not necessary to remove the regulator arm 4.
2 Refer to **FIG 12:9** and at the front of the quarter vent frame, pull away the weatherstrips to expose two pop rivets 9. Drill out the rivets.
3 Lift out the vent assembly from the door frame.

Refitting:

4 Reverse the operations 1 to 3 using new pop rivets.

Removing rear door glass:

1 Remove the door trim pad as described in **Section 12:2**.
2 Refer to **FIG 12:10** and unscrew the three screws 2 which secure the glass stop (early models only).

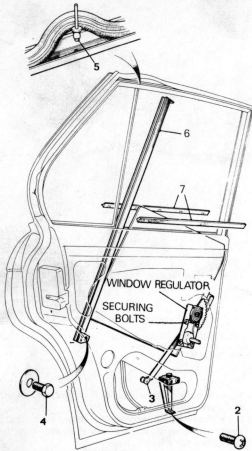

FIG 12:10 Removing rear door glass and window regulator

Key to Fig 12:10   2 Glass stop screws   3 Regulator arm   4 Bolt   5 Pop-rivet   6 Channel   7 Waist seals

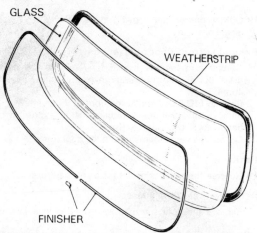

FIG 12:11 Windscreen glass, weather strip and finisher trim

3 Wind the glass fully down and detach the regulator arm 3 from the channel.

4 Remove the bolt and plain washer 4. Pull away the weatherstrip at the top of the door as shown to expose the single pop rivet 5. Drill out the rivet and detach the channel 6.

5 Pull the inner and outer door waist seals 7 out of their securing clips.

6 Turn the glass sideways and lift it upwards and out of the window frame. Take care not to scratch the glass on the seal support clips.

Refitting:

7 Reverse the instructions 1 to 6 using a new pop rivet.

Removing rear door quarter light:

1 Follow the instructions 1 to 5 for removing the rear door glass.

2 Break the weatherstrip seal around the quarter light using a suitably blunt tool.

3 Pull the glass out of its frame.

Refitting:

4 If necessary, renew the weatherstrip and apply Seelastik to the mating surfaces before fitting. Make sure all the old traces of weatherstrip are removed, using a scraper and spirit cleaner.

5 Reverse the operations 1 to 3.

Removing window regulator:

1 Refer to FIGS 12:8 and 12:10. Complete operations 1 to 3 for removing front and rear door windows.

2 Remove the four bolts which secure the regulator mechanism support bracket to the door and withdraw the mechanism.

Refitting:

3 Lightly grease the mechanism before replacing in the reverse order of removal.

12:4 The windscreen

Before removing or replacing the windscreen remove the windscreen wiper arms. The instructions for removing and refitting the windscreen apply equally to the back light except that the backlight has no finisher strip (see FIG 12:11) and it may incorporate a heating system.

To remove the glass, use a blunt screwdriver or wedge of wood to break the seal between the rubber weatherstrip and the flange on the body. Keep the tool firmly pressed under the lip of the weatherstrip to avoid damaging the paint as the tool is worked around the weatherstrip. Apply firm hand pressure at the lower corners of the glass from the inside of the car to push the glass out, and have an assistant outside the car to take the glass as it comes free. Remove the cover, finisher and weatherstrip noting the positions for refitting.

If the glass has been broken it is essential to remove all the particles of glass. For the windscreen the demister duct should be removed and cleaned out, otherwise particles of glass may be blown out when the heater is operated. If glass has broken it is most advisable to obtain a new weatherstrip with the replacement glass, as the old weatherstrip is sealed to both the glass and aperture and it will most likely be damaged on removal.

1 Refit the weatherstrip around the glass and inject sealant between the weatherstrip and the glass. Remove surplus sealant using a piece of cloth dampened in petrol or white spirits, but do not use much solvent that it seeps into the join.

2 Remove old sealant from around the glass aperture, again using petrol or white spirits. Check that the flange is true. Dress out any dents using a hammer and block. Any protrusion should be filed smooth with the rest of the flange, otherwise they may cause the new glass to fracture after fitting.

3 Insert a long length of thick cord all the way around the channel in the weatherstrip, leaving the ends protruding freely from the lower centre of the weatherstrip. Lubricate the aperture flange with soap solution and lay the glass and weatherstrip assembly into position on the outside of the car with the ends of the cord passed in through the aperture. While an assistant firmly presses the glass into place, pull out the cord as shown in **FIG 12:12** so that the lip of the

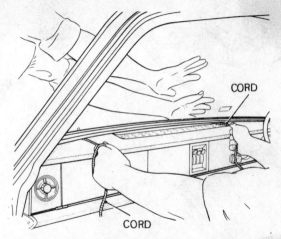

FIG 12:12 Whilst an assistant presses the glass into position, pull out the cord so that the lip of the weather strip is drawn over the body flange

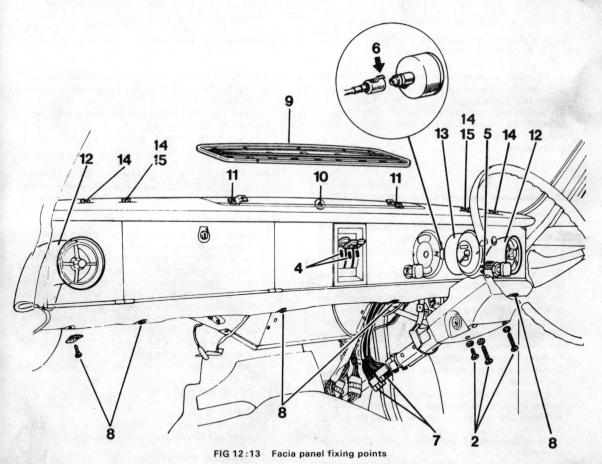

FIG 12:13 Facia panel fixing points

Key to Fig 12:13   2 Nacelle screws   4 Grub screws   5 Screen washer control   6 Speedometer cable connectionn   7 Wiring harness plugs   8 Lower fixing screws   9 Demister grille   10 Upper fixing screws   11 Brackets   12 Ducting hoses   13 Speedometer   14 Upper securing nuts   15 Studs

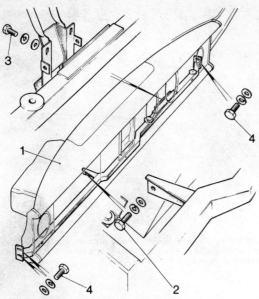

FIG 12:14 Removing facia panel support rail

Key to Fig 12:14 1 Facia panel 2 Bolt 3 Front bracket bolts 4 Side bracket bolts

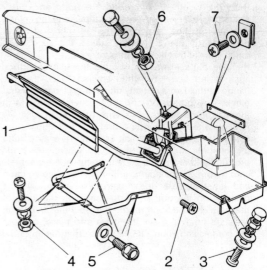

FIG 12:15 Removing front parcel shelf

Key to Fig 12:15 1 Trim board 2 to 7 Retaining screws and bolts

weatherstrip is drawn over the flange. It may be necessary to use a rubber hammer to drive the windscreen fully into place.

4 With the cord completely removed, inject sealant between the weatherstrip and flange, wiping away surplus sealant with a cloth moistened in petrol or white spirits.

12:5 Removing the facia panel and support rail

1 Disconnect the battery.
2 Refer to **FIG 12:13**, remove the three screws 2 and detach the steering column nacelles.
3 Refer to **Chapter 2** and remove the choke control from the facia.
4 Unscrew the heater control knob grubscrews 4 where fitted and pull off the control knobs. Disconnect the screen washer tubes from the control 5, mark them with tape so that they can be replaced correctly.
5 Refer to the inset 6 and press the connector button on the speedometer cable to disengage it from the drive. Disconnect the wiring harness plugs 7.
6 Remove the five screws 8 and collect the fix nuts.
7 Unwind the six screws around the demister grille 9 and remove it.
8 Remove the single screw and washer 10 and the screws and washers retaining the brackets 11.
9 Pull the ducting hoses 12 off the vents from behind the facia.
10 Refer to **Chapter 11** and remove the speedometer indicator 13.
11 Unscrew the four nuts 14, collect the spring and plain washers, lift the two centre studs 15 and pull the facia assembly clear.

12 If it is necessary to remove the facia support rail, refer to **FIG 12:14** and remove the single bolt 2 and its spring and plain washer.
13 Remove the two bolts 3 and the four bolts 4 with spring and plain washers.
14 Lift out the support rail.

Refitting:

15 Refit the support rail in the reverse order of 12 to 14 and the facia panel in the reverse order of 1 to 11. Ensure no leads are trapped by the wipers linkage.

12:6 Removing front parcel shelf

Before removing or refitting the parcel shelf make sure the air distribution lever is in the 'OFF' position.

1 Refer to **FIG 12:15** and remove the trim board 1 by prising it away from the four securing clips.
2 Unwind the three screws 2 to remove the finisher frame. Remove the four screws 3 complete with nuts, cap nuts, lockwashers and eight plain washers.
3 Remove the two screws 4, washers and nuts and the two bolts 5 and plain washers.
4 Remove the two nuts 6, collect the spring and plain washers and extract the bolts.
5 Unwind the two screws 7, collect the washers and the strap.
6 Pull the parcel shelf clear.

Refitting:

7 Make sure the air distribution lever is in the 'OFF' position and reverse the removal operations.

12:7 The front bonnet

Removing:

Details in removing the bonnet are given in **Chapter 1**.

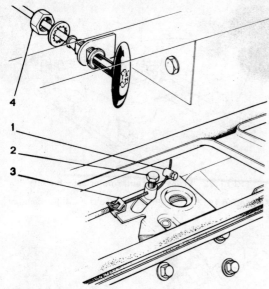

FIG 12:16 Bonnet release handle and attachment cable to bonnet catch

Key to Fig 12:16   1 Trunnion and bolt   2 Release catch post   3 Clip   4 Handle retaining nut

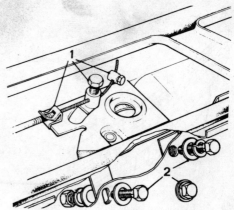

FIG 12:17   Bonnet lock attachment

Key to Fig 12:17   1 Trunnion, bolt and clip   2 Securing bolts

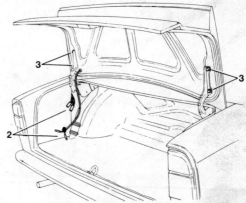

FIG 12:18   Boot lid fixing points

Key to Fig 12:18   2 Wiring harness   3 Hinge bolts

Bonnet release cable:

To renew the bonnet release cable, refer to **FIG 12:16** and lift the bonnet, loosen and remove the trunnion 1, slacken the pinch bolt 2 and pull the cable and clip 3 from the catch plate.

From inside the car, unscrew nut 4 and pull the cable out.

At this stage do not close the bonnet with the cable removed.

Fit the cable in the reverse order, make sure the cable is secure and fairly taut before closing the bonnet. With the bonnet still open, check the action of the releasing mechanism, if it appears to be satisfactory, test it with the bonnet closed.

Bonnet lock:

To remove the bonnet lock, lift the bonnet, refer to **FIG 12:17** and release the cable as previously described. Unscrew and withdraw the nuts, bolts and spring and plain washers.

On lefthand drive models the fan motor must be removed before the lock can be removed (see **Section 12:11**).

12:8 The boot lid and lock

Removing boot lid:

1 Disconnect the battery, refer to **FIG 12:18** and disconnect the number plate lamp cables 2. Mark the position of the hinges in relation to the lid.
2 Unscrew and remove the four bolts 3 complete with spring and plain washers.
3 Refit the lid to the previously made marks.

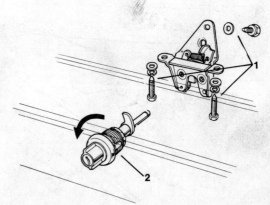

FIG 2:19   Boot lock details

Key to Fig 12:19   1 Lock attachment   2 Lock

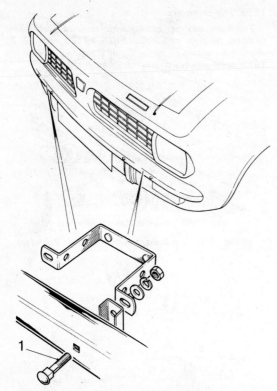

FIG 12:20 Front bumper fixing points (pre-1973 models)

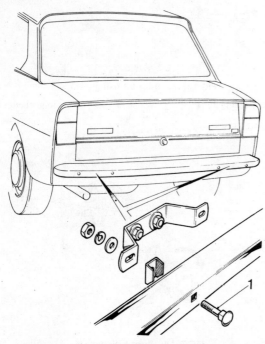

FIG 12:21 Rear bumper fixing points (pre-1973 models)

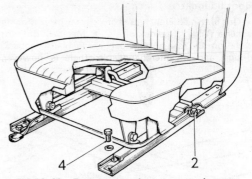

FIG 12:22 Front seat and runner attachments

Key to Fig 12:22 2 Runner rear bolts 4 Runner front bolts

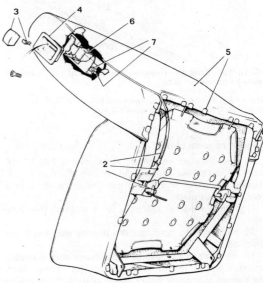

FIG 12:23 Tilt catch release and cable (2-door only)

Key to Fig 12:23 2 Trunnion screw, clip and cable 3 Release knob 4 Escutcheon 5 Squab cover 6 Bolt 7 Clip and cable lever assembly

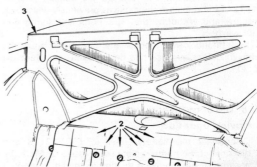

FIG 12:24 Rear seating area with squab and cushion removed

Key to Fig 12:24 2 Rubber plugs 3 Trim panel

Boot lid lock:

One of two different makes of lock may be incorporated, either a Wilmot Breeden or a C. E. Marshall. Both locks work on the same principal, are almost identical in design, and are interchangeable. There is, however, a slight difference in the method of removing and fitting.

1 Open the boot lid, refer to **FIG 12:19** and remove the three bolts 1 complete with spring and plain washers. Lift off the latch.

2 Wilmot Breeden: Rotate the locking ring through 90 deg. (rotation of arrow) and withdraw the lock assembly 2 and sealing ring. Refit in the reverse order.

3 C. E. Marshall: Disengage the retaining spring by tapping the end of the spindle lightly with a wood or hide mallet. Withdraw the lock. When refitting, locate the lock in the aperture slots and press firmly to engage the retaining spring.

12:9 The bumpers

The front and rear bumpers are secured by brackets retained by nuts and bolts. **FIGS 12:20** and **12:21** show the method of removal and fitting. Since October 1972 'wrap-around' type bumpers are fitted.

12:10 The seats

Front:

Removing:

1 Lift the release lever at the front righthand side and push the seat fully forward. Refer to **FIG 12:22** and remove the two bolts 2.

2 Push the seat fully rearward and remove the two bolts 4.

3 Lift out the seat complete with runners.

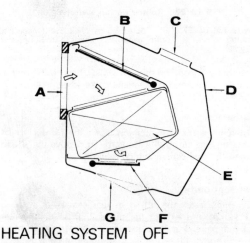

HEATING SYSTEM OFF

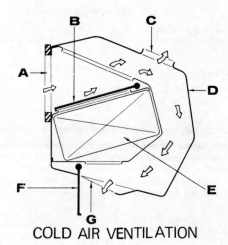

COLD AIR VENTILATION

WHITE ARROWS-COLD
BLACK ARROWS-WARM

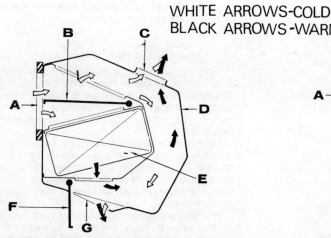

WARM AIR VENTILATION

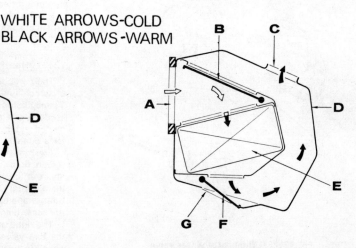

WINDSCREEN DEFROSTING

FIG 12:25   Working principle of heating and ventilating distribution box

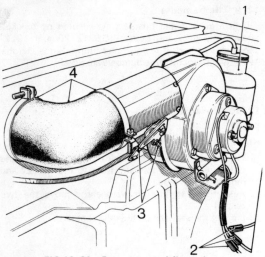

FIG 12 : 26   Fan motor and flap valve

Key to Fig 12 : 26   1 Windscreen washer container
2 Wiring snap connectors   3 Flap operating lever
4 Hose clips

Refitting :

4 Ensure that the packing washers are correctly positioned and reverse the sequence of operations.

Catch release cable (2 door saloons) :

To renew the catch release cable, remove the seats as previously described. Refer to **FIG 12 : 23**, slacken the trunnion screw 2, pull off the clip and detach the cable. Pull off the release knob 3, take out the two screws to extract the escutcheon 4 and remove the squab cover 5

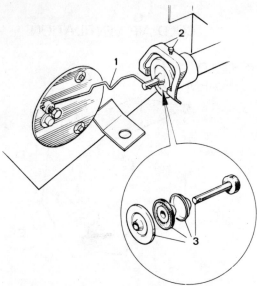

FIG 12 : 28   The heater water valve

Key to Fig 12 : 28   1 Control rod   2 Retainer screw
3 Valve details

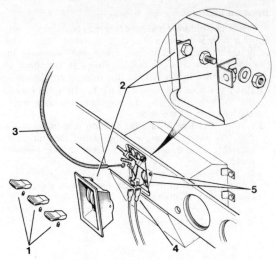

FIG 12 : 27   Removing fan switch

Key to Fig 12 : 27   1 Control knobs   2 Escutcheon and
securing bolts   3 Control cable   4 Leads   5 Supporting
screws

by releasing it from the thirteen clips. Unscrew the bolt 6, pull off the clip and remove the cable lever assembly 7.

Rear seats :

To remove the rear cushion, raise the front clear of the spring clip and pull it forward. To remove the squab unwind the two screws which retain it.

Rear seat belts :

To prepare for the fitting of rear seat belts, refer to **FIG 12 : 24** and extract the plugs 2. Prise up the rear deck trim panel 3 to expose the fixing points. Cut through the trim above these points if shoulder strap type belts are being fitted.

Fit the seat belts in accordance with the manufacturers instructions.

12 : 11 Heating and ventilating system

The combined heater and ventilating distribution unit, of which four stages of distribution are shown in **FIG 12 : 25**, comprises a water heated element **E** mounted inside a casing **D**. Two flap valves **B** and **F** are connected independently to the three control levers on the facia panel.

Fresh air, from an air intake at the base of the windscreen, flows into the distribution box through the inlet **A** and out by moving the control levers, either through the aperture **C** and on to the windscreen, or through the bottom aperture **G** to the car interior; or through both at the same time.

The righthand control lever on the facia panel operates the flap valve **B**. When the lever is moved to the 'hot' position, the air is directed through the heating element **E**. As the lever is moved further down the quadrant it gradually closes the flap to give a varying mixture of hot and cold air. At the bottom position the heating element is excluded and the water valve is shut off, only cold air enters the interior.

The lefthand control lever on the facia panel operates the flap valve **F**. When the lever is in the 'off' position the flap seals off the heating element. As it is moved down the quadrant, air is first directed onto the screen, until further downward movement of the lever directs the flow to both screen and car interior.

The central control lever governs the volume of the air stream into the distribution box. When the lever is in the 'off' position, the passage of air through the inlet **A** is cut off. Movement of the lever downwards gradually opens the flap valve allowing air to enter the chamber. Further movement downwards operates a two-speed blower to give high or low speed air flow as required.

The swivelling fresh air vents at each end of the facia can be opened or closed by turning the central knob in the desired direction.

Removing fan motor:

1 Take out the screen washer bottle (righthand drive only) and refer to **FIG 12 : 26**.
2 Disconnect the three leads at the snap connectors 2.
3 Detach the cable and clip by slackening the trunnion bolt 3.
4 Slacken the two clips and remove the air tube 4.
5 Undo the three bolts securing the fan motor to the bulkhead, collect the spring and plain washers.

Refitting:

6 Use Seelastik SR51 to seal the fan motor to the bulkhead. Before refitting the control cable, make sure the central control lever is in the 'off' position and the fan motor flap lever 3 is positioned fully to the left (righthand drive) or fully to the right (lefthand drive).

Removing fan switch:

1 Refer to **FIG 12 : 27** and remove the three grubscrews securing the control knobs 1. Later models are secured by clips.
2 To withdraw the escutcheon 2 undo the two nuts, bolts and plain washers. Later models have four clips.
3 Disconnect the control cable 3 and the two leads 4, mark the leads or note the colours for correct replacement.
4 Take out the two screws 5 and remove the switch.

Refitting:

5 Reverse the operations 1 to 4.

Removing air flow control cable:

1 Refer to **FIG 12 : 26** and detach the cable.
2 Carry out operations 1 and 2 for removing fan switch.
3 Disconnect the cable and pull it through the bulkhead.

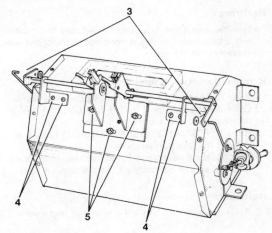

FIG 12 : 29   The control assembly

Key to Fig 12 : 29   3 Control rods   4 Pop-rivets
5 Retaining screws

Refitting:

4 Reverse operations 1 to 3. Before refitting the control cable, make sure the central control lever is in the 'off' position and the fan motor flap lever, 3 in **FIG 12 : 26** is positioned fully to the left (righthand drive) or fully to the right (lefthand drive).

Removing heater water valve:

1 The heater water valve is situated on the righthand side of the distributor unit. It may be more convenient to remove the parcel shelf to carry out this work (see **Section 12 : 6**).
2 Refer to **FIG 12 : 28** and uncouple the control rod 1. Slacken the screw 2 and remove the retainer.
3 Withdraw the valve assembly.

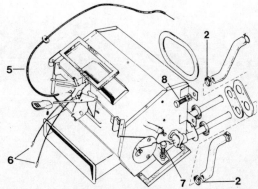

FIG 12 : 30   Removing heater element from distribution box

Key to Fig 12 : 30   2 Hose clips   5 Control cable
6 Leads   7 Securing bolts   8 Securing bolts

Refitting:

4 Reverse operations 1 to 3 and make sure the control rod is positioned so that it does not obstruct the free movement of the valve.

Removing control assembly:

1 Refer to **Section 12:5** and remove the facia panel.
2 Carry out operations 2 and 3 for removing the air flow control cable, but disconnecting it only.
3 Refer to **FIG 12:29**, detach the control rods 3 and drill out the four pop-rivets 4.
4 Take out the three screws 5 and manoeuvre the lever, rods and switch assembly off the distribution box.

Refitting:

5 Reverse operations 1 to 4. Fit two new pop-rivets.

Removing heater element:

1 Refer to **Chapter 4** and drain the cooling system.
2 Refer to **FIG 12:30**, slacken the clips 2 and disconnect the hoses.
3 Refer to **Section 12:5** and remove the facia panel and support rail.
4 Disconnect the control cable 5 from the central lever and the two leads 6. Note the colour of the leads and their positions.
5 Undo the two nuts, bolts and plain washers 7 and the four nuts, bolts, spring and plain washers 8.
6 Taking care to avoid spilling coolant, which has remained in the matrix, pull the heater unit clear.

Refitting:

7 Reverse operations 1 to 9 and apply Seelastik SR 51 to the dash seals and rear fixing brackets.

APPENDIX

TECHNICAL DATA

Engine   Fuel system   Ignition system   Cooling system
Clutch   Transmission   Brakes   Steering
Suspension   Electrical   Capacities   Wheels and tyres
Dimensions   Torque wrench settings

WIRING DIAGRAMS

FIG 13:1   Toledo wiring diagram, righthand drive, 1970-72
FIG 13:2   Toledo wiring diagram, lefthand drive with minimum equipment
FIG 13:3   Toledo wiring diagram, lefthand drive with maximum equipment
FIG 13:4   Toledo wiring diagram, righthand drive, 1973 on

METRIC CONVERSION TABLE

HINTS ON MAINTENANCE AND OVERHAUL

GLOSSARY OF TERMS

NOTES

TECHNICAL DATA

Dimensions in inches, millimetres in brackets

ENGINE

Type	4-cylinder in-line, OHV water-cooled
Cylinder bore	2.90 (73.70)
Stroke, 1300	2.99 (76.00)
1500	3.44 (87.50)
Capacity, 1300	1296 cc
1500	1493 cc
Compression ratio, 1300 ...	8.5:1
1500	9:1
Firing order	1-3-4-2
Maximum power, 1300	58 bhp net at 5300 rev/min
1500 single carburetter ...	61 bhp net at 5000 rev/min
1500 twin carburetter ...	65 bhp net at 5500 rev/min
Ventilation	Closed circuit breathing from rocker cover to depression side of carburetter
Crankshaft	Three main journals, integral balance weights
Main journal diameter	2.3115 to 2.3120 (58.713 to 58.725)
Regrind undersides	—.010 (—.25), —.020 (—.51), —.030 (—.76) stamped on crankshaft web
Crankpin diameter	1.8750 to 1.8755 (47.625 to 47.638)
Regrind undersides	As main journals
End float	.006 to .014 (.1524 to .3556)
Thrust washer oversizes	.005 (.13)
Maximum runout of centre journal (with front and rear supported)	.003 (.076)
Maximum out of balance with key and dowel fitted	.3 oz/inch (3.36 g/cm)
Main and big-end bearings	Steel backed, lead-bronze with lead-indium overlay
Undersizes available	—.010 (—.25), —.020 (—.51), —.030 (—.76) stamped on undersize of shell
Cylinder block	Chromium iron
Original size bore, Grade F	2.8995 to 2.9000 (73.64 to 73.66)
Grade G	2.9001 to 2.9005 (73.66 to 73.77)
Maximum rebore size	+.020 (+.51)
Camshaft	Chilled cast iron, 4 bearing, chain driven
Journal diameter	1.9649 to 1.9654 (49.91 to 49.92)
End float	.0042 to .0085 (.110 to .216)
Bore in block	1.9680 to 1.9695 (49.980 to 50.025)
Timing chain	.375 (9.52) pitch x 62 pitches)
Pistons	Aluminium alloy, solid skirt
Diameter, top, Grade F	2.875 to 2.880 (73.03 to 73.15)
bottom, Grade F	2.8976 to 2.8981 (73.59 to 73.61)
top, Grade G	2.875 to 2.880 (73.03 to 73.15)
bottom, Grade G ...	2.8982 to 2.8987 (73.617 to 73.620)
Oversizes	+.020 (+.52)
Groove width, bottom	.1578 to .1588 (3.99 to 4.01)
centre and top ...	.064 to .065 (1.625 to 1.650)
Piston rings:	
Width, centre and top compression ...	.0620 to .0625 (1.575 to 1.5787)
oil control (3 part)	.1540 to .1560 (3.90 to 3.96)
Oversizes	+.010 (+.25), +.020 (+.51), +.030 (+.76)
Gaps	.012 to .020 (.30 to .50)

Connecting rods ... ... 45 ton steel forging. Obliquely split big-end, solid small-end

Small-end bush diameter (fitted)	.8126 to .8129 (20.64 to 20.65)
Maximum rod bend	.0015 (.04)
Maximum rod twist	.0045 (.114)

Gudgeon pins ... ... Fully floating
Diameter ... ... .8123 to .8125 (20.63 to 20.64)

Connecting rod and piston assemblies:
Weight variation between heaviest and lighest assembly ... ... Maximum 4 drams

Cylinder head ... ... Cast iron, individual ports

Valves:

Head diameter, 1500, inlet	1.429 to 1.433 (36.31 to 36.38)
1300, inlet	1.304 to 1.308 (33.12 to 33.22)
from engine No. DG25001	1.437 to 1.443 (36.49 to 36.65)
1500, exhaust	1.230 to 1.234 (31.24 to 31.34)
from engine No. DM5001, DS 5001	1.168 to 1.172 (29.66 to 29.76)
1300, exhaust	1.168 to 1.172 (29.68 to 29.76)
Stem diameter, inlet	.3107 to .3112 (7.87 to 7.90)
exhaust	.3100 to .3105 (7.874 to 7.887)
Seat face angle	90 deg. total inclusive angle
Stem to guide clearance, inlet	.0008 to .0023 (.02 to .06)
exhaust... ...	.0015 to .0030 (.03 to .07)

Valve guides:

Length	2.0625 (52.387)
Bore	.312 to .313 (7.92 to 7.95)
Outside diameter	.501 to .502 (12.72 to 12.75)
Height above cylinder head	.749 to .751 (19.025 to 19.075)

Valve springs:

	Type A	Type B
Internal diameter ...	0.795 in (20.193 mm)	0.795 in (20.193 mm)
Working coils ...	3¼	3½
Load at length ...	1.36 in at 27 to 30 lb (34.54 mm at 12.25 to 13.61 kg)	1.074 in at 105 to 115 lb (27.28 mm at 47.3 to 52.2 kg)
Free length ...	1.61 in (40.9 mm)	1.59 in (40.4 mm)
Solid length ...	0.93 in (23.6 mm)	0.96 in (24.4 mm)
Rate	150 lb/in (2679 kg/m)	235 lb/in (4196 kg/m)

	Type C
Internal diameter	0.795 in (20.193 mm)
Working coils	3¾
Load at length	0.989 in at 123 to 133 lb (25.1 mm at 55.8 to 60.3 kg)
Free length	1.52 in (38.6 mm)
Solid length	0.875 in (22.2 mm)
Rate	240 lb/in (4286 kg/m)

Note: Type A fitted to 1300 cc engines up to engine number DG 25001 with the exception of engines within the following three groups: DG 10731 to 10750, DG 10786 to 10909, DG 11116 to 11622

Type B fitted to 1300 cc engines of the above three groups and 1500 cc engines up to DM 5001 and DS 5001.

Type C fitted to 1300 cc engines from DG 25001 and 1500 cc engines from DM 5001 and DS 5001.

	1300, 1500 SC and 1500 TC *Engine No. 5001 onwards*	1500 TC *Up to Engine No. 5001*
Valve timing:		
Inlet opens	18° BTDC	25° BTDC
closes	58° ABDC	65° ABDC
Exhaust opens	58° BBDC	65° BBDC
closes	18° ATDC	25° ATDC

Rocker gear clearances:
Standard, cold ... ... .010 (.25)
Valve timing only, No. 7 and 8 ... ... .050 (1.27)

Lubrication:
Oil pump ... ... High capacity rotor type
Clearance between inner and outer rotor ... .010 (.25) maximum
Clearance between outer rotor and body ... .008 (.20) maximum
Rotor end float ... ... .004 (.10) maximum
Oil filter ... ... Fullflow replaceable element
Warning light goes out at ... ... 3 to 5 lb/sq inch (.21 to .35 kg/sq cm) oil
pressure

FUEL SYSTEM

Fuel pump:
Type ... ... Mechanically operated, diaphragm type
Pressure ... ... 2.5 to 3.5 lb/sq inch

	Before eng. No. DG 25001 DM 5001 DS 5001	*From eng. No. to eng. No. DG 25001 DH 1 DM 5001 DM 10001 DS 5001 DS 10001*	*After eng. No. DH 1 DM 10001 DS 10001*
Carburetter:			
Make/type, single carburetter engine ...	S.U. HS4	S.U. HS4E	S.U. HS4E
twin carburetter engine ...	S.U. HS2	S.U. HS2E	S.U. HS2E
Main jet	0.090 in	0.090 in	0.090 in
Venturi, single carburetter engine	1.500 in	1.500 in	1.500 in
twin carburetter engine	1.250 in	1.250 in	1.250 in
Needle, 1300 single carburetter engine ...	AAK	AAW	ABF or ABQ
1500 single carburetter engine ...	AAK	AAK	ABG
1500 twin carburetter engine	AAN	AAX	AAX

Air filter:
Type, 1300 and 1500 two-door ... ... Combined cleaner and silencer with single
renewable element
1500 four-door ... ... Combined cleaner and silencer with
twin renewable elements

Idling speed:
1300 and 1500 two-door ... ... 700 to 750 rev/min
1500 four-door ... ... 700 to 800 rev/min

IGNITION SYSTEM

Distributor:

Type ... ... Lucas 25D4 or 45D4 with centrifugal and vacuum automatic advance control

Contact points gap ... ... .014 to .016 (.36 to .41)

Dwell angle, 25D4 ... ... 60 ± 3 deg.

45D4 ... ... 51 + 5 deg.

Rotor rotation ... ... Anticlockwise

Capacitor... ... ... .20 mfd

Coil:

Type ... ... Lucas 16C6

Winding resistance ... ... 1.43 to 1.58 ohms

Ballast resistor:

Type ... ... Lucas 3BR

Resistance ... ... 1.3 to 1.4 ohms

Sparking plugs ... ... Champion N-9Y

Gap ... ... .024 to .026 (.625 to .66)

	Before engine No.	*After engine No.*
	DG 25001	*DG 25001*
	DM 5001	*DM 5001*
Ignition timing:	*DS 5001*	*DS 5001*
1300	9 deg. BTDC	10 deg. BTDC
1500, single carburetter	9 deg. BTDC	10 deg. BTDC
twin carburetter	5 deg. BTDC	10 deg. BTDC

Distributor applicability chart:

1300 Single carburetter. Fitted up to engine number DG25000 H or L ... ... Stanpart No. 212292

1500 Twin carburetter. Fitted up to engine number DS 5000 H or L ... ... Stanpart No. 217613

All types following the above mentioned engine numbers ... ... Stanpart No. 218106

COOLING SYSTEM

Type ... ... Water no-loss system incorporating a separate pressurized expansion tank.

Circulation ... ... Impeller type pump driven by V-belt. Thermostatically controlled flow

Fan ... ... 7 blade, $11\frac{1}{2}$ inch (292 mm) diameter. Belt driven

Pressure ... ... 13 lb/sq inch (.91 kg/sq cm)

Anti-freeze specification ... ... BSI 3151 or 3152

CLUTCH

Type ... ... Borg and Beck diaphragm type. Single dry plate hydraulically operated

Driven plate diameter, 1300... ... ... $6\frac{1}{2}$ (165 mm)

1500... ... ... $7\frac{1}{4}$ (184 mm)

Facing material ... ... Mintex M19

Number of damper springs 4

Spring colours ... ... Violet/Pink (2)

White/Yellow (2)

Clutch release bearing ... ... Ball journal

Hydraulic fluid ... ... Castrol/Girling Brake and Clutch Fluid (Green) or UNIPART 550 Brake Fluid

TRANSMISSION

Gearbox	Four forward speeds, one reverse with silent helical gears. Synchromesh on all forward gears. Remote control gear selection

Gear ratios:

Top, 1:1	Overall: 1300 4.11:1
	1500 3.89:1
Third, 1.394:1	1300 5.74:1
	1500 5.42:1
Second, 2.158:1	1300 8.88:1
	1500 8.39:1
First, 3.504:1	1300 14.41:1
	1500 13.65:1
Reverse, 3.988:1	1300 16.39:1
	1500 15.53:1
Final drive	Live axle via hypoid bevel gears and 2 pinion differential
Rear axle ratio, 1300	4.11:1
1500	3.89:1
Propeller shaft	All metal shaft, universal joints with needle roller bearings

BRAKES

Type:

Early 1300 and 1500 two-door (front) ...	Hydraulically operated, drum type with two leading shoes
Drum size	9 x 1¾ (228 x 44.45)
1300 and 1500 two-door (rear)	Foot hydraulically operated drum type with one leading and one trailing shoe. Handbrake operates mechanically
Drum size	8 x 1½ (204 x 38)
1500 four-door, later two-door and later 1300 models (front)	Hydraulically operated and self-adjusting caliper disc type with servo assistance
Disc diameter	8¾ (222 mm)
1500 four-door (rear)	Foot hydraulically operated drum type with one leading and one trailing shoe. Servo assistance. Handbrake operates mechanically and automatically adjusts brake shoes
Drum size	8 x 1½ (204 x 38)
Hydraulic fluid	Castrol/Girling Clutch and Brake Fluid (Green) or UNIPART 550 Brake Fluid

STEERING

Type	Alford and Alder rack and pinion. Impact absorbing steering column and anti-theft locking device
Steering wheel diameter	16 inch (407)
Turns, lock to lock	3
Turning circle	29 ft 9 inch (9.1 m) between kerbs

Steering geometry (kerb condition):

Camber angle, up to ADG11512 and ADS-648 only	1½ deg. + to ½ deg. −
from ADG11512, ADS648, and other models ...	2¼ deg. + to ¼ deg. +
from ADH 1 and ADF 50,001	0 deg. to 2 deg. +

Castor angle	$2\frac{1}{4}$ deg. $\pm$ 1 deg.
Swivel pin inclination, up to ADG 11512 and ADS 648 only	$6\frac{1}{2}$ deg. $\pm$ 1 deg.
from ADG 11512, ADS 648, and other models ...	$5\frac{3}{4}$ deg. $\pm$ 1 deg.
Wheel alignment	0 to $\frac{1}{16}$ inch (0 to 1.59 mm) toe-in

SUSPENSION

Type:

Front	Independent with coil springs and telescopic hydraulic dampers. Upper wishbone and lower transverse link. Trailing radius rods
Rear	Combined coil springs and telescopic hydraulic dampers operating in the four link system. All connections rubber bushed
Spares	Consult authorized dealer, referenced colour codes

ELECTRICAL

Battery:

Type	12-volt. Negative earth
Capacity	40 ampere hours, 20 hour rate

Alternator:

Type	Lucas 15 ACR, ventilated 318 watts

Starter:'

Type	Lucas M35J, inertia or M35JPE, pre-engaged type
Light running current	65 amp
Running torque current	260 to 275 amp
Brush length, minimum	.375 (9.53)

Windscreen wiper:

Type	AC Delco single speed or two-speed
Single speed, righthand drive	Stanpart 215751
lefthand drive	Stanpart 215750
Two-speed, righthand drive	Stanpart 216720
lefthand drive	Stanpart 215588
Normal speed	1.5 amp, single speed
	2.3 amp, two-speed
High speed	3.0 amp, two speed
Armature end float	None

CAPACITIES

Fuel tank	$10\frac{1}{2}$ gall. (48 litres)
Engine sump, drain and refill	7 pints (4 litres)
with filter change	8 pints ($4\frac{1}{2}$ litres)
Gearbox, dry	$1\frac{1}{2}$ pints (.85 litre)
Rear axle, dry	$1\frac{1}{2}$ pints (.85 litre)
Cooling system, with heater	$8\frac{1}{2}$ pints (4.8 litres)

WHEELS AND TYRES

Wheels	13 x 4J steel disc rims
Tyres, crossply, pre-October 1972	5.20 x 13 tubeless. Later models, 5.60 x 13
radial	155 SP-13 tubeless

Pressures:

Crossply, 5.20 x 13, 1 to 4 up, front ...	25 lb/sq inch (1.76 kg/sq cm)
rear ...	30 lb/sq inch (2.11 kg/sq cm)
fully laden, front	26 lb/sq inch (1.83 kg/sq cm)
rear	32 lb/sq inch (2.25 kg/sq cm)
Remainder, all conditions, front	22 lb/sq inch (1.55 kg/sq cm)
rear	26 lb/sq inch (1.83 kg/sq cm)

Do not fit a mixture of crossply and radial tyres on the car. Fit all of one type only including the spare

DIMENSIONS

Length	13 ft $\frac{1}{8}$ inch (3965 mm)
Width	5 ft 1$\frac{3}{4}$ inch (1568 mm)
Height, unladen	4 ft 6 inch (1372 mm)
Track, front	4 ft 5 inch (1346 mm)
rear	4 ft 2 inch (1270 mm)
Ground clearance	4$\frac{1}{2}$ inch (108 mm)

Weights:

Dry, excluding extra equipment:

1300 and 1500 two-door	16 cwt (815 kg)
1300, four-door	16$\frac{1}{4}$ cwt (825 kg)
1500 four-door TC	16$\frac{3}{4}$ cwt (850 kg)

Basic kerb (including tools, fuel, oil and water):

1300 and 1500 two-door	17 cwt (865 kg)
1500 four-door TC	17$\frac{3}{4}$ cwt (900 kg)

Gross, maximum:

1300 and 1500 two-door	24 cwt (1230 kg)
1500 four-door TC	24$\frac{3}{4}$ cwt (1265 kg)

TORQUE WRENCH SETTINGS

Engine 1300:

		kgf m	lbf ft
Alternator to mounting bracket and front engine plate	$\frac{5}{16}$ in UNF	2.8	20
Alternator to adjusting link	$\frac{5}{16}$ in UNC	2.8	20
Cylinder block oil gallery	$\frac{1}{4}$ in Dryseal plug	1.9	14
Cylinder block oil gallery seals	$\frac{5}{16}$ in UNF	2.8	20
Cylinder block drain plug	$\frac{1}{2}$ in × 20 NPT	5.2	38
Crankshaft pulley to crankshaft	1 in × 16 TPI	20.7	150
Connecting rod bolt	$\frac{3}{8}$ in UNF { colour dyed	6.9	50
	phosphated	6.4	46
Cylinder head to block	$\frac{3}{8}$ in UNF	6.4	46
Clutch to flywheel	$\frac{5}{16}$ in UNF	2.8	20
Flywheel to crankshaft	$\frac{3}{8}$ in UNF { parkarised	6.2	45
	cad. plated	5.5	40

		kgf m	lbf ft
Gearbox and rear engine plate to block ...	$\frac{5}{16}$ in UNF	1.9	14
Manifold inner to head	$\frac{3}{8}$ in UNF	3.5	25
Manifold outer to head	$\frac{3}{8}$ in UNF	3.5	25
Oil filters attachment	Proprietary	1.4	10
Oil sump drain plug	$\frac{3}{8}$ in Dryseal	3.5	25
Rocker pedestal to cylinder head	$\frac{3}{8}$ in UNF	4.7	34
Rocker oil feed to block	$\frac{5}{16}$ in UNF	2.8	20
Main bearing cap bolts	$\frac{7}{16}$ in UNF	9.0	65
Rear crankshaft seal	$\frac{5}{16}$ in UNF	2.8	20
Sealing block to engine plate	$\frac{5}{16}$ in UNF	2.8	20
Sealing block to cylinder block	$\frac{5}{16}$ in UNF	1.9	14
Starter motor attachment	$\frac{3}{8}$ in UNF	4.7	34

Engine 1500:

		kgf m	lbf ft
Air cleaner attachment...	$\frac{5}{16}$ in UNC	1.1	8
Alternator to mounting bracket and front engine plate	$\frac{5}{16}$ in UNF	2.8	20
Alternator to adjusting link	$\frac{5}{16}$ in UNC	2.8	20
Bearing caps to block	$\frac{7}{16}$ in UNF	9.0	65
Clutch to flywheel	$\frac{1}{4}$ in UNF	1.5	11
*Cylinder head to block	$\frac{3}{8}$ in UNF	6.4	46
Crankshaft nut...	1 in × 16 TPI	20.7	150
Exhaust manifold to head	$\frac{5}{16}$ in UNF	1.9	14
Flywheel to crankshaft	$\frac{3}{8}$ in UNF {parkarized cad.	6.2	45
	plated	5.5	40
Gearbox and rear engine plate to block ...	$\frac{5}{16}$ in UNF	1.9	14
Manifold inner to cylinder head	$\frac{3}{8}$ in UNF	3.5	25
Manifold outer to cylinder head	$\frac{3}{8}$ in UNF	3.5	25
Oil sump drain plug	$\frac{3}{8}$ in, 18 Dryseal	3.5	25
Oil filter attachment	Proprietary	2.8	20
Sealing block to cylinder block	$\frac{5}{16}$ in UNF	1.9	14
Sealing block to engine plate	$\frac{5}{16}$ in UNF	2.8	20

*Studs to be tightened into block to 1.9 kgf m (14 lbf ft)

Gearbox:

		kgf m	lbf ft
Extension to gearbox	$\frac{5}{16}$ in UNF	2.8	20
Filler plug	$\frac{3}{8}$ in NP	3.5	25
Gearbox case to clutch housing	$\frac{3}{8}$ in UNF	4.7	34

Rear axle:

		kgf m	lbf ft
Hypoid housing bearing cap retainer	$\frac{3}{8}$ in UNF	5.2	38
Crown wheel retainer	$\frac{3}{8}$ in UNF	6.4	46
Drain plug	$\frac{3}{8}$ in, 18 Dryseal	3.5	25
Hypoid housing attachment	$\frac{5}{16}$ in UNF	2.8	20
Hypoid flange to pinion	$\frac{5}{8}$ in UNF	16.6	120
Hub to axle shaft	$\frac{5}{8}$ in UNF	16.6	120
Propeller shaft attachment front and rear ...	$\frac{5}{16}$ in UNF	2.8	20
Propeller shaft centre bearing bracket to floor ...	$\frac{5}{16}$ in UNF	2.8	20
Rear shaft to pinion flange	$\frac{3}{8}$ in UNF	4.7	34

Front suspension:

		kgf m	lbf ft
Brake backplate to vertical link	$\frac{3}{8}$ in UNF	4.7	34
Brake drum retaining screw	$\frac{1}{4}$ in UNF	1.0	7
Ball pin to vertical link...	$\frac{1}{2}$ in UNF	7.0	50
Brake backplate to vertical link	$\frac{5}{16}$ in UNF	2.8	20
Damper to damper plate on upper wishbone ...	$\frac{3}{8}$ in UNF	4.7	34
Front sub-frame mounting bracket to body member	$\frac{1}{2}$ in UNF	6.6	48

		kgf m	lbf ft
Front damper and road spring assembly ...	$\frac{5}{16}$ in UNF	2.8	20
Hub to stub axle	$\frac{1}{2}$ in UNF Tighten to 0.7 kgf m (5 lbf ft), turn back one flat and install splitpin to give 0.003 to 0.005 in (0.076 to 0.127 mm) hub end float		
IFS mounting bracket to front sub-frame, upper attachment	$\frac{5}{16}$ in UNF	1.9	14
IFS mounting bracket to front sub-frame, lower attachment	$\frac{3}{8}$ in UNF	3.5	25
Lower ball pin attachment	$\frac{7}{16}$ in UNF	6.2	45
Lower wishbone attachments	$\frac{3}{8}$ in UNF	4.7	34
Rear mounting sub-frame to body	$\frac{1}{2}$ in UNF	6.6	48
Rear damper assembly to lower link ...	$\frac{7}{16}$ in UNF	5.2	38
Strut to front sub-frame	$\frac{7}{16}$ in UNF	5.2	38
Strut to lower wishbone	$\frac{7}{16}$ in UNF	9.0	65
Stub axle to vertical link	$\frac{7}{16}$ in UNF	11.1	80
Tie rod to vertical link	$\frac{7}{16}$ in UNF	8.3	60
Upper ball joint and damper plate to upper wishbone	$\frac{3}{8}$ in UNF	4.7	34
Upper wishbone to fulcrum shaft	$\frac{7}{16}$ in UNF	5.2	38
Upper wishbone to fulcrum shaft	$\frac{7}{16}$ in UNF jam nut	4.7	34
Upper wishbone to fulcrum shaft	$\frac{7}{16}$ in UNF nyloc nut	5.2	38
Wheel to hub	$\frac{3}{8}$ in UNF	6.6	48

Rear suspension:

		kgf m	lbf ft
Damper assembly to body	$\frac{1}{4}$ in UNF	1.1	8
Damper assembly to lower link	$\frac{7}{16}$ in UNF	5.2	38
Lower link to axle	$\frac{7}{16}$ in UNF	5.2	38
Lower link to body	$\frac{7}{16}$ in UNF	6.6	48
Rear damper detail	$\frac{1}{4}$ in UNF	1.1	8
Rear suspension mounting bracket forward fixing	$\frac{5}{16}$ in UNF	2.8	20
Upper link to axle	$\frac{7}{16}$ in UNF	5.2	38
Upper link to body bracket	$\frac{7}{16}$ in UNF	5.2	38
Wheel to hub	$\frac{3}{8}$ in UNF	6.6	48

Steering:

		kgf m	lbf ft
Clamp to steering column	$\frac{1}{4}$ in UNF	1.1	8
Lower coupling pinch bolts	$\frac{5}{16}$ in UNF	2.8	20
Lower support tube to body	$\frac{5}{16}$ in UNF	2.8	20
Rack to sub-frame	$\frac{5}{16}$ in UNF U-bolt	1.9	14
Shoulder bolts lower coupling	$\frac{1}{4}$ in UNF	1.1	8
Steering column clamp to steering column ...	$\frac{1}{4}$ in UNF shear-head bolt	Tighten to shear	
Steering column lock to housing	$\frac{5}{16}$ in UNC shear-head bolt	Tighten to shear	
Steering column support to lower rail	$\frac{1}{4}$ in UNF	1.1	8
Steering wheel retaining nut	$\frac{9}{16}$ in UNF nut	4.7	34
Support bracket to dash front	$\frac{1}{4}$ in UNF	1.1	8
Tie rod end ball joint assembly	$\frac{1}{2}$ in UNF	4.4	32
Tie rod end locknuts	$\frac{1}{2}$ in UNF (thin locknut)	5.2	38
Universal joint to steering column	$\frac{5}{16}$ in UNF	2.8	20

Chassis, engine mountings:

		kgf m	lbf ft
Engine and rear engine plate to transmission unit	$\frac{5}{16}$ in UNF	2.8	20

		kgf m	lbf ft
Engine and rear engine plate to transmission unit ...	$\frac{3}{8}$ in UNF	4.7	34
Rubber to crossmember front engine mounting	$\frac{5}{16}$ in UNF	2.8	20
Rear engine rubber to mounting plate ...	$\frac{3}{8}$ in UNF	3.5	25

Chassis, brake and clutch systems:

		kgf m	lbf ft
Brake cable to abutment bracket	$\frac{1}{4}$ in UNF	1.0	7
Brake pedal mounting details ...	$\frac{3}{8}$ in UNF	2.8	20
Brake pedal support bracket to scuttle	$\frac{3}{8}$ in UNF	4.7	34
Brake pedal support bracket to scuttle	$\frac{1}{4}$ in UNF	1.1	8
Clutch pedal to support bracket	$\frac{5}{16}$ in UNF	2.8	20
Clutch pedal to support bracket	$\frac{3}{8}$ in UNF	4.7	34
Clutch pedal support bracket to scuttle	$\frac{5}{16}$ in UNF	2.8	20
Handbrake and bracket clamp plate to floor	$\frac{1}{4}$ in UNF	1.1	8
Handbrake fulcrum pin	$\frac{3}{8}$ in UNF	3.5	25
Master cylinder support bracket to turret	$\frac{5}{16}$ in UNF	2.8	20
Plate to body ...	$\frac{5}{16}$ in UNF	2.8	20
Union four-way to body	$\frac{1}{4}$ in UNF	1.1	8

Chassis, brake pipe:

		kgf m	lbf ft
Brake hose front ($12\frac{1}{2}$ in long)	$\frac{3}{8}$ in UNF	1.2	9
Clutch master cylinder to plate	$\frac{5}{16}$ in UNF	2.8	20
Clutch pipe to slave and master cylinder	$\frac{3}{8}$ in UNF	1.0	7
Pipe (bent) double-ended unit to rear hose	$\frac{3}{8}$ in UNF	1.2	9
Pipe (bent) four-way to righthand front hose	$\frac{3}{8}$ in UNF	1.0	7
Pipe (bent) four-way to lefthand front hose	$\frac{3}{8}$ in UNF	1.0	7
Pipe (bent) rear hose to righthand wheel cylinder	$\frac{3}{8}$ in	1.2	9
Pipe (bent) righthand wheel cylinder to lefthand wheel cylinder	$\frac{3}{8}$ in	1.0	7
Union double-ended ...	$\frac{3}{8}$ in	1.2	9

Body (exhaust system, radiator, fuel tank):

		kgf m	lbf ft
Fuel tank drain plug ...	$\frac{5}{8}$ in UNF	5.2	38

Body:

		kgf m	lbf ft
Front seat tilt mechanism lever to bracket on seat ...	$\frac{1}{4}$ in UNF	1.0	8
Front seat safety harness eye bolt	$\frac{7}{16}$ in UNF	3.5	25
Front seat slide to floor	$\frac{5}{16}$ in UNF	1.9	14
Lock to truck lid	$\frac{1}{4}$ in UNF	1.1	8
Rear seat safety harness eyebolt	$\frac{7}{16}$ in UNF	3.5	25
Spring assembly to front bumper	$\frac{3}{8}$ in UNF	3.5	25
Spring bracket to front and rear bumper bar	$\frac{3}{8}$ in UNF	3.5	25
Safety harness pivot bolt	$\frac{7}{16}$ in UNF	3.5	25
Torsion bar to rear parcel shelf	$\frac{1}{4}$ in UNF	1.0	7

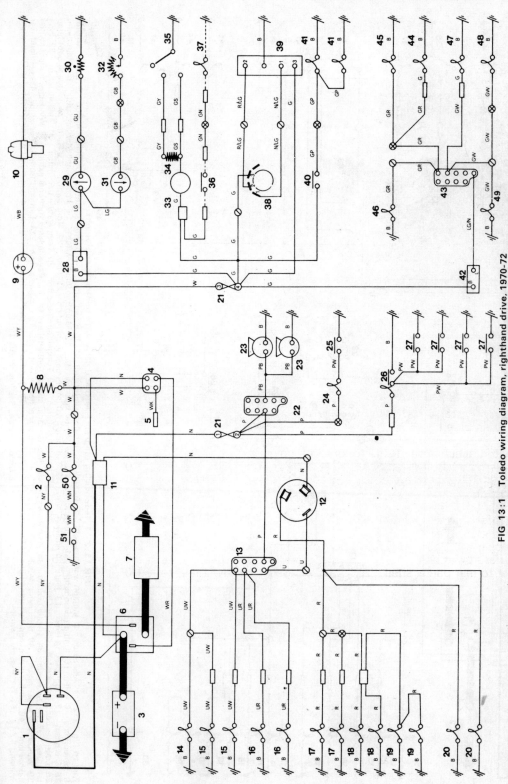

FIG 13:1 Toledo wiring diagram, righthand drive, 1970-72

Key to Fig 13:1 1 Alternator 2 Ignition warning light 3 Battery 4 Ignition/starter switch 5 Radio supply 6 Starter solenoid 7 Starter motor 8 Ballast resistor 9 Ignition coil—6-volt 10 Ignition distributor 11 Connector block 12 Master light switch 13 Main/dip/flash switch 14 Main beam warning light 15 Main beam 16 Dip beam 17 Front parking lamp 18 Plate illumination lamp 19 Tail lamp 20 Instrument illumination 21 Fuse 22 Horn 23 Horn switch 24 Luggage boot lamp 25 Luggage boot lamp switch 26 Roof lamp 27 Door switch 28 Voltage stabilizer 29 Temperature indicator 30 Temperature transmitter 31 Fuel indicator 32 Fuel tank unit 33 Heater resistor 34 Heater switch 35 Heater motor 36 Reverse lamp (optional extra) 37 Reverse lamp switch (optional extra) 38 Windscreen wiper switch 39 Windscreen wiper motor 40 Stop lamp 41 Stop lamp switch 42 Turn signal flasher unit 43 Turn signal flasher switch 44 Lefthand front flasher lamp 45 Lefthand rear flasher lamp 46 Lefthand turn signal warning light 47 Righthand front flasher lamp 48 Righthand rear flasher lamp 49 Righthand turn signal warning light 50 Oil pressure warning light 51 Oil pressure switch

Key to colour code N Brown U Blue R Red P Purple G Green W White Y Yellow S Slate B Black LG Light green

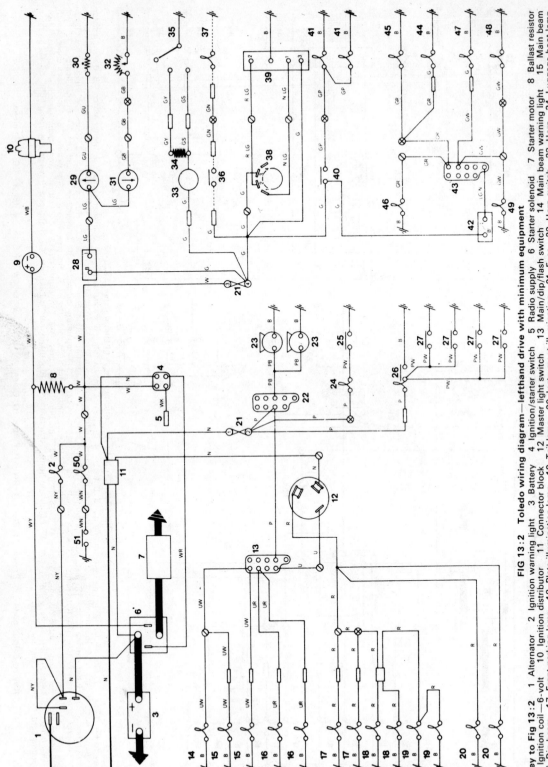

FIG 13 : 2 Toledo wiring diagram—lefthand drive with minimum equipment

Key to Fig 13 : 2: 1 Alternator 2 Ignition warning light 3 Battery 4 Ignition/starter switch 5 Radio supply 6 Ignition/starter switch 7 Starter motor 8 Ballast resistor 9 Ignition coil—6-volt 10 Ignition distributor 11 Connector block 12 Master light switch 13 Main/dip/flash switch 14 Main beam warning light 15 Main beam 16 Dip beam 17 Front parking lamp 18 Plate illumination lamp 19 Tail lamp 20 Instrument illumination 21 Fuse 22 Horn switch 23 Horn 24 Luggage boot lamp 25 Luggage boot lamp switch 26 Roof lamp 27 Door switch 28 Voltage stabilizer 29 Temperature indicator 30 Temperature transmitter 31 Fuel indicator 32 Fuel tank unit 33 Heater motor 34 Heater resistor 35 Heater switch 36 Reverse lamp switch (optional extra) 37 Reverse lamp (optional extra) 38 Windscreen wiper switch 39 Windscreen wiper motor 40 Stop lamp switch 41 Stop lamp 42 Turn signal flasher unit 43 Turn signal switch 44 Lefthand front flasher lamp 45 Lefthand rear flasher lamp 46 Lefthand turn signal warning light 47 Righthand front flasher lamp 48 Righthand rear flasher lamp 49 Righthand turn signal warning light 50 Oil pressure warning light 51 Oil pressure switch

Colour code: See key to FIG 13 : 1

174

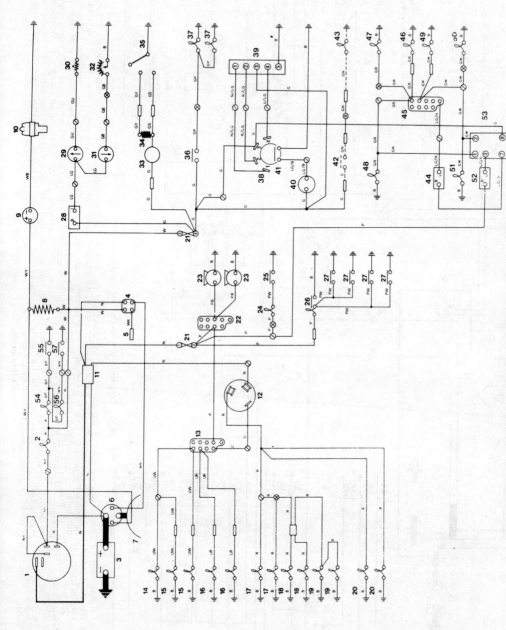

FIG 13:3   Toledo wiring diagram—lefthand drive with maximum equipment

Key to Fig 13:3 : 1 Alternator   2 Ignition warning light   3 Battery   4 Ignition/starter switch   5 Radio supply   6 Starter solenoid   7 Starter motor   8 Ballast resistor
9 Ignition coil—6-volt   10 Ignition distributor   11 Connector block   12 Master light switch   13 Main/dip/flash switch   14 Main beam warning light   15 Main beam
16 Dip beam   17 Front parking lamp   18 Plate illumination lamp   19 Tail lamp   20 Instrument illumination   21 Fuse   22 Horn switch   23 Horn   24 Luggage boot lamp
25 Luggage boot lamp switch   26 Roof lamp   27 Door switch   28 Voltage stabilizer   29 Temperature transmitter   30 Temperature indicator   31 Fuel indicator   32 Fuel
tank unit   33 Heater motor   34 Heater resistor   35 Heater switch   36 Stop lamp switch   37 Stop lamp   38 Windscreen wiper switch   39 Windscreen wiper motor
40 Windscreen washer pump   41 Windscreen washer switch   42 Reverse lamp switch (optional extra)   43 Reverse lamp (optional extra)   44 Turn signal flasher unit
45 Turn signal switch   46 Lefthand front flasher lamp   47 Lefthand rear flasher lamp   48 Lefthand turn signal warning light   49 Righthand front flasher lamp   50 Righthand
rear flasher lamp   51 Righthand turn signal warning light   52 Hazard flasher unit   53 Hazard switch   54 Brake line failure warning light   55 Brake line failure switch
56 Oil pressure warning light   57 Oil pressure switch   **Colour code:** See Key to **FIG 13:1**

TOLEDO 1300/1500

175

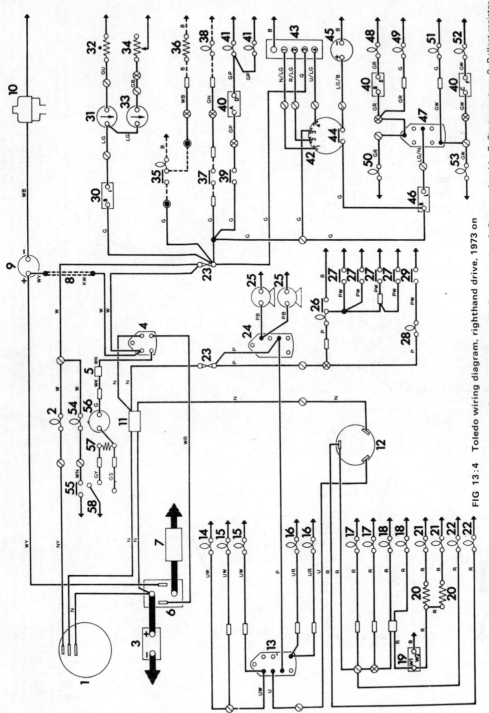

FIG 13:4 Toledo wiring diagram, righthand drive, 1973 on

Key to Fig 13:4 1 Alternator 2 Ignition warning light 3 Battery 4 Ignition/starter switch 5 Radio supply 6 Starter solenoid 7 Starter motor 8 Ballast resistor wire 9 Ignition coil, 6-volt 10 Ignition distributor 11 Connector block 12 Master light switch 13 Main/dip/flash switch 14 Main beam warning light 15 Main beam 16 Dip beam 17 Front parking lamp 18 Plate illumination lamp 19 Night dimming relay winding 20 Tail lamp resistor 21 Tail lamp 22 Instrument illumination 23 Fuse 24 Horn switch 25 Horn 26 Roof lamp 27 Door switch 28 Luggage boot lamp 29 Luggage boot lamp switch, when fitted 30 Voltage stabiliser 31 Temperature indicator 32 Temperature transmitter 33 Fuel indicator 34 Fuel transmitter 35 Heated backlight switch, when fitted 36 Heated backlight, when fitted 37 Reverse lamp switch, when fitted 38 Reverse lamp, when fitted 39 Stop lamp switch 40 Night dimming relay contacts 41 Stop lamp 42 Windscreen wiper switch 43 Windscreen wiper motor 44 Windscreen washer switch 45 Windscreen washer pump 46 Turn signal flasher unit 47 Turn signal switch 48 Lefthand rear flasher lamp 49 Lefthand front flasher lamp 50 Lefthand turn signal warning light 51 Righthand front flasher lamp 52 Righthand rear flasher lamp 53 Righthand turn signal warning light 54 Oil pressure warning light 55 Oil pressure switch 56 Heater motor 57 Heater resistor 58 Heater switch

For colour code: See Key to FIG 13:1

Inches	Decimals	Millimetres	Inches to Millimetres — Inches	Inches to Millimetres — mm	Millimetres to Inches — mm	Millimetres to Inches — Inches
1/64	.015625	.3969	.001	.0254	.01	.00039
1/32	.03125	.7937	.002	.0508	.02	.00079
3/64	.046875	1.1906	.003	.0762	.03	.00118
1/16	.0625	1.5875	.004	.1016	.04	.00157
5/64	.078125	1.9844	.005	.1270	.05	.00197
3/32	.09375	2.3812	.006	.1524	.06	.00236
7/64	.109375	2.7781	.007	.1778	.07	.00276
1/8	.125	3.1750	.008	.2032	.08	.00315
9/64	.140625	3.5719	.009	.2286	.09	.00354
5/32	.15625	3.9687	.01	.254	.1	.00394
11/64	.171875	4.3656	.02	.508	.2	.00787
3/16	.1875	4.7625	.03	.762	.3	.01181
13/64	.203125	5·1594	.04	1.016	.4	.01575
7/32	.21875	5.5562	.05	1.270	.5	.01969
15/64	.234375	5.9531	.06	1.524	.6	.02362
1/4	.25	6.3500	.07	1.778	.7	.02756
17/64	.265625	6.7469	.08	2.032	.8	.03150
9/32	.28125	7.1437	.09	2.286	.9	.03543
19/64	.296875	7.5406	.1	2.54	1	.03937
5/16	.3125	7.9375	.2	5.08	2	.07874
21/64	.328125	8.3344	.3	7.62	3	.11811
11/32	.34375	8.7312	.4	10.16	4	.15748
23/64	.359375	9.1281	.5	12.70	5	.19685
3/8	.375	9.5250	.6	15.24	6	.23622
25/64	.390625	9.9219	.7	17.78	7	.27559
13/32	.40625	10.3187	.8	20.32	8	.31496
27/64	.421875	10.7156	.9	22.86	9	.35433
7/16	.4375	11.1125	1	25.4	10	.39370
29/64	.453125	11.5094	2	50.8	11	.43307
15/32	.46875	11.9062	3	76.2	12	.47244
31/64	.484375	12.3031	4	101.6	13	.51181
1/2	.5	12.7000	5	127.0	14	.55118
33/64	.515625	13.0969	6	152.4	15	.59055
17/32	.53125	13.4937	7	177.8	16	.62992
35/64	.546875	13.8906	8	203.2	17	.66929
9/16	.5625	14.2875	9	228.6	18	.70866
37/64	.578125	14.6844	10	254.0	19	.74803
19/32	.59375	15.0812	11	279.4	20	.78740
39/64	.609375	15.4781	12	304.8	21	.82677
5/8	.625	15.8750	13	330.2	22	.86614
41/64	.640625	16.2719	14	355.6	23	.90551
21/32	.65625	16.6687	15	381.0	24	.94488
43/64	.671875	17.0656	16	406.4	25	.98425
11/16	.6875	17.4625	17	431.8	26	1.02362
45/64	.703125	17.8594	18	457.2	27	1.06299
23/32	.71875	18.2562	19	482.6	28	1.10236
47/64	.734375	18.6531	20	508.0	29	1.14173
3/4	.75	19.0500	21	533.4	30	1.18110
49/64	.765625	19.4469	22	558.8	31	1.22047
25/32	.78125	19.8437	23	584.2	32	1.25984
51/64	.796875	20.2406	24	609.6	33	1.29921
13/16	.8125	20.6375	25	635.0	34	1.33858
53/64	.828125	21.0344	26	660.4	35	1.37795
27/32	.84375	21.4312	27	685.8	36	1.41732
55/64	.859375	21.8281	28	711.2	37	1.4567
7/8	.875	22.2250	29	736.6	38	1.4961
57/64	.890625	22.6219	30	762.0	39	1.5354
29/32	.90625	23.0187	31	787.4	40	1.5748
59/64	.921875	23.4156	32	812.8	41	1.6142
15/16	.9375	23.8125	33	838.2	42	1.6535
61/64	.953125	24.2094	34	863.6	43	1.6929
31/32	.96875	24.6062	35	889.0	44	1.7323
63/64	.984375	25.0031	36	914.4	45	1.7717

UNITS	Pints to Litres	Gallons to Litres	Litres to Pints	Litres to Gallons	Miles to Kilometres	Kilometres to Miles	Lbs. per sq. In. to Kg. per sq. Cm.	Kg. per sq. Cm. to Lbs. per sq. In.
1	.57	4.55	1.76	.22	1.61	.62	.07	14.22
2	1.14	9.09	3.52	.44	3.22	1.24	.14	28.50
3	1.70	13.64	5.28	.66	4.83	1.86	.21	42.67
4	2.27	18.18	7.04	.88	6.44	2.49	.28	56.89
5	2.84	22.73	8.80	1.10	8.05	3.11	.35	71.12
6	3.41	27.28	10.56	1.32	9.66	3.73	.42	85.34
7	3.98	31.82	12.32	1.54	11.27	4.35	.49	99.56
8	4.55	36.37	14.08	1.76	12.88	4.97	.56	113.79
9		40.91	15.84	1.98	14.48	5.59	.63	128.00
10		45.46	17.60	2.20	16.09	6.21	.70	142.23
20				4.40	32.19	12.43	1.41	284.47
30				6.60	48.28	18.64	2.11	426.70
40				8.80	64.37	24.85		
50					80.47	31.07		
60					96.56	37.28		
70					112.65	43.50		
80					128.75	49.71		
90					144.84	55.92		
100					160.93	62.14		

UNITS	Lb ft to kgm	Kgm to lb ft	UNITS	Lb ft to kgm	Kgm to lb ft
1	.138	7.233	7	.967	50.631
2	.276	14.466	8	1.106	57.864
3	.414	21.699	9	1.244	65.097
4	.553	28.932	10	1.382	72.330
5	.691	36.165	20	2.765	144.660
6	.829	43.398	30	4.147	216.990

NOTES

HINTS ON MAINTENANCE AND OVERHAUL

There are few things more rewarding than the restoration of a vehicle's original peak of efficiency and smooth performance.

The following notes are intended to help the owner to reach that state of perfection. Providing that he possesses the basic manual skills he should have no difficulty in performing most of the operations detailed in this manual. It must be stressed, however, that where recommended in the manual, highly-skilled operations ought to be entrusted to experts, who have the necessary equipment, to carry out the work satisfactorily.

Quality of workmanship:

The hazardous driving conditions on the roads to-day demand that vehicles should be as nearly perfect, mechanically, as possible. It is therefore most important that amateur work be carried out with care, bearing in mind the often inadequate working conditions, and also the inferior tools which may have to be used. It is easy to counsel perfection in all things, and we recognize that it may be setting an impossibly high standard. We do, however, suggest that every care should be taken to ensure that a vehicle is as safe to take on the road as it is humanly possible to make it.

Safe working conditions:

Even though a vehicle may be stationary, it is still potentially dangerous if certain sensible precautions are not taken when working on it while it is supported on jacks or blocks. It is indeed preferable not to use jacks alone, but to supplement them with carefully placed blocks, so that there will be plenty of support if the car rolls off the jacks during a strenuous manoeuvre. Axle stands are an excellent way of providing a rigid base which is not readily disturbed. Piles of bricks are a dangerous substitute. Be careful not to get under heavy loads on lifting tackle, the load could fall. It is preferable not to work alone when lifting an engine, or when working underneath a vehicle which is supported well off the ground. To be trapped, particularly under the vehicle, may have unpleasant results if help is not quickly forthcoming. Make some provision, however humble, to deal with fires. Always disconnect a battery if there is a likelihood of electrical shorts. These may start a fire if there is leaking fuel about. This applies particularly to leads which can carry a heavy current, like those in the starter circuit. While on the subject of electricity, we must also stress the danger of using equipment which is run off the mains and which has no earth or has faulty wiring or connections. So many workshops have damp floors, and electrical shocks are of such a nature that it is sometimes impossible to let go of a live lead or piece of equipment due to the muscular spasms which take place.

Work demanding special care:

This involves the servicing of braking, steering and suspension systems. On the road, failure of the braking system may be disastrous. Make quite sure that there can be no possibility of failure through the bursting of rusty brake pipes or rotten hoses, nor to a sudden loss of pressure due to defective seals or valves.

Problems:

The chief problems which may face an operator are:
1 External dirt.
2 Difficulty in undoing tight fixings
3 Dismantling unfamiliar mechanisms.
4 Deciding in what respect parts are defective.
5 Confusion about the correct order for reassembly.
6 Adjusting running clearances.
7 Road testing.
8 Final tuning.

Practical suggestion to solve the problems:

1 Preliminary cleaning of large parts—engines, transmissions, steering, suspensions, etc.,—should be carried out before removal from the car. Where road dirt and mud alone are present, wash clean with a high-pressure water jet, brushing to remove stubborn adhesions, and allow to drain and dry. Where oil or grease is also present, wash down with a proprietary compound (Gunk, Teepol etc.,) applying with a stiff brush—an old paint brush is suitable—into all crevices. Cover the distributor and ignition coils with a polythene bag and then apply a strong water jet to clear the loosened deposits. Allow to drain and dry. The assemblies will then be sufficiently clean to remove and transfer to the bench for the next stage.

On the bench, further cleaning can be carried out, first wiping the parts as free as possible from grease with old newspaper. Avoid using rag or cotton waste which can leave clogging fibres behind. Any remaining grease can be removed with a brush dipped in paraffin. If necessary, traces of paraffin can be removed by carbon tetrachloride. Avoid using paraffin or petrol in large quantities for cleaning in enclosed areas, such as garages, on account of the high fire risk.

When all exteriors have been cleaned, and not before, dismantling can be commenced. This ensures that dirt will not enter into interiors and orifices revealed by dismantling. In the next phases, where components have to be cleaned, use carbon tetrachloride in preference to petrol and keep the containers covered except when in use. After the components have been cleaned, plug small holes with tapered hard wood plugs cut to size and blank off larger orifices with grease-proof paper and masking tape. Do not use soft wood plugs or matchsticks as they may break.

2 It is not advisable to hammer on the end of a screw thread, but if it must be done, first screw on a nut to protect the thread, and use a lead hammer. This applies particularly to the removal of tapered cotters. Nuts and bolts seem to 'grow' together, especially in exhaust systems. If penetrating oil does not work, try the judicious application of heat, but be careful of starting a fire. Asbestos sheet or cloth is useful to isolate heat.

Tight bushes or pieces of tail-pipe rusted into a silencer can be removed by splitting them with an open-ended hacksaw. Tight screws can sometimes be started by a tap from a hammer on the end of a suitable screwdriver. Many tight fittings will yield to the judicious use of a hammer, but it must be a soft-faced hammer if damage is to be avoided, use a heavy block on the opposite side to absorb shock. Any parts of the steering system which have been damaged should be renewed, as attempts to repair them may lead to cracking and subsequent failure, and steering ball joints should be disconnected using a recommended tool to prevent damage.

3   If often happens that an owner is baffled when trying to dismantle an unfamiliar piece of equipment. So many modern devices are pressed together or assembled by spinning-over flanges, that they must be sawn apart. The intention is that the whole assembly must be renewed. However, parts which appear to be in one piece to the naked eye, may reveal close-fitting joint lines when inspected with a magnifying glass, and, this may provide the necessary clue to dismantling. Left-handed screw threads are used where rotational forces would tend to unscrew a right-handed screw thread.

Be very careful when dismantling mechanisms which may come apart suddenly. Work in an enclosed space where the parts will be contained, and drape a piece of cloth over the device if springs are likely to fly in all directions. Mark everything which might be reassembled in the wrong position, scratched symbols may be used on unstressed parts, or a sequence of tiny dots from a centre punch can be useful. Stressed parts should never be scratched or centre-popped as this may lead to cracking under working conditions. Store parts which look alike in the correct order for reassembly. Never rely upon memory to assist in the assembly of complicated mechanisms, especially when they will be dismantled for a long time, but make notes, and drawings to supplement the diagrams in the manual, and put labels on detached wires. Rust stains may indicate unlubricated wear. This can sometimes be seen round the outside edge of a bearing cup in a universal joint. Look for bright rubbing marks on parts which normally should not make heavy contact. These might prove that something is bent or running out of truth. For example, there might be bright marks on one side of a piston, at the top near the ring grooves, and others at the bottom of the skirt on the other side. This could well be the clue to a bent connecting rod. Suspected cracks can be proved by heating the component in a light oil to approximately 100°C, removing, drying off, and dusting with french chalk, if a crack is present the oil retained in the crack will stain the french chalk.

4   In determining wear, and the degree, against the permissible limits set in the manual, accurate measurement can only be achieved by the use of a micrometer. In many cases, the wear is given to the fourth place of decimals; that is in ten-thousandths of an inch. This can be read by the vernier scale on the barrel of a good micrometer. Bore diameters are more difficult to determine. If, however, the matching shaft is accurately measured, the degree of play in the bore can be felt as a guide to its suitability. In other cases, the shank of a twist drill of known diameter is a handy check.

Many methods have been devised for determining the clearance between bearing surfaces. To-day the best and simplest is by the use of Plastigage, obtainable from most garages. A thin plastic thread is laid between the two surfaces and the bearing is tightened, flattening the thread. On removal, the width of the thread is compared with a scale supplied with the thread and the clearance is read off directly. Sometimes joint faces leak persistently, even after gasket renewal. The fault will then be traceable to distortion, dirt or burrs. Studs which are screwed into soft metal frequently raise burrs at the point of entry. A quick cure for this is to chamfer the edge of the hole in the part which fits over the stud.

5   **Always check a replacement part with the original one before it is fitted.**

If parts are not marked, and the order for reassembly is not known, a little detective work will help. Look for marks which are due to wear to see if they can be mated. Joint faces may not be identical due to manufacturing errors, and parts which overlap may be stained, giving a clue to the correct position. Most fixings leave identifying marks especially if they were painted over on assembly. It is then easier to decide whether a nut, for instance, has a plain, a spring, or a shakeproof washer under it. All running surfaces become 'bedded' together after long spells of work and tiny imperfections on one part will be found to have left corresponding marks on the other. This is particularly true of shafts and bearings and even a score on a cylinder wall will show on the piston.

6   Checking end float or rocker clearances by feeler gauge may not always give accurate results because of wear. For instance, the rocker tip which bears on a valve stem may be deeply pitted, in which case the feeler will simply be bridging a depression. Thrust washers may also wear depressions in opposing faces to make accurate measurement difficult. End float is then easier to check by using a dial gauge. It is common practice to adjust end play in bearing assemblies, like front hubs with taper rollers, by doing up the axle nut until the hub becomes stiff to turn and then backing it off a little. Do not use this method with ballbearing hubs as the assembly is often preloaded by tightening the axle nut to its fullest extent. If the splitpin hole will not line up, file the base of the nut a little.

Steering assemblies often wear in the straight-ahead position. If any part is adjusted, make sure that it remains free when moved from lock to lock. Do not be surprised if an assembly like a steering gearbox, which is known to be carefully adjusted outside the car, becomes stiff when it is bolted in place. This will be due to distortion of the case by the pull of the mounting bolts, particularly if the mounting points are not all touching together. This problem may be met in other equipment and is cured by careful attention to the alignment of mounting points.

When a spanner is stamped with a size and A/F it means that the dimension is the width between the jaws and has no connection with ANF, which is the designation for the American National Fine thread. Coarse threads like Whitworth are rarely used on cars to-day except for studs which screw into soft aluminium or cast iron. For this reason it might be found that the top end of a cylinder head stud has a fine thread and the lower end a coarse thread to screw into the cylinder block. If the car has mainly UNF threads then it is likely that any coarse threads will be UNC, which are not the same as Whitworth. Small sizes have the same number of threads in Whitworth and UNC, but in the $\frac{1}{2}$ inch size for example, there are twelve threads to the inch in the former and thirteen in the latter.

7 After a major overhaul, particularly if a great deal of work has been done on the braking, steering and suspension systems, it is advisable to approach the problem of testing with care. If the braking system has been overhauled, apply heavy pressure to the brake pedal and get a second operator to check every possible source of leakage. The brakes may work extremely well, but a leak could cause complete failure after a few miles.

Do not fit the hub caps until every wheel nut has been checked for tightness, and make sure the tyre pressures are correct. Check the levels of coolant, lubricants and hydraulic fluids. Being satisfied that all is well, take the car on the road and test the brakes at once. Check the steering and the action of the handbrake. Do all this at moderate speeds on quiet roads, and make sure there is no other vehicle behind you when you try a rapid stop.

Finally, remember that many parts settle down after a time, so check for tightness of all fixings after the car has been on the road for a hundred miles or so.

8 It is useless to tune an engine which has not reached its normal running temperature. In the same way, the tune of an engine which is stiff after a rebore will be different when the engine is again running free. Remember too, that rocker clearances on pushrod operated valve gear will change when the cylinder head nuts are tightened after an initial period of running with a new head gasket.

Trouble may not always be due to what seems the obvious cause. Ignition, carburation and mechanical condition are interdependent and spitting back through the carburetter, which might be attributed to a weak mixture, can be caused by a sticking inlet valve.

For one final hint on tuning, never adjust more than one thing at a time or it will be impossible to tell which adjustment produced the desired result.

NOTES

GLOSSARY OF TERMS

Allen key — Cranked wrench of hexagonal section for use with socket head screws.

Alternator — Electrical generator producing alternating current. Rectified to direct current for battery charging.

Ambient temperature — Surrounding atmospheric temperature.

Annulus — Used in engineering to indicate the outer ring gear of an epicyclic gear train.

Armature — The shaft carrying the windings, which rotates in the magnetic field of a generator or starter motor. That part of a solenoid or relay which is activated by the magnetic field.

Axial — In line with, or pertaining to, an axis.

Backlash — Play in meshing gears.

Balance lever — A bar where force applied at the centre is equally divided between connections at the ends.

Banjo axle — Axle casing with large diameter housing for the crownwheel and differential.

Bendix pinion — A self-engaging and self-disengaging drive on a starter motor shaft.

Bevel pinion — A conical shaped gearwheel, designed to mesh with a similar gear with an axis usually at 90 deg. to its own.

bhp — Brake horse power, measured on a dynamometer.

bmep — Brake mean effective pressure. Average pressure on a piston during the working stroke.

Brake cylinder — Cylinder with hydraulically operated piston(s) acting on brake shoes or pad(s).

Brake regulator — Control valve fitted in hydraulic braking system which limits brake pressure to rear brakes during heavy braking to prevent rear wheel locking.

Camber — Angle at which a wheel is tilted from the vertical.

Capacitor — Modern term for an electrical condenser. Part of distributor assembly, connected across contact breaker points, acts as an interference suppressor.

Castellated — Top face of a nut, slotted across the flats, to take a locking splitpin.

Castor — Angle at which the kingpin or swivel pin is tilted when viewed from the side.

cc — Cubic centimetres. Engine capacity is arrived at by multiplying the area of the bore in sq cm by the stroke in cm by the number of cylinders.

Clevis — U-shaped forked connector used with a clevis pin, usually at handbrake connections.

Collet — A type of collar, usually split and located in a groove in a shaft, and held in place by a retainer. The arrangement used to retain the spring(s) on a valve stem in most cases.

Commutator — Rotating segmented current distributor between armature windings and brushes in generator or motor.

Compression ratio — The ratio, or quantitative relation, of the total volume (piston at bottom of stroke) to the unswept volume (piston at top of stroke) in an engine cylinder.

Condenser — See capacitor.

Core plug — Plug for blanking off a manufacturing hole in a casting.

Crownwheel — Large bevel gear in rear axle, driven by a bevel pinion attached to the propeller shaft. Sometimes called a 'ring gear'.

'C'-spanner — Like a 'C' with a handle. For use on screwed collars without flats, but with slots or holes.

Damper — Modern term for shock-absorber, used in vehicle suspension systems to damp out spring oscillations.

Depression — The lowering of atmospheric pressure as in the inlet manifold and carburetter.

Dowel — Close tolerance pin, peg, tube, or bolt, which accurately locates mating parts.

Drag link — Rod connecting steering box drop arm (pitman arm) to nearest front wheel steering arm in certain types of steering systems.

Dry liner — Thinwall tube pressed into cylinder bore.

Dry sump — Lubrication system where all oil is scavenged from the sump, and returned to a separate tank.

Dynamo — See Generator.

Electrode — Terminal, part of an electrical component, such as the points or 'Electrodes' of a sparking plug.

Electrolyte — In lead-acid car batteries a solution of sulphuric acid and distilled water.

End float — The axial movement between associated parts, end play.

EP — Extreme pressure. In lubricants, special grades for heavily loaded bearing surfaces, such as gear teeth in a gearbox, or crownwheel and pinion in a rear axle.

Fade	Of brakes. Reduced efficiency due to overheating.
Field coils	Windings on the polepieces of motors and generators.
Fillets	Narrow finishing strips usually applied to interior bodywork.
First motion shaft	Input shaft from clutch to gearbox.
Fullflow filter	Filters in which all the oil is pumped to the engine. If the element becomes clogged, a bypass valve operates to pass unfiltered oil to the engine.
FWD	Front wheel drive.
Gear pump	Two meshing gears in a close fitting casing. Oil is carried from the inlet round the outside of both gears in the spaces between the gear teeth and casing to the outlet, the meshing gear teeth prevent oil passing back to the inlet, and the oil is forced through the outlet port.
Generator	Modern term for 'Dynamo'. When rotated produces electrical current.
Grommet	A ring of protective or sealing material. Can be used to protect pipes or leads passing through bulkheads.
Grubscrew	Fully threaded headless screw with screwdriver slot. Used for locking, or alignment purposes.
Gudgeon pin	Shaft which connects a piston to its connecting rod. Sometimes called 'wrist pin', or 'piston pin'.
Halfshaft	One of a pair transmitting drive from the differential.
Helical	In spiral form. The teeth of helical gears are cut at a spiral angle to the side faces of the gearwheel.
Hot spot	Hot area that assists vapourisation of fuel on its way to cylinders. Often provided by close contact between inlet and exhaust manifolds.
HT	High Tension. Applied to electrical current produced by the ignition coil for the sparking plugs.
Hydrometer	A device for checking specific gravity of liquids. Used to check specific gravity of electrolyte.
Hypoid bevel gears	A form of bevel gear used in the rear axle drive gears. The bevel pinion meshes below the centre line of the crownwheel, giving a lower propeller shaft line.
Idler	A device for passing on movement. A free running gear between driving and driven gears. A lever transmitting track rod movement to a side rod in steering gear.
Impeller	A centrifugal pumping element. Used in water pumps to stimulate flow.
Journals	Those parts of a shaft that are in contact with the bearings.
Kingpin	The main vertical pin which carries the front wheel spindle, and permits steering movement. May be called 'steering pin' or 'swivel pin'.
Layshaft	The shaft which carries the laygear in the gearbox. The laygear is driven by the first motion shaft and drives the third motion shaft according to the gear selected. Sometimes called the 'countershaft' or 'second motion shaft.'
lb ft	A measure of twist or torque. A pull of 10 lb at a radius of 1 ft is a torque of 10 lb ft.
lb/sq in	Pounds per square inch.
Little-end	The small, or piston end of a connecting rod. Sometimes called the 'small-end'.
LT	Low Tension. The current output from the battery.
Mandrel	Accurately manufactured bar or rod used for test or centring purposes.
Manifold	A pipe, duct, or chamber, with several branches.
Needle rollers	Bearing rollers with a length many times their diameter.
Oil bath	Reservoir which lubricates parts by immersion. In air filters, a separate oil supply for wetting a wire mesh element to hold the dust.
Oil wetted	In air filters, a wire mesh element lightly oiled to trap and hold airborne dust.
Overlap	Period during which inlet and exhaust valves are open together.
Panhard rod	Bar connected between fixed point on chassis and another on axle to control sideways movement.
Pawl	Pivoted catch which engages in the teeth of a ratchet to permit movement in one direction only.
Peg spanner	Tool with pegs, or pins, to engage in holes or slots in the part to be turned.
Pendant pedals	Pedals with levers that are pivoted at the top end.
Phillips screwdriver	A cross-point screwdriver for use with the cross-slotted heads of Phillips screws.
Pinion	A small gear, usually in relation to another gear.
Piston-type damper	Shock absorber in which damping is controlled by a piston working in a closed oil-filled cylinder.
Preloading	Preset static pressure on ball or roller bearings not due to working loads.
Radial	Radiating from a centre, like the spokes of a wheel.

Radius rod	Pivoted arm confining movement of a part to an arc of fixed radius.
Ratchet	Toothed wheel or rack which can move in one direction only, movement in the other being prevented by a pawl.
Ring gear	A gear tooth ring attached to outer periphery of flywheel. Starter pinion engages with it during starting.
Runout	Amount by which rotating part is out of true.
Semi-floating axle	Outer end of rear axle halfshaft is carried on bearing inside axle casing. Wheel hub is secured to end of shaft.
Servo	A hydraulic or pneumatic system for assisting, or, augmenting a physical effort. See 'Vacuum Servo'.
Setscrew	One which is threaded for the full length of the shank.
Shackle	A coupling link, used in the form of two parallel pins connected by side plates to secure the end of the master suspension spring and absorb the effects of deflection.
Shell bearing	Thinwalled steel shell lined with anti-friction metal. Usually semi-circular and used in pairs for main and big-end bearings.
Shock absorber	See 'Damper'.
Silentbloc	Rubber bush bonded to inner and outer metal sleeves.
Socket-head screw	Screw with hexagonal socket for an Allen key.
Solenoid	A coil of wire creating a magnetic field when electric current passes through it. Used with a soft iron core to operate contacts or a mechanical device.
Spur gear	A gear with teeth cut axially across the periphery.
Stub axle	Short axle fixed at one end only.
Tachometer	An instrument for accurate measurement of rotating speed. Usually indicates in revolutions per minute.

TDC	Top Dead Centre. The highest point reached by a piston in a cylinder, with the crank and connecting rod in line.
Thermostat	Automatic device for regulating temperature. Used in vehicle coolant systems to open a valve which restricts circulation at low temperature.
Third motion shaft	Output shaft of gearbox.
Threequarter floating axle	Outer end of rear axle halfshaft flanged and bolted to wheel hub, which runs on bearing mounted on outside of axle casing. Vehicle weight is not carried by the axle shaft.
Thrust bearing or washer	Used to reduce friction in rotating parts subject to axial loads.
Torque	Turning or twisting effort. See 'lb ft'.
Track rod	The bar(s) across the vehicle which connect the steering arms and maintain the front wheels in their correct alignment.
UJ	Universal joint. A coupling between shafts which permits angular movement.
UNF	Unified National Fine screw thread.
Vacuum servo	Device used in brake system, using difference between atmospheric pressure and inlet manifold depression to operate a piston which acts to augment brake pressure as required. See 'Servo'.
Venturi	A restriction or 'choke' in a tube, as in a carburetter, used to increase velocity to obtain a reduction in pressure.
Vernier	A sliding scale for obtaining fractional readings of the graduations of an adjacent scale.
Welch plug	A domed thin metal disc which is partially flattened to lock in a recess. Used to plug core holes in castings.
Wet liner	Removable cylinder barrel, sealed against coolant leakage, where the coolant is in direct contact with the outer surface.
Wet sump	A reservoir attached to the crankcase to hold the lubricating oil.

NOTES

INDEX

NOTES

Alfa Romeo Giulia 1600, 1750, 2000 1962 on
Aston Martin 1921-58
Auto Union Audi 70, 80, Super 90, 1966-72
Audi 100 1969 on
Austin, Morris etc. 1100 Mk. 1 1962-67
Austin, Morris etc. 1100 Mk. 2, 3, 1300 Mk. 1, 2, 3 America 1968 on
Austin A30, A35, A40 Farina 1951-67
Austin A55 Mk. 2, A60 1958-69
Austin A99, A110 1959-68
Austin J4 1960
Austin Allegro 1973 on
Austin Maxi 1969 on
Austin, Morris 1800 1964 on
Austin, Morris 2200 1972 on
Austin Kimberley, Tasman 1970 on
Austin, Morris 1300, 1500 Nomad 1969 on
BMC 3 (Austin A50, A55 Mk. 1, Morris Oxford 2, 3 1954-59)
Austin Healey 100/6, 3000 1956-68
Austin Healey, MG Sprite, Midget 1958 on
Bedford CA Mk. 2 1964-69
Bedford CF Vans 1969 on
Bedford Beagle HA Vans 1964 on
BMW 1600 1966 on
BMW 1800 1964-71
BMW 2000, 2002 1966 on
Chevrolet Corvair 1960-69
Chevrolet Corvette V8 1957-65
Chevrolet Corvette V8 1965 on
Chevrolet Vega 2300 1970 on
Chrysler Valiant V8 1965 on
Chrysler Valiant Straight Six 1963 on
Citroen DS 19, ID 19 1955-66
Citroen ID 19, DS 19, 20, 21 1966 on
Citroen Dyane Ami 1964 on
Daf 31, 32, 33, 44, 55 1961 on
Datsun Bluebird 610 series 1972 on
Datsun Cherry 100A, 120A 1971 on
Datsun 1000, 1200 1968 on
Datsun 1300, 1400, 1600 1968 on
Datsun 240C 1971 on

Datsun 240Z Sport 1970 on
Fiat 124 1966 on
Fiat 124 Sport 1966 on
Fiat 125 1967-72
Fiat 127 1971 on
Fiat 128 1969 on
Fiat 500 1957 on
Fiat 600, 600D 1955-69
Fiat 850 1964 on
Fiat 1100 1957-69
Fiat 1300, 1500 1961-67
Ford Anglia Prefect 100E 1953-62
Ford Anglia 105E, Prefect 107E 1959-67
Ford Capri 1300, 1600 OHV 1968 on
Ford Capri 1300, 1600, 2000 OHC 1972 on
Ford Capri 2000 V4, 3000 V6 1969 on
Ford Classic, Capri 1961-64
Ford Consul, Zephyr, Zodiac, 1, 2 1950-62
Ford Corsair Straight Four 1963-65
Ford Corsair V4 1965-68
Ford Corsair V4 2000 1969-70
Ford Cortina 1962-66
Ford Cortina 1967-68
Ford Cortina 1969-70
Ford Cortina Mk. 3 1970 on
Ford Escort 1967 on
Ford Falcon 6 1964-70
Ford Falcon XK, XL 1960-63
Ford Falcon 6 XR/XA 1966 on
Ford Falcon V8 (U.S.A.) 1965-71
Ford Falcon V8 (Aust.) 1966 on
Ford Pinto 1970 on
Ford Maverick 6 1969 on
Ford Maverick V8 1970 on
Ford Mustang 6 1965 on
Ford Mustang V8 1965 on
Ford Thames 10, 12, 15 cwt 1957-65
Ford Transit V4 1965 on
Ford Zephyr Zodiac Mk. 3 1962-66
Ford Zephyr Zodiac V4, V6, Mk. 4 1966-72
Ford Consul, Granada 1972 on
Hillman Avenger 1970 on
Hillman Hunter 1966 on
Hillman Imp 1963-68
Hillman Imp 1969 on
Hillman Minx 1 to 5 1956-65
Hillman Minx 1965-67

Hillman Minx 1966-70
Hillman Super Minx 1961-65
Jaguar XK120, 140, 150, Mk. 7, 8, 9 1948-61
Jaguar 2.4, 3.4, 3.8 Mk. 1, 2 1955-69
Jaguar 'E' Type 1961-72
Jaguar 'S' Type 420 1963-68
Jaguar XJ6 1968 on
Jowett Javelin Jupiter 1947-53
Landrover 1, 2 1948-61
Landrover 2, 2a, 3 1959 on
Mazda 616 1970 on
Mazda 808, 818 1972 on
Mazda 1200, 1300 1969 on
Mazda 1500, 1800 1967 on
Mazda RX-2 1971 on
Mazda R100, RX-3 1970 on
Mercedes-Benz 190b, 190c, 200 1959-68
Mercedes-Benz 220 1959-65
Mercedes-Benz 220/8 1968 on
Mercedes-Benz 230 1963-68
Mercedes-Benz 250 1965-67
Mercedes-Benz 250 1968 on
Mercedes-Benz 280 1968 on
MG TA to TF 1936-55
MGA MGB 1955-68
MGB 1969 on
Mini 1959 on
Mini Cooper 1961-72
Morgan Four 1936-72
Morris Marina 1971 on
Morris (Aust) Marina 1972 on
Morris Minor 2, 1000 1952-71
Morris Oxford 5, 6 1959-71
NSU 1000 1963-72
NSU Prinz 1 to 4 1957-72
Opel Ascona, Manta 1970 on
Opel GT 1900 1968 on
Opel Kadett, Olympia 993 cc 1078 cc 1962 on
Opel Kadett, Olympia 1492, 1698, 1897 cc 1967 on
Opel Rekord C 1966-72
Peugeot 204 1965 on
Peugeot 304 1970 on
Peugeot 404 1960 on
Peugeot 504 1968 on
Porsche 356A, B, C 1957-65
Porsche 911 1964 on
Porsche 912 1965-69
Porsche 914 S 1969 on
Reliant Regal 1952-73

Renault R4, R4L, 4 1961 on
Renault 5 1972 on
Renault 6 1968 on
Renault 8, 10, 1100 1962-71
Renault 12, 1969 on
Renault 15, 17 1971 on
Renault R16 1965 on
Renault Dauphine Floride 1957-67
Renault Caravelle 1962-68
Rover 60 to 110 1953-64
Rover 2000 1963-73
Rover 3 Litre 1958-67
Rover 3500, 3500S 1968 on
Saab 95, 96, Sport 1960-68
Saab 99 1969 on
Saab V4 1966 on
Simca 1000 1961 on
Simca 1100 1967 on
Simca 1300, 1301, 1500, 1501 1963 on
Skoda One (440, 445, 450) 1955-70
Sunbeam Rapier Alpine 1955-65
Toyota Carina, Celica 1971 on
Toyota Corolla 1100, 1200 1967 on
Toyota Corona 1500 Mk. 1 1965-70
Toyota Corona Mk. 2 1969 on
Triumph TR2, TR3, TR3A 1952-62
Triumph TR4, TR4A 1961-67
Triumph TR5, TR250, TR6 1967 on
Triumph 1300, 1500 1965-73
Triumph 2000 Mk. 1, 2.5 PI Mk. 1 1963-69
Triumph 2000 Mk' 2, 2.5 PI Mk. 2 1969 on
Triumph Dolomite 1972 on
Triumph Herald 1959-68
Triumph Herald 1969-71
Triumph Spitfire, Vitesse 1962-68
Triumph Spitfire Mk. 3, 4 1969 on
Triumph GT6, Vitesse 2 Litre 1969 on
Triumph Stag 1970 on
Triumph Toledo 1970 on
Vauxhall Velox, Cresta 1957-72
Vauxhall Victor 1, 2, FB 1957-64
Vauxhall Victor 101 1964-67
Vauxhall Victor FD 1600, 2000 1967-72

Continued on following page

Vauxhall Victor 3300,
  Ventora 1968-72
Vauxhall Victor FE
  Ventora 1972 on
Vauxhall Viva HA 1963-66
Vauxhall Viva HB 1966-70

Vauxhall Viva, HC Firenza
  1971 on
Volkswagen Beetle 1954-67
Volkswagen Beetle 1968 on
Volkswagen 1500 1961-66

Volkswagen 1600 Fastback
  1965-73
Volkswagen Transporter
  1954-67
Volkswagen Transporter
  1968 on

Volkswagen 411 1968-72
Volvo 120 series 1961-70
Volvo 140 series 1966 on
Volvo 160 series 1968 on
Volvo 1800 1960-73